The Dark of the Soul

CPA Seminar Series

The Dark of the Soul

Psychopathology in the Horoscope

Liz Greene

Centre for Psychological Astrology Press
London

First published 2003 by the CPA Press, BCM Box 1815, London WC1 3XX, United Kingdom, Tel/Fax +44 20 8749 2330.

THE DARK OF THE SOUL

Copyright © 2003 by Liz Greene

Liz Greene asserts the moral right to be identified as the author of this work.

ISBN 978-1-900869-28-7

British Library Cataloguing-in-Publication Data. A catalogue record for this book is available from the British Library.

Printed in the United Kingdom by CPI Antony Rowe, Chippenham, Wiltshire SN14 6LH.

Table of Contents

Part One: The Psychopath

Part Two: Sanity and Madness

Part Three: The Scapegoat

Part One: The Psychopath

This seminar was given on 1 July 2001 at Regents College, London as part of the Summer Term of the seminar programme of the Centre for Psychological Astrology.

Introduction

A rose by any other name

We have a difficult and highly emotionally charged theme to discuss today. To begin, it might be useful to consider the ways in which the term "psychopath" is colloquially used. When we think of psychopaths, we tend to think of serial killers like Hannibal the Cannibal from *The Silence of the Lambs*: people who are terrifyingly cold, destructive and violent. Or we think of ruthless dictators like Hitler or Stalin, who commit acts of genocide without even a glimmer of remorse. But when we examine the clinical descriptions of psychopathy, which I will cover in some detail in a few minutes, we will discover that only a very small percentage of what is understood as psychopathic behaviour exhibits this kind of florid violence. The majority of individuals who display psychopathic behavioural patterns do so under the guise of "normal life". They have made what James Masterson calls "a superficial social adaptation".[1] They often have excellent professional qualifications, and they can be found in the upper echelons of religious as well as corporate hierarchies. They may run governments without committing obvious criminal acts, or own chains of newspapers, or head the boards of museums, hospitals or charitable organisations. They may even be found in the helping professions and the esoteric community. In fact, they may be anywhere at all. Psychopathic behaviour, because it is not always violent, is not always immediately identifiable.

---

[1] James F. Masterson, *The Narcissistic and Borderline Disorders*, Bruner/Mazel, New York, 1981.

It is also useful to look at the evolution of our definitions of psychopathy, and the etymology of the term. The term "psychopath" is not in clinical favour any more, and it hadn't even been invented a century ago. Psychopathy was known as "moral insanity" or "moral inferiority", the implication being that the psychopath has a diseased moral sense: an incapacity to distinguish between right and wrong. As our ideas about right and wrong became more relative over the decades, the concept of moral inferiority became questionable, and "psychopath" was the preferred psychiatric term for a great many years. The roots of the word are *psyche* and *pathos*: the suffering of the soul. In practice it seems to be other people's souls which suffer at the hands of the psychopath, rather than the soul of the psychopath himself or herself, about which we still know very little. More recently, the term "sociopath" has come into vogue, the implication being that the antisocial features of psychopathy are the relevant issue, not the internal state of the psychopathic individual. That is, of course, in keeping with the current *Zeitgeist*, which is more concerned with the collective than with the inner world of the individual.

Illness or personality disorder?

In Britain we still use the term "sociopath", although it is increasingly being replaced by an American term, "APD", an abbreviation of "antisocial personality disorder". This is a very specific clinical term. When psychiatry refers to something as a personality disorder, it is making a careful distinction between illness and something which is fundamental to character. Illness is something "extra" that distorts basic character and may involve the possibility of a "cure". Illness may be linked to physical or psychological factors or both, but it is an "altered" state, rather than innate. In contrast, inherent character qualities are not "curable" because that is simply how the person is made. It is now generally thought that psychopathy is not "curable" because there is no illness to cure. This distinction immediately takes us into very tricky terrain. One of the questions we will be dealing with throughout the day is whether psychopathic behaviour is created by the environment or is something innate, almost certainly exacerbated by the environment but already there in potential. If it is innate, then there should be some reflection of it in the natal horoscope.

The social services are always attempting statistical assessments of violent criminals with antisocial behaviour and, as we all know, there are lies, damned lies and statistics. However, statistical results can occasionally be interesting, and every now and then they can even be helpful. For example, according to recent statistics, 80% of psychopaths are male. Now, please remember that 80% is not the same as 100%. Women are allowed to join this club, and they often do. But it may be useful to keep this statistic in mind when we begin to explore more deeply what psychopathy is all about. We should, however, bear in mind that statistics on psychopathy are inevitably based on people who are in high-security prisons or psychiatric wards. It isn't very helpful to stop people in the street and say, "Are you a psychopath? Very good. Would you mind answering the following questions?" Statistical assessments of psychopathy are limited to that small percentage of psychopaths who have been incarcerated because of criminal behaviour. But of this group, it is interesting to note that 84% suffered childhood abuse. This figure apparently supports the psychopaths-are-made-not-born argument, although it does not necessarily contradict the possible presence of genetic or constitutional "tendencies". Sexual or violent physical abuse in childhood seems to be a major component – or a major trigger – in the development of violent psychopathic tendencies. Of course, this should come as no surprise.

On the psychopaths-are-born-not-made side, a number of brain tests have been performed on various groups of criminals with psychopathic behaviour, and around 65% of them have frontal lobe abnormalities of one kind or another. Now, primates have the largest frontal lobe of all the animals, and humans have the largest frontal lobe of all the primates. The frontal lobe of the brain is connected with faculties such as judgement, self-control, the ability to plan into the future and the ability to balance individual needs with the needs of the group. Frontal lobe abnormalities are sometimes related to actual physical damage, caused by factors such as tumours, accidents, birth traumas or hereditary conditions. The behaviour patterns arising from this kind of physical damage can certainly look like psychopathy. But of the 65% showing frontal lobe abnormalities, a large proportion showed no actual physical brain damage. The "abnormality" is revealed in the way the frontal lobe responds to emotional triggers. In other words, if one is presented with an emotive trigger, like a film depicting a child being tortured, one would ordinarily react with horror, and one's emotional reaction would by reflected in increased frontal lobe activity. The psychopath appears not to respond. The brain, although physically normal, does not react in the usual way to visual or verbal emotional triggers.

This raises a very important question. Is this disturbed activity in the brain a physiological factor that causes psychopathic behaviour, or does the psychology of the individual create this kind of brain response? We don't know the answer. In any exploration of psychological suffering, we are always faced with the eternal conundrum of mind and body: which affects which? As with the chicken and the egg, when we think causally about the human being, we wind up going around in circles. Does the brain affect, or even dictate, human psychology and behaviour? Or does human psychology and behaviour produce effects in the brain? Or are they both part of a single package, inseparable and acausal? Jung's term "psychoid" describes the unifying ground which contains both physical and psychic reality, and this is the perspective that we, as psychological astrologers, also tend to take. An astrological symbol describes both levels of human existence, and we often cannot differentiate from the birth chart alone on what level a particular astrological configuration will be expressed. It isn't that the body is affecting the mind, or that the mind is affecting the body. Rather, they are mirrors of each other: simultaneous, synchronous and part of the same unified individual reality.

The ineffectuality of therapy

Here is another interesting statistical snippet. Psychopaths, or APDs if you prefer, do not seem to respond to therapeutic intervention. In other words, forget the "with the right sort of understanding and compassion, every wound can be healed" stuff. James Masterson, in his book, *The Narcissistic and Borderline Disorders*,[2] mentions the case of an adolescent boy who had been diagnosed as "borderline" but who, after six months of treatment, had managed to baffle every therapist with whom he worked, because he showed no improvement whatsoever. Masterson states laconically, "I observed that he hadn't gotten better because he was not going to get better, that there had been a misdiagnosis; he was a psychopath." Apparently, we cannot work therapeutically with psychopathy, no matter what approach we take. All that happens is that the psychopath shamelessly manipulates the therapist, and refuses to form what is called the "working alliance". There is no real wish to be helped. It was once thought that psychopaths did not become anxious or depressed, but this is not actually the case. If a psychopath is cornered and cannot remove himself from the "hot seat" by manipulation, he often gets depressed, and may even attempt suicide as a way of getting himself out of the trap. But this evidently does not reflect real suffering or remorse. When these people come out of prison, they tend to repeat their crimes. Nothing changes, and there is no improvement. Punishment – whether in the form of deprivation or physical pain – does not help, nor do rewards for good behaviour. There is no "fear trigger".

Most of us would like to think that we are moral people, and that we obey social rules because we are good and decent. Nevertheless, while this is no doubt partly true, a large component of our goodness and decency is based on the fear of what will happen if we don't obey the rules. Our goodness is a very human mixture of genuine empathy for others and a realistic appraisal, based on what we have learned from past experience, of the price we will have to pay if we display our impulses in an uncontrolled way. The ability to learn from past experience seems to be missing in psychopathic behaviour. There is no capacity to learn from earlier punishment – only an overwhelming obsession with not getting caught. There is a marked absence of the socialised individual's fear of ostracism and the punishment of society if its laws are broken.

Psychopathy is a frightening area to explore. A seminar on this subject will inevitably stir up awkward responses, and many people

---

[2] *Ibid.*

would prefer to simply not think about it. Yet the media rubs the issue in our faces all the time. At the moment we in Britain are grappling with the terrifying dilemma of whether or not to set Jamie Bulger's murderers free.[3] How can we begin to understand children who deliberately and cold-bloodedly murder other children? Are they endemic psychopaths, or are they the victims of terrible parenting or a corrupt society? According to the psychiatric establishment, it is possible to diagnose psychopathy in the early teens, and the behaviour patterns are visible to the discerning eye even in childhood. There is often a history of torturing animals, cruelty to other children, violent rebellion against the parents, truancy and constant lying. This may be observable even in very young children.

But what are we dealing with? Are we looking at psychopathy, or are we looking at a deeply damaged child who, with the right kind of support and help, could move beyond such compulsive patterns? Or are we dealing with a child who, like the "identified patient" in family therapy, acts out the rage he or she absorbs from the family or the larger collective environment? Some psychiatrists believe that psychopaths usually have at least one parent who is himself or herself psychopathic, but who has managed to make that "superficial social adaptation" I mentioned earlier. The parents may provoke, condone or even support the child's acting out. This is common enough with children who are violent and disruptive at school, and whose parents "side" with the child against the school authorities. I don't have answers to any of these questions. At the end of the day you will not go away with a nice, neat formula whereby you can say, "Yes, I can now see psychopathy in the chart – it's when someone has thingey quintile whatnot." The best we can hope to do today is gain a deeper understanding of this problem and its possible psychological and astrological colourations.

---

[3] For those readers unfamiliar with this case, on 12 February 1993 two ten-year-old boys, Jon Venables and Robert Thompson, cold-bloodedly murdered a two-and-a-half-year-old toddler called Jamie Bulger. They were given an eight-year sentence, and on 26 October 2000 the court declared they had served this sentence. On 22 June 2001 they were given new legal identities and, amidst a great public outcry, were freed. This seminar was given on 1 July 2001, when discussion about Venables and Thompson, and whether they were psychopaths who should have been given a twenty-year sentence, was at its height.

Psychopathic behaviour appears to be on the increase. Conservative estimates suggest that 4% of the population has psychopathic tendencies, if not full blown psychopathic behaviour. Whether there really is an increase, or whether we are just noticing it more, is another important but unanswerable question. Also, it depends on the culture in which we are living. There are cultures where it is acceptable to chop off a person's hand if they steal a tomato from a market stall, and where it is acceptable to execute a woman if she commits adultery, or mutilate her with a clitorectomy in order to ensure her fidelity. There are cultures in which it is acceptable to blow up lots of people, and even oneself, if one disagrees with the official political or religious stance. We need to be very careful about how we define psychopathic behaviour, because the apparently fixed and immovable categories of right and wrong vary from one culture to another and from one epoch of history to another. Some people believe there is a fundamental and intrinsic human morality which psychopathic behaviour violates. Others believe that psychopathy is relative to the cultural milieu. I have no definitive answer to this question, so you will have to discover your own, although we will no doubt be circling around the issue throughout the day.

The clinical picture

Now I would like to talk about the clinical definitions of psychopathy in some detail. Clinical definitions are always suspect because they change according to prevailing social and political attitudes, the prevailing dominance of particular medications on the market, and the prevailing moral climate. We need to take these definitions with a certain amount of healthy cynicism. However, they make a useful beginning, and they can open up the question of what might really be going on from a deeper psychological perspective. We can also start thinking about what sort of astrological factors we might be looking at. Is psychopathy a Mars issues? Is it a Moon issue? No matter how much we search, I don't believe we will ever find a "psychopathic configuration" in the birth chart. But we might at least get a feeling of what general astrological factors we might need to think about. Then we can start looking at some individual charts.

In most of our seminars, lots of you want your charts discussed in the group, and there is never enough time to cover them all. I don't know whether any of you have brought a chart for discussion today. If you have brought your own, you may already be having second thoughts. If you have brought someone else's, you may need to think about why you want it discussed. Because the majority of diagnosed psychopaths are male, many psychologically semi-literate people tend to label as psychopathic any man who doesn't respond to their emotional needs. If your lover or partner has rejected you, that does not mean he is psychopathic. We can easily accuse someone of being psychopathic when they have hurt us emotionally. But how do we define someone who lacks feeling? Does it mean someone who lacks feeling in general, or does it mean someone who lacks feeling for us personally? These considerations apart, it would be very useful to look at some examples from the group as well as the rather florid ones I have brought. First, let's work our way through this interesting list of characteristics which, according to the psychiatric establishment, define the psychopath in our midst.

Charm

Charm appears on all the clinical lists describing psychopathic behaviour. It is the characteristic means by which the psychopathic personality navigates social situations. Try to remember that not every criminal is a psychopath, and not every psychopath is a criminal. People can commit murder and other brutal crimes in a state of extreme emotional distress, or because they are mad. But psychopaths are not mad. They have a remarkable ability to manipulate with great astuteness the actual situation in which they are placed, which is one of the reasons why psychopathy is called a personality disorder and not an illness. In the psychopathic personality, charm is a highly sophisticated form of social adaptation, which paradoxically reflects both emotional dissociation and a realistic relationship with outer reality. The ability to be charming while one is coldly planning to manipulate or even destroy another individual is one of the chief behavioural characteristics of psychopathy. While we examine the other characteristics on the list, think about how we might see charm astrologically, and what we mean by the word.

Grandiose sense of self-worth

The second characteristic on the list is a grandiose sense of self-worth. We might also call it inflation. Inflation is usually linked with clinical narcissicism, which may give us a hint of the deeper psychological dynamics at work beneath the surface of psychopathy. A grandiose sense of self-worth has a lot of behavioural implications. The psychopathic individual may be convinced that he or she has a mission – to murder prostitutes, to convert the world to a particular religion, or to destroy the American government. The psychopath needs to feel very, very important, and this mythic sense of mission – or even the assumption of superiority over other people – provides the justification for an incredible amount of destructiveness. We could also call the sense of grandiosity "identification with an archetype". There is often a messianic element in psychopathy. It also means that the psychopath feels himself or herself exempt from ordinary laws. Laws apply to common people, who have to put up with speed limits and queues in banks and supermarkets. These people have to work for a living and pay for what they want. But if one is special and intrinsically superior, one can lie, cheat, steal and take what one wants whenever one wants it. In psychopathy there is no social conscience, no community feeling at all. But there is often an irresistible inclination to boast in order to feed the inflation, and this is how many psychopathic criminals are apprehended. They cannot resist sending taunting letters to the police, or dropping hints to someone they meet in a pub.

Now, we know that narcissism, which is another way of describing this kind of inflation, is the opposite of genuine self-appreciation and self-respect. Narcissistic inflation is the compensation for a hollow core. It is like a polo mint: there is no real sense of individual identity in the middle. Narcissism is a form of suffering which springs from no sense of self; delusions of greatness then form as a defence around a terrifying feeling of emptiness and worthlessness. In what is called narcissistic personality disorder, this problem can respond to psychotherapy, although it is often a long haul. In psychopathy, the problem seems to be irrevocable and irreversible. The grandiose sense of self-worth in psychopathic behaviour is not genuine self-confidence taken past reasonable limits. This latter behaviour pattern is sometimes the case with a preponderance of planets in fire signs. Psychopathy reflects a deeply infantile character structure: that of the tiny baby around whom the world orbits, but who might be consigned to oblivion at any moment.

Audience: Is that the same as megalomania?

Liz: You could use that term if you like, but it doesn't suggest any of the deeper patterns at work in psychopathy. It's simply an insult. The term narcissism can give us a sense of one of the astrological factors we might look at, because narcissism is, in large part, a solar problem. It involves too little rather than too much Sun. Many people, perhaps even most people, suffer from some degree of narcissistic wounding, so if we are looking for psychopathic patterns, we need to look at a number of astrological factors. It is even possible that all people carry some elements of psychopathy, to one degree or another. There are certain pointers in the chart which suggest that the Sun is struggling, and if this is mixed up with certain kinds of environmental pressures and other astrological factors which we will explore later, it is possible that we might discern a danger that the psychopathic elements of the personality could take over. But then again, we might not.

Low boredom threshold

The third characteristic on the list is a low boredom threshold. The psychopath needs constant stimulation. What might this mean?

Audience: Does it mean you need to be distracted from yourself?

Liz: It can reflect a need to be distracted from oneself, if one is carrying a lot of pain which seems intolerable. This is a common enough defence, and many people attempt to escape unhappiness by flitting from one subject or thought to another in order to avoid an unbearable inner conflict. There may be contributing social factors as well. As a collective, our attention span is becoming very short. We no longer have the patience to read long novels or listen to lengthy expositions on a particular subject. The Monty Python team gently but astutely encapsulated this problem in a sketch called "the Summarise Proust Contest". We can't be bothered to write long letters any more, but prefer e-mail or text messages. We want instant information and instant solutions to problems. Recently I received a complaint from an American astrology student, who was upset because I used words in my book, *The Astrological Neptune*, which had more than three syllables and required the help of a dictionary.

Audience: That sounds to me like a Mercury problem.

Liz: It may be connected with Mercury. But the inability to focus the mind also has to do with an emotional response to ideas, things and people. We tend to stay interested in something if it stirs us emotionally and imaginatively. When we engage with the "object" on these non-rational levels – even if our apparent interest is intellectual – we can concentrate. We become bored if a subject doesn't touch our feelings. If we absolutely adore taking apart car engines, then a manual on car engines will be riveting, but if we aren't interested, it's as exciting as watching paint dry.

People who are interested in other people tend to be interesting, because the emotional empathy we feel from them draws us out and makes us want to find out about ourselves as well as about them. People who are uninterested, even if they have a pleasant persona, tend to be boring because they talk about themselves all the time, and leave us feeling vaguely denigrated for no apparent reason. This has more to do with the Moon than with Mercury, and the Moon, as we will see, is another important astrological factor we need to explore. The Mercury sign and aspects can certainly reflect one's degree of mental flexibility. Mercury in the mutable signs obviously likes lots of variety, while

Mercury in the fixed signs has a greater capacity for concentration. Mercury aspecting Neptune requires imaginative stimulation and expression, while Mercury aspecting Saturn is better related to facts and structures in the material world. But no Mercury problem will, in itself, make someone a psychopath.

Audience: Does a short attention span also come from a fear of intimacy, of getting too close?

Liz: Yes, that is part of it, and we are back to the Moon. But the psychopath's low boredom threshold doesn't only apply to other human beings. The mind simply will not subject itself to the discipline of sticking deeply with something. It needs to be stimulated from the outside because there is nothing inside. We are once again in the realm of narcissism. If one is empty inside, one has no inner resources, and one must find one's stimulation from the outside. Like the problem of narcissistic wounding, the problem of a short attention span is on the increase, and we should not be surprised that psychopathy, too, is on the increase. How many of you were raised watching television from your very early life? Some of you don't have your hands up. What did you do to amuse yourselves as children, if there was no television?

Audience: I read books.

Audience: I went into my imagination a lot. I played games which I made up, or I invented stories.

Liz: Exactly. You exercised your imaginative muscles, and once developed, these imaginative muscles are always available as an inner resource. Reading also exercises the imagination, because we have to come up with our own images when we read a book. Television and films provide these images ready-made, so there is no room for fantasy. If, from infancy onward, there is a screen sitting in front of you all the time which gives you all your images, thoughts and ideas, of course the capacity to generate ideas and images from within is lost. We are producing generation after generation of people who have lost the capacity to stimulate themselves mentally and imaginatively. They don't know how to do it because they have been trained to receive someone else's images. I am not suggesting that we go on a campaign to ban TV and films, but it is a question of balance. In some respects, the best thing we may get out of exploring the disturbing subject of psychopathy is what we might give to our children to help ensure that they remain connected to their inner life.

Audience: This is making me think of so many social factors. For example, we have so many mothers now who are single parents, and they can't always deal with the responsibility. So they park their children in front of the television. The rise of single motherhood is becoming a huge issue. It is not a moral issue. It is just that you have got one person who has to cope with everything, and TV and video games seem to be the way through.

Liz: Yes, there are many social factors which could be relevant, and I don't doubt that this is one of them. Many external pressures may feed into the psychopathic character structure. But we need to look at why some individuals are peculiarly receptive to these kinds of pressures. Otherwise we would all be psychopaths. Maybe we are, on one level or another. But we would be a lot more florid in exhibiting the characteristics. Exploring social factors is always useful, but in the end, even if we were capable of doing all we could do on the purely practical level, we are left with the mystery of individual character. Some individuals respond to social problems much more severely than others, and this is what we need to look at astrologically. The astrologer cannot deal with society as a whole, and even if we explore collective trends, in the end we must deal with people one by one if we want to make any kind of creative contribution through our work. It is possible that we might get a psychopath coming for a chart reading. We probably won't know it if we do, unless the cheque bounces afterward. What is much more relevant is the kind of parenting people give their children, and the client who has children is the one who may benefit most from whatever insights come out of this seminar.

Pathological lying

Number four on the clinical list is pathological lying. Lying is something that everyone does at some point in their lives. Is there anyone here who is brazen enough to say that they have never lied? No, I thought not. When we lie, why do we lie?

Audience: To protect ourselves from others.

Liz: Yes, we lie to conceal something, to protect ourselves, to get away with something. Or we are ashamed about something that we don't want others to know about.

Audience: Speaking as a parent, if your child lies, he is either afraid of you or he is four.

Liz: Yes, children of a certain age will lie for no apparent reason, because they need to feel they have the power to keep secrets. It's a form of preserving something for oneself, and expresses what Freud called the anal stage of development – the building of a sense of autonomy through holding back. Fear of authority, whether parental or educational, naturally causes many children to lie, even if there is no actual punishment waiting. "I didn't do it, *he* did!" is a favourite way out, achieving the additional bonus of implicating a sibling or classmate toward whom the child feels envy. There is also an ingenious range of excuses for unfinished schoolwork, and these are often more than mere lies: they are works of considerable creative imagination. But children know they are lying in such circumstances, and they also know why.

In the ordinary run of things, we reserve our lies for specific situations where they serve an end which we feel justifies the lie. A man lies and tells his wife he is working late at the office. The purpose of this lie is to conceal the affair he's having, so that he can continue to enjoy the extramarital sex without destroying his family life. The motive for our lying may often seem mean and selfish to outside eyes, but sometimes the purpose is more altruistic. Sometimes we lie in order to avoid hurting someone, not because we stand to gain from it. Or we lie to protect loved ones from unjust treatment at the hands of others. But whether we are being mean or noble, we lie to achieve a specific end. Pathological lying is distinguished by the fact that it serves no particular purpose. One lies because it is so much fun to dupe people. It is not delusional in the sense that the person is unable to distinguish truth from fantasy. That is something different, and it does not apply to psychopathic behaviour. The psychopath lies, not only in order to avoid getting caught but, more importantly, because there is a kick in knowing that he or she has fooled someone.

Audience: Having spent several years in the legal profession, I can tell you that most of these attributes would apply to my colleagues. They would list them on their CV rather than hide them, because these traits are highly useful in the practice of law.

Liz: I don't doubt it. I would like to mention an article on psychopathy from the American press. The article is called, "America's New Corporate Pastime: Spot the Psychopath". The writer states that psychopaths can be extremely useful in certain professions because of their manipulative capacities and their ruthlessness.

Audience: There was a review in the British papers two years ago, of senior managers in the City and in industry. The article stated that something like 70% were psychopathic, in that their behaviour fit all the clinical pictures. It wasn't necessarily that they could take tough decisions or stick to a plan. But they were very useful because they had no qualms about making as much money as possible without caring about who got damaged or ruined.

Liz: Many of the characteristics linked with psychopathy are rewarded in certain professions and spheres of society. The implications of this are very disturbing. I would like to read you another comment, relevant what you are saying. This is a quote from a psychologist writing on psychopathy: "There are psychopathic personalities in the highest echelons of society, and even within religious hierarchies in America. You can't just assume that a person with the title 'Judge' or 'Hospital Orderly' got there honestly and won't manipulate the hell out of you." Once we have gone through our list of clinical characteristics, we need to have a good, hard look at what – if anything – distinguishes the rest of us from someone who might be deemed clinically psychopathic.

The psychopath lies because it is so much fun. You can all see the power issues involved here. Covering one's tracks is obviously part of any criminal activity, and since criminal activity is often part of the psychopathic individual's lifestyle, he or she will lie in order to avoid getting caught. But these people will also lie because there is a desire to demean and humiliate others, even if the others don't realise they're being lied to. This in turn relates to the grandiose sense of self which we've already looked at, and the intractable wound that underpins it. Why should one need to feel so superior to others, unless one feels utterly small, wretched and worthless somewhere underneath?

Conning

The fifth characteristic on the list is allied to pathological lying, and it is called "conning". This word is derived from the term "confidence artist". William James, taking a little swipe at what he called the "oppressions of the purveyors of religion", once said: "'Faith', after all, is a synonym for 'trust me', and like that phrase, is the con artist's credo." Conning means the ability to seduce other people into having confidence in one's lies and scams. Successful conning utilises the weapon of charm. In the hands of the psychopath, conning is used not only for personal gain, but also for the pleasure of tricking other people and making them into fools. It is connected to a grandiose sense of self in the same way pathological lying is: other people are duped and thus one feels superior. It also provides a solution to the problem of a low boredom threshold, because conning other people keeps one occupied and makes life more interesting: "Who will be next? Can I get away with it again?" The more important the victim, the more powerful and superior the psychopath feels. Conning the police is often a favourite pastime. Conning the public is also popular. As P. T. Barnum once said, "There's a sucker born every minute."

We make it easy for psychopaths to con us, because we are very easily conned. We are conned through our emotional and spiritual longings, our material desires and our social conscience. We are conned by politicians who promise us a better world, and by advertisers who promise that we will be happier, more beautiful and more fulfilled if we buy their products. There is a school of thought, to which William James belonged, which postulates that we are also conned by religious and spiritual leaders who play on our fear of meaninglessness and death, and promise us immortality or enlightenment if we buy *their* products. We are very easily made to feel bad if we are selfish or politically incorrect, or if we are not thinking in accord with the prevailing definition of loving human behaviour. We play into the psychopath's hands in a frighteningly gullible way, and that has some uncomfortable implications. It is as though the psychopathic behaviour pattern is the dark side of our unrealistic aspirations toward individual and social perfection. The more disconnected and unreal we become as a collective in our efforts to be something other than authentic, whole individuals, the more psychopathy breeds in the darkness.

Lack of remorse

Now we have reached the most important characteristic on the list: lack of remorse. In the ordinary run of things, when we hurt someone we feel bad about it. Sometimes an act performed out of vengeance seems free of remorse, but the psychopath does not act out of vengeance – at least, not vengeance toward the individuals or groups who are injured or destroyed by his or her actions. There is often a kind of abstract or displaced vengeance at work in psychopathy, and this is suggested by some of the more famous psychopaths in history, such as Hitler. But it is a cold, dissociated sort of vengeance, which has become utterly disconnected from its personal emotional roots and is vastly out of proportion to whatever the original sense of hurt might have been.

Historians and biographers are always trying to explain Hitler's consuming hatred toward the Jews with the suggestion that he might have had some kind of painful or humiliating experience at the hands of a Jewish teacher at school, or was embarrassed by a grandparent who was part Jewish. Perhaps that's true. But a revenge which involves murdering six million people is, shall we say, somewhat over the top. When relatively stable individuals seek vengeance, it is usually a vengeance fuelled by emotional affect and proportionate to what is perceived as the "crime". Thus we hear innumerable stories about the betrayed wife who cuts her husband's suits to ribbons with a razor blade, or the jilted boyfriend who beats up his ex-lover's new man while drunk at the pub. Sometimes the individual is free of remorse after such acts – at least for a while – and there may even be a temporary sense of pride and satisfaction. But this kind of vengeance has a heart, even if it is ugly and ultimately senseless.

Usually, if we have inadvertently injured someone, or even if we have deliberately injured someone, we feel distressed afterward. Our sense of remorse may be partly rooted in an ethical code, a religious view or a set of ideals, but it also springs from our ability to identify with and feel what another person feels. Even if it is necessary to inflict hurt, there is still a feeling of reluctance, and a sense of sadness and shame afterward. But in psychopathic behaviour there is no remorse, because there is no compassion. Psychopaths are usually able to imagine themselves in another person's shoes, because they are often of above average intelligence. They can see what the world looks like from another person's perspective. They *know* what it would feel like. But they don't *feel* what it would feel like. In other words, the ability for psychological insight is present, but the feeling of empathy is not.

I would like all of you to think about this paradox, because it is not easy to grasp. We tend to think of psychopathic personalities as hard, brutish, and lacking the capacity to understand others' feelings. But they understand all too well. Let's say that we are driving somewhere very late at night, and the car breaks down. There is only one house within miles. We go to the house and knock on the door, and the door is reluctantly opened by a little old lady living on her own. We can all recognise that this lady's reluctance to open the door springs from the fact that she is isolated, frightened and very vulnerable. The psychopath can recognise this too. We might then seek to reassure her by saying very gently, "Please, may I ask you for some help? My car broke down, and I desperately need to use your phone. Here is my driving license, so you can see my name and address." The psychopath will do the same. We can put ourselves in the old lady's shoes. We know that we need to proceed carefully to assuage her fear. We all have some idea of what it might be like to be a lonely old lady disturbed by a stranger knocking at the door late at night. So does the psychopath. But the difference is that we will feel empathy for her, and the psychopath will not. While the rest of us would use the phone, thank her with genuine gratitude, and then leave, the psychopath stays, plays on her need to have human contact by engaging her in conversation, hits her over the head and steals her savings, and feels no remorse.

The ability to understand another person is often quite acute in the psychopathic personality, but there is no remorse, no empathy, no pity for the other person. It is like a missing organ. This is why psychopathy is so frightening. When we are faced with someone's anger or potential violence, we try to appeal to their sense of decency and empathy. We want to believe that even very violent people can be rehabilitated, rather than simply subjected to execution or brutal prison treatment. But rehabilitation depends on there being something at the core which can respond with remorse. How do you help someone to take emotional responsibility for what they have done when they couldn't care less? It is this blankness, this inner void, which is so terrifying. Because of the charm and the ability to lie with skill, it is often not visible in the outer personality. We don't see it because the psychopath can be so very convincing. That is why we often find these people in politics, especially when a country is weak and looking for a strong leader to restore its pride. It is not only our gullibility which opens the door to the psychopath's conning. It is also our desperate need to find someone or something outside ourselves which will redeem us.

Lack of empathy

The next characteristic on the list, lack of empathy, is closely related to lack of remorse, as I have just explained. There was actually another heading on this list called "callousness", but callousness, along with lack of remorse and lack of empathy, is part of the same package. Astrologically speaking, I believe it is a lunar package. Does anyone want to comment on that? No? As astrologers, we can see that callousness, lack of remorse and lack of empathy are all issues concerned with emotional response and the ability to identify with others' feelings. Empathy belongs to the lunar realm. Despite the importance of the Sun in narcissistic problems, we will find throughout the day that lunar disturbances, more than any other astrological factor, lie at the core of psychopathic behaviour.

Audience: How about a lack of water in the chart?

Liz: Lack of water in a birth chart describes a lack of adaptation in the feeling function, rather than an inability to empathise. The functions of consciousness do not describe our fundamental human drives. They describe how we adapt to life according to our innate strengths and weaknesses. The lack of any element doesn't mean that the person is incapable of experiencing or expressing the element. Lack of earth, for example, doesn't mean one lacks sensuality, and lack of air doesn't mean one lacks intelligence. It's often quite the opposite. But with a weak or missing element, the responses are not adapted, and are therefore unsophisticated and even archaic. Sometimes the ego tries to disconnect because of the power of that missing element, but the disconnection is never absolute. It comes and goes in an autonomous way. A lack of water can indicate tremendously strong emotional responses, and feelings of empathy can be so powerful that they sometimes seem overwhelming. But the feelings are not refined or sophisticated, and they are not within the control of the ego. They come and go as they wish, not as consciousness wishes, and they often have an inflexible, intense and rather primitive quality.

It is important to remember that the zodiac signs describe qualities of expression, not psychological motivations. Water signs do not describe our ability to feel. They describe the manner in which any planet placed in those signs is experienced and expressed. Having Mercury or Saturn in water says nothing about whether or not an individual can feel empathy. Mercury in water makes a statement about a way of processing and understanding information: it is done through the feeling *function*, rather than through abstract concepts, as is the case with air, or intuitive hunches, as is the case with fire, or observable facts, as is the case with earth. But the Moon, whatever its sign, describes a fundamental drive within us. It is a planet, not a sign. The Moon is our organ of contact with others, and the means by which we empathise with other people. That is why our experiences with mother have such a profound effect on the way the Moon is expressed later in life. Mother is our first contact with another human on an emotional level. We learn how to use, or abuse, our Moon through this primal bond.

Audience: When you say "lack of adaptation", do you mean the person doesn't know how to use the element?

Liz: Yes, that is what I mean. It is not within the control of the conscious ego. If there is lots of air in a chart, the ability to reason logically comes easily. In other words, the thinking *function* is sophisticated and is a primary means of adaptation. It is under the control of consciousness. But this says nothing about intelligence. Watery people are usually conscious of what they are feeling, although they may not always be able to articulate it on demand in a logical way. Even though they may exhibit dramatic emotions in front of the right audience, the ego is in control of the feelings – not in a rational, calculated way, but in a conscious way. Watery people use their feelings as a tool of adaptation to life. That is why they often excel at diplomacy, and also why they often do just the opposite. When the emotional situation requires anger or a rebellious stance, they will provide that, too, with the same sophisticated sense of timing. When there is a lack of water, the ego can't use the feelings; the feelings use the ego. They just erupt, and one is taken over by them. They are raw and unsophisticated.

Someone lacking air may be very brilliant, and ideas may erupt with incredible clarity and creativity. But there is often an inability to sit down and plan ahead on an ordinary day-to-day level, and perspective is sometimes lacking. I have known many watery people who are brilliant with computers, but they "feel" how to work with them rather than logically understanding them. They never read the instruction manual and can't explain the steps, although they may get superb results. The idea comes or it doesn't come, and when it does, it has a power and inflexibility that reflect its archaic nature. The same applies to a lack of water. This is a very different thing from the state which is described by this clinical list of psychopathic characteristics. You will see later, when I put up some example charts, that water, in fact, predominates in the charts of a great many psychopaths. But somehow, for some reason, the Moon isn't working. Something has gone horribly wrong with the lunar responses, and the ability to connect with another human being in an empathetic way is absent or severely impaired.

Parasitic lifestyle

This is an interesting characteristic. It is linked to the grandiose sense of self. The psychopath's attitude is: "Why should I have to work for a living like all these ordinary, boring, inferior people? Somebody else should provide for me because I'm so special. It's owed to me." There is a fundamental assumption that other people should give the psychopath whatever he wants and needs. There is no sense of self-responsibility. Partners, friends, lovers, work colleagues or the state should make everything easy – not because one lacks the skills to find a job, but because one doesn't feel one should have to. One is "entitled". Here we are back to the narcissistic personality structure. There is no wish to achieve real self-sufficiency.

Lack of self-control

Now we come to a group of characteristics which are all related, so I'll amalgamate them under the heading, "Lack of self-control". This includes characteristics such as extreme impulsiveness and the inability to tolerate frustration. This last is very important, because our capacity to tolerate frustration is a Saturn function. Mars is obviously also involved with this group of characteristics. The inability to tolerate frustration means that, for the psychopath, rage becomes a way of life. Sooner or later we all wind up in a slow queue at the bank, or our train leaves an hour late, or there are road works on the M25, or a cheque we are eagerly awaiting doesn't arrive because there is a postal strike, or it rains on the day we've invited twenty people to a barbecue in the garden. This is Sod's Law: life is full of big and little frustrations. In the main, we tend to deal with such events reasonably well, displaying nothing worse than a bit of irritability: "Oh, bloody hell, why did it have to rain today?" Then we get over it. We exhibit self-control to a greater or lesser degree, and adapt to circumstances.

But the psychopathic personality has no tolerance for frustration. If another driver cuts in front on the M25, the psychopath may display a lethal case of road rage. Rather than hooting the horn, shouting abuse and then forgetting about it, the psychopath forces the other driver off the road and slits their throat. He has no remorse at having actually killed another human being. It was merely some fool who cut in front and deserved what they got. This disproportionate rage in response to the minor frustrations of life is characteristic of psychopathic responses. The rage is enormous, and there is no self-control. There is no capacity to count to ten, no ability to say to oneself, "Why I am getting so upset? What's the big deal?" This inability to tolerate frustration, combined with the inability to control one's affects, has terrifying implications. You can see how closely connected it is with violence. You can also see how connected it is with the grandiose sense of self-importance. "Why should I have to endure these frustrations?" says the psychopath. "I am so much more important than everyone else." Ordinary people might have to stand in queues or tolerate other people's stupidity. Why should a superior being submit to such things?

Audience: But there's something deeper there.

Liz: Yes, there's something deeper. Narcissistic inflation masks a sense of utter worthlessness, emptiness and impotence. From that place, every minor frustration hammers home these terrible feelings of emptiness and powerlessness. The violent, murderous response is the psychopath's way of restoring an illusory sense of power. And there are even deeper issues related to mother, which we will explore in due course.

Lack of relatedness

This characteristic should be obvious, given what we have already seen. The psychopathic personality displays an inability to form close relationships, as these are only possible when there is a capacity for emotional empathy. What appears to be relatedness is really manipulation for narcissistic gratification. Sex is used by the psychopath as a means of manipulation, and promiscuity is usually a way of life, unless there is complete impotence – which is not uncommon. There is frequently an exaggerated emphasis on sexual technique, but this fulfils ends other than the emotional and physical gratification of either partner, and may also mask serious sexual problems. Power rather than sensual satisfaction, domination rather than sharing, cruelty rather than tenderness, and the acquisition of money or information are all served by the psychopath's short-lived "relationships". To put it simply, the psychopath exploits others sexually. If such an individual marries – which is a common enough occurrence, especially when there is a prospect of financial gain – the promiscuity continues without conscience or remorse, often involving the psychopath's own children or step-children.

Failure to accept responsibility

Like lack of remorse, this last characteristic on the list is extremely important. It is a much bigger issue than the parasitic lifestyle which requires others to pay for everything. Psychopathic behaviour, when confronted, is invariably blamed on someone else. There seems to be no capacity to say, "I committed this act by choice. I must take responsibility." Masterson says in his book, "The patient himself tends to be unaware of, as well as to deny, his behaviour." If the behaviour is acknowledged at all, its cause is always attributed to an external source. Because many psychopaths are highly intelligent, they often understand enough about psychology to present a convincing case about their actions being "caused" by parental abuse or social ills, and in a courtroom or a therapist's consulting room, this can be a highly effective piece of theatre. We collude with and believe in this kind of performance because we, too, want to believe that human destructiveness is always "caused" by external factors rather than residing in the individual's own heart and soul.

Recently we seem to have developed into a society which always seeks to blame external factors for our violence and cruelty as well as the messes we land ourselves in. If we are dumb enough to drive with a cup of hot coffee in our lap, and it spills and burns us, we sue Macdonalds rather than saying, "What a bloody stupid thing to do." We have become obsessed with lawsuits, financial compensation for every human ill, and witch-hunts to find the culpable party for every disaster that befalls us, even if our own idiocy is flagrantly the cause. We encourage a mental attitude of taking no responsibility for our mistakes. This plays into the hands of the psychopath, who is doing nothing more than voicing the general view when he claims it wasn't his fault. The psychopath aggressively fobs off responsibility on others, and this is one of the reasons why it is virtually impossible to work therapeutically with the psychopathic personality.

Any effective therapeutic process depends on the patient assuming self-responsibility. There has to be a point where he or she says, "I have contributed to my own mess. I had the freedom to choose and I chose badly. I am part of the equation, consciously or unconsciously, even if others are also involved." The psychopath never reaches this point. The blame lands on society, the police, the government, the educational establishment, parents, rich people, poor people, Christians, Jews, Muslims, Asians, whites, blacks, immigrants, gays, smokers, research laboratories, fashion magazines – anything at all that comes to hand. Like skirt lengths, the collective perception of culpability for social ills goes through cycles of fashion, and the psychopath is usually very clever at selecting whatever group, law, habit or ideology is currently in vogue to blame.

Will the real psychopath please stand up?

Now we have worked through the list, which gives you a good albeit simple clinical picture of psychopathic behaviour. Although I have suggested some deeper issues that might be at work, the clinical picture does not really touch on them. But we can make our own deductions as we go along, both psychologically and astrologically. As we have seen, there are several planets that seem to be relevant. The Sun, Saturn and Mars are obviously important, and we will deal with these later. But the Moon is clearly critical, since so many of the psychopath's issues concern lack of relatedness and the absence of empathy. If we think in terms of developmental problems and are looking for anything in the chart that suggests that a response to early suffering might move along psychopathic rather than other possible behavioural lines, we need to keep our eyes on the Moon.

Whatever conclusions we might draw from the chart, we will always be looking at a chemical mix between inherent personality and environment. This is the case with all psychological patterns. Whatever the nature of an individual's suffering or pathology, the chart, which describes inherent character, always interacts with the environment, both family and social. Are psychopaths born or made? Perhaps both. And if it is indeed both, a certain kind of early environmental experience is necessary, combined with a certain kind of temperament. The temperament may be similar to that of many other people who do not display psychopathic behaviour. But if that temperament is put together with precisely the right sort of social and parental environment, the resulting chemical mix may produce what we call psychopathy. There may be a genetic component involved. But what does that mean? What is a genetic predisposition? Is it physiological or psychological? And if it is psychological, why does current research focus solely on the physical dimension of genetic inheritance? As astrologers, we don't yet know whether the chart configurations which we associate with inherent temperament also describe genetic inheritance of a physiological and/or psychological kind. But given the way in which astrological patterns repeat in families, it is highly likely.

Audience: Does psychopathic behaviour always include all those factors on the list? Or is it a question of having three or four of the characteristics?

Liz: All the factors on the list are present in psychopathy. It is highly likely that all of us have at least one if not more of these factors in our own nature, but it is the total picture which reveals psychopathy. There is one characteristic I didn't include, which is usually part of the clinical picture: frequent breaking of the law, or violent criminal activity. I didn't include it because, although it is common in psychopathic behaviour, it is not inevitable. Otherwise, every one of the characteristics on the list is present to one degree or another. We obviously have to be careful with this clinical picture. Just because someone lacks self-control, or can't tolerate frustration, or tends to live off other people, or needs constant mental stimulation, or lacks empathy for certain kinds of people, it doesn't make them a psychopath. Lots of people with a fiery Mars aspecting Uranus can't tolerate frustration, and lots of people with hard Sun-Neptune aspects adopt a parasitic lifestyle. Mercury-Jupiter people may have trouble concentrating, and Venus-Saturn people can be highly selective in their empathy. These configurations simply describe character qualities which can be expressed on many levels, positive or negative. They are not, in themselves, indicators of psychopathy.

The clinical picture is based on the experiences of therapists and psychiatrists working with psychopaths over a long period of time, during which all the characteristics become visible. A brief encounter with a psychopathic personality may not reveal all of them. As I said, most if not all people display one or more of the characteristics on the list. Can we therefore call someone a "partial" psychopath? When we read the clinical descriptions, it might seem as if there is a creature called a psychopath who is different from everyone else because they display these components while the rest of us are "normal". Is there anyone here today who can claim never to have exhibited any of the characteristics on the list?

Psychopathy and the infant personality

Audience: All of those traits can be displayed by a child in a "hot spot". In a difficult situation, children lie through their teeth. They hit people and then they say, "It was your fault. I'm not sorry."

Liz: Most, if not all, of the characteristics on the list could describe the infant personality. Even promiscuity has its infant equivalent in what Freud called "polymorphous perverse" – receptivity to sensual pleasure whatever the source. But when the infant personality remains infantile while the body and persona grow up, something rather more sinister is heralded. The most important difference, which we will explore in more depth later, is the psychopath's wish to destroy, which is cold and without affect. Children, when they become destructive, do it with heat. They get furious, and they want to kill their little brother because Daddy loves him best, or they want to hurt Mummy badly because she won't allow an extra portion of ice cream. The emotions are certainly violent and often cruel, and sometimes the behaviour is, too. But the chilling lack of affect in the psychopath reflects a predator's mentality, not a child's.

Audience: I teach children, and I know I have taught some psychopathic children, one of whom takes pleasure in coldly destroying. It is quite scary to be around.

Liz: At the moment, as I mentioned, we are having to contemplate the freeing of the two boys who coldly murdered Jamie Bulger. We are staring something in the face that we do not wish to look at. A statement is being made about all of us and the world which we are creating, and we would prefer to either look the other way or resort to violent emotional responses which help no one. As I said, all the characteristics on this list describe elements which may appear in anyone. And most of them are typical of children's behaviour when the child is under stress.

Audience: Another thing about children: the ones who exhibit the most difficult behaviour are parented by people who don't feel that the child is bad. The mother feels guilty, so the child is massively indulged and is not allowed to be disciplined. The mother believes that she is bad, not the child.

Liz: I would like to go into this more deeply later. Perhaps you could raise these points then. Now I would like to start exploring the birth chart in relation to psychopathy, and work on some examples. As we examine issues of bonding and the attitude of the mother toward the child, we are going to see some very interesting patterns coming up. As I mentioned earlier, the Moon seems to play a critical role in the charts of psychopaths. This is connected with lack of empathy and the inability to relate to others. Many people display an ability to dissociate from their feelings. That does not make them psychopaths, although dissociation is a fundamental characteristic of psychopathy. It may be a question of degree, and whether one can "re-associate" after dissociating, or whether we are looking at a permanent state of dissociation, which seems to be the case in psychopathy. Clinical studies indicate that there appear to be two underlying triggers for dissociation, which may appear individually or together in the psychopathic personality: fear of engulfment and fear of abandonment. Both of these are obviously lunar issues, and I would like you to keep these in mind as we begin to explore the astrological pictures.

Was he or wasn't he: the "Oklahoma Bomber"

Let's look at our first example chart. It might have been better to look at this chart anonymously, so that you couldn't immediately say, "Of course he did all those terrible things. You can see he's a psychopath from the retrograde Moon." But the fact that I have brought the chart to this particular seminar immediately tells you the person might be psychopathic, so there is no point in hiding his identity. Of course, I could fool you and put up Tony Blair's chart without a name, and until you realised who it was, you might find all kinds of psychopathic signatures in it. Never mind. What kind of feeling do you get from this chart?

Audience: It isn't Tony Blair, is it?

Liz: No. But they're both Taureans with Venus in Aries. Make of that what you will.

Audience: There's a lot of infantile frustration, with all those Aries planets.

Liz: Do you mean that everyone with Aries planets suffers infantile frustration? Try phrasing that again.

Timothy McVeigh
23 April 1968, 5.24 am, Pendleton, New York

Audience: It's the combination of Chiron and Saturn acting as a dampener on the Aries impulsiveness.

Liz: Yes, his sense of personal potency might be impaired, which is suggested by both Chiron and Saturn in Aries. And they are all hidden away in the 12th house, and Venus in Aries is inhibited by its conjunction with Saturn. Look at the aspects to this conjunction. Venus and Saturn are both trine Jupiter, which is in Leo in the 5th.

Audience: That would make it really combustible.

Liz: Why combustible? Once again, think about how you phrase your interpretations. If this seminar were on the subject of the artist, you wouldn't think in terms of psychopathy. You would say, "Oh, look at those lovely trines to the 5th house Jupiter. What a lot of creative inspiration!" Be very careful. Hindsight is a great hindrance as well as a great help to astrological interpretation. I once put up the Pope's chart during a seminar, and we were discussing his Mercury-Neptune square. Someone in the group who wasn't overly fond of the Catholic Church said, "Oh, it's obvious from that Mercury-Neptune that he's a liar." Now, if I had put up Proust's or Goethe's chart and you saw Mercury square Neptune, you would probably say, "What a wonderful imagination!" Or if you saw it in Dane Rudyhar's chart, you might say, "What fine intuition and spiritual perception!" All these things, of course, may be true about all these people, but they are all colours in a spectrum, and we don't know which part of the spectrum will be expressed through the individual personality.

The compensation of inflation

Jupiter in the 5th in Leo trine an exact Venus-Saturn conjunction in Aries looks bad to you because you know that it's Timothy McVeigh's configuration. Try to view the configuration more objectively. What does Venus-Saturn say to you?

Audience: Very low self-esteem.

Liz: Yes, there is some very deep isolation and hurt here – a feeling of having no value and no capacity to find self-value, because his sense of impotence is too great. This exact Venus-Saturn conjunction is in the 12th, the house of the ancestors. The pattern of isolation, inhibition of affection and conditional or limited love has probably been at work in the family psyche for many generations.

Audience: So the trines to Jupiter might make it easier to escape the loneliness and self-denigration by having fantasies about his great importance.

Liz: Yes, exactly. That might also be true of an artist with this configuration, and it might fuel the artist's creative work. It might lead to an inflated sense of self-importance in any person, psychopathic or not, because Jupiter is the only outlet for the pain of the Venus-Saturn conjunction. If McVeigh had been able to find a creative vehicle, we could speculate that things might have been different. But creative endeavour requires an ego, and there seems to be some difficulty here in building a strong ego. The Sun is right on the Ascendant, and the need to make an impact on the world is very powerful, but apart from the conjunction to Mercury, the Sun makes no aspects except a trine to Jupiter. Jupiter is like the tap through which all the currents of the 12th house flow. And it is exactly square Neptune, within 4' of arc. Inflation – a grandiose sense of self – is certainly implied. That alone does not make a psychopath, but it is one of the ingredients in the recipe.

Audience: So it would be easy for him to convince himself that he was completely justified in what he did.

Liz: It would be easy for him to imagine himself as a kind of messiah. Trines are lovely aspects, but they do make things too easy at times, and they are not conducive to the struggle required for real ego-consciousness. McVeigh had a natural ability to self-mythologise. Now, that's fine if there is an ego that can utilise the fantasy world creatively and keep a sense of humour about it at the same time. But if there is a severely damaged sense of self, then the gift of self-mythologising, the gift of seeing oneself as a hero in a grand cosmic drama, will be used to compensate for the feeling of having no value. This configuration doesn't tell us that McVeigh is a psychopath. But it tells us he had a problem with self-aggrandisement, fuelled by a low sense of self-worth.

Audience: The Jupiter-Neptune square may have made it easy for him to delude himself.

Liz: Jupiter-Neptune has a great range of expressions. It is often associated with a propensity for mysticism. It can be rather gullible and overly redemption-minded: the individual believes in miracles, and may either attempt to be a saviour or go around looking for a saviour. Jupiter-Neptune can work very positively in an individual who seeks some kind of transcendent reality to which they can offer themselves. It reflects a devotional quality and a need to serve a higher unifying principle. In itself, it is not a negative aspect. Like all aspects, it is neutral, and everything depends on whether there is a well-grounded ego. If the ego is weak and the emotional responses are distorted, Jupiter-Neptune may produce a messianic element which, combined with other factors, can be very problematic and even dangerous, to oneself or to others.

The Uranus-Pluto generation

Audience: With the Moon in the 12th in Pisces opposite Uranus-Pluto in the 6th in Virgo, I don't think the mother cuddled this baby. He would be very vulnerable and need a lot of cuddling, contact and touching. I sense this baby was never touched.

Liz: The lunar oppositions to Uranus and Pluto are certainly relevant. Remember the two "triggers" for dissociation that I mentioned earlier: fear of abandonment and fear of engulfment. Here we can see the signature of both. As a baby, McVeigh may well have been ignored much of the time, or if he was held and cuddled, there may have been some powerful emotional undercurrents which made it feel dangerous or "unclean". But before we explore these lunar aspects psychologically, do remember that they are not uncommon. I am sure there are many of you here today who were born into this 1960s Uranus-Pluto generation group, with the Moon making a hard aspect to the conjunction. We cannot assume that every person born with the Moon in hard aspect to Uranus-Pluto was never touched, let alone that they are psychopaths.

What we can say is that McVeigh's experience of safety and consistent emotional contact in early life was probably unstable. There could be many reasons for this which the chart does not tell us, and instability in the early environment, as described by the Moon opposite Uranus-Pluto, can be caused by the mother's illness or financial anxieties rather than a lack of love or physical affection. Or the affection may be intermittent rather than consistent, or overly intense but alternating with times of coldness and lack of contact. The psychiatrist John Bowlby, in an essay called "The Nature of the Child's Tie to His Mother" which was published in 1958 in the *International Journal of Psychiatry*, talks about the responses of children removed from their mothers – physically or psychologically – during the early separation stage of development, at only a few months old. He describes three stages: protest and the wish for reunion with the mother; despair; and finally, detachment or dissociation if the mother is not "restored". In other words, after a certain level of deprivation, the child removes all emotional investment from the object, and this sets the pattern for all future relationships, which are devoid of any real relatedness.

Obviously the deprivation must be severe, and the chart alone cannot tell us how severe it was. And the basic character must also be one which cannot cope well with this kind of experience. A child with Moon in Cancer or Pisces will cope less well with separation than a child with Moon in Capricorn or Aquarius. Remember that we are looking for a particular chemical mix. Let's go back to our astrological basics. What kind of person is described by Sun in Taurus and Moon in Pisces? As one of you has pointed out, McVeigh must have been a very tactile child who needed a lot of physical affection and closeness. That is his basic temperament, based on the Sun-Moon combination: a sensuous, affectionate, emotionally needy and receptive child. With Moon in the 12th in Pisces, he must also have been a highly imaginative child, very "porous" and open to the collective psyche. What does it mean if someone is open to the collective psyche? Would you say that is a positive or a negative thing?

Audience: If they can't mediate those energies, then it would be negative, because the ego would be overwhelmed. If they could mediate them, it would be very creative.

Liz: Yes, the key lies with the formation of a solid ego. The individual needs to be able to consciously mediate collective energies, and that means having a childhood environment where enough support is given to the development of the ego. The Uranus-Pluto conjunction marks a whole generation group, doesn't it? Everyone born during the 1960s feels its pressure, although it is stronger in those who have the Sun or Moon aspecting the conjunction. Uranus and Pluto are a rather anarchistic combination, reflecting an urgent need for change, renewal, cleaning up the environment and transforming world consciousness. During the 1960s the world erupted in social, political and spiritual movements that were fuelled by a spirit of revolution. The children born during the 1960s have a feeling of urgency inside them, and a very strong sense of the importance of doing something to transform the world. They can't avoid being involved in some way. That in itself is not a negative thing, although it does produce a tremendous awareness of the collective, which not every generation group possesses. The "nimbies"[4] of the world are not very interested in the state of the collective, as long as their family, their village, their community is safe. But the Uranus-Pluto generation, especially if the Sun or Moon is connected, can't forget about the state of the world. They are carrying a collective revolution inside them. The mother may be experienced as the focus of danger and instability, but she is carrying something for the whole of the society around her.

The role of the Moon in psychopathy

Are you familiar with Winnicott's description of the mother who is alternatively too possessive and then too detached?[5] This aptly fits Moon opposite Uranus-Pluto. The child is first smothered and then abandoned, and then smothered and then abandoned again. This is not necessarily because the mother is "bad" or unloving. It may be due to circumstances or her own insecurity. And we also need to remember that this configuration describes something within the child: an inherent tendency to alternate between extreme neediness and extreme independence. But it is experienced first through the mother, and the

---

[4] For those unfamiliar with this term, "nimby" is the abbreviation for "not in *my* back yard".

[5] See D. W. Winnicott, *Playing and Reality*, Penguin Books, 1974.

child feels repeatedly swallowed up and repudiated: engulfed and then abandoned. This creates enormous anxiety, aggravated by the tension occurring in the collective. If there is "good enough" bonding with the mother, such a pattern may, at worst, generate cyclical anxiety states and various kinds of relationship problems. But it does not "cause" psychopathy. However, it is likely that McVeigh's early bonding was severely disrupted or non-existent. In such a case, the chemical mix can become lethal. From this picture, you can begin to get a sense of the nature of this man's inner landscape. There was nowhere safe, nowhere to hide, nowhere to go, and eventually that extreme anxiety – combined with the resentful isolation of Venus-Saturn, the frustration of Saturn and Chiron in Aries, the inflation fantasies of Jupiter in Leo, the sense of impotence of Mars-Neptune, and the reformist zeal of his Uranus-Pluto generation group – led to the flowering of a callous and enraged terrorist.

Timothy McVeigh, the "Oklahoma Bomber", was just executed in the USA. To the very end, he expressed no remorse. He remained totally convinced that he had done the right thing. It didn't matter how many times he was reminded of the number of children whom he had murdered. He believed that he had a mission. His enemy was the American government. Now, disliking the American government doesn't mean a person is psychopathic. It may even reflect a high degree of sanity and intelligence. In any event, McVeigh saw the American government as a monster, and he felt the need to make a big statement which involved killing a great many innocent people. No doubt he would have gone on with his bombing campaign if he had not been caught. In keeping with the clinical description of psychopathic behaviour, he exhibited absolutely no feelings of regret or remorse of any kind.

Was he a psychopath? Possibly. But we cannot be certain whether this label is appropriate, and we have a lot of ingredients to sift through here. One of the most important ingredients is that McVeigh was a vessel for the collective in which he lived. We are all part of the collective, but some individuals are more open to it than others. This man was not only damaged; he was open to collective forces around and within him which he acted out as a personal mission. Why him? Why not someone else? This is where we have to consider factors such as the exact Venus-Saturn conjunction, the exact Jupiter-Neptune square, and the opposition between Mars and Neptune. Mars is in the 1st house and is the dispositor of the three Aries planets, yet it is in detriment in Taurus and it forms a T-cross with Jupiter and Neptune. It makes apparently benign trines to the Uranus-Pluto conjunction, so it can act only through that outer planet conjunction rather than through personal desire. In other words, McVeigh can only express personal anger by adopting a collective cause which seems to justify it. Remember some of the things on our list which are linked with Mars, such as the inability to tolerate frustration, and the impulsive, even violent behaviour when thwarted or frustrated.

Once again, these are aspects which occur in many birth charts. None are, in themselves, psychopathic significators. With hindsight, we can say, "Of course he feels impotent, with Mars opposite Neptune. That combines with the impatience and irritability of Mars square Jupiter and the self-will of Mars trine Uranus-Pluto. And with Venus conjunct Saturn, he feels no one loves him." And so on. When we add all these factors together, it certainly starts looking a bit funny. But it is only with hindsight that we can do that. And however revealing McVeigh's chart might be, we need to see a selection of charts before we can form any sort of picture. Something in the psychopathic personality dissociates from feeling, and the Moon is connected with this in some way. Now we need to ask whether it is possible to see a propensity for this kind of absolute dissociation in a birth chart. Emotional distancing, when conscious, gives detachment, and that is not a negative thing. Detachment is a very valuable capacity, in the right place at the right time. But when taken to extremes, it can become permanent dissociation or, as Bowlby puts it, a permanent incapacity for emotional relatedness. What would we look for astrologically?

The Moon and Neptune

Audience: The Moon aspecting the outer planets.

Liz: That covers a lot of people. Any outer planet?

Audience: Well, Uranus and Pluto.

Liz: The Moon describes our ability to make feeling contact, to empathise, to identify emotionally with others. Think about what is likely to happen if that "organ" of relating to others is put under extreme pressure. How do you react when you are really cornered emotionally, or threatened with an extremely painful experience such as rejection, abandonment or the death of someone you love? Every human being has their own individual means of coping with this kind of stress, and each person's Moon will respond differently according to its house, sign and aspects. We can learn a lot about any planet in the chart by considering how that planet will respond if the person is in a situation where the planet is threatened or its needs cannot be met. For example, we all have Mars in the chart. If someone attacks us, our reaction will be described by our Mars, because Mars is the fighter, the defender who mobilises to ensure our survival. The Mars house, sign and aspects will say something about how we meet attack. If Mars is in Aries opposite Pluto, it will react very differently from Mars in Pisces square Neptune. McVeigh has the Moon in Pisces in the 12th, trine Neptune and opposite Uranus and Pluto. What happens if this Moon's emotional requirements are blocked, injured or threatened?

Audience: It would dissociate.

Liz: Moon opposite Uranus tends to disconnect when under stress, and we will look at this in a few minutes. But it is not the only lunar aspect in this chart. We need to think in terms of a combination of responses, rather than only one, in order to make any sense of McVeigh's emotional landscape. Moon opposite Pluto doesn't dissociate, nor does Moon in Pisces in the 12th trine Neptune. A Neptunian Moon – and here the Neptunian theme is stated three times, by sign, house and aspect – is more likely to create a fantasy world as an alternative reality. That is why it is often linked with creative talent. Also, a Piscean Moon readily adopts the posture of the victim. Some people, when they are hurt, get really pissed off and strike back. Moon in Aries does this, and so does Moon in Scorpio, although it may seethe for a while first. But Moon in Pisces is more likely to say, "Of course I got hurt. Everyone is always hurting me. It's just my lot in life." Passivity and victimisation come naturally to an injured Piscean Moon, especially if it's trine Neptune.

Audience: Would Moon in Pisces also say, "It's not my fault, somebody else is to blame"?

Liz: Yes, that can also be characteristic of a Piscean Moon. It is another expression of the victim's pattern. Culpability lies either in one's own utter worthlessness or in the cruelty of others, but there is often little sense of real responsibility based on freedom of choice. Nevertheless, Moon in Pisces does not tend to dissociate. We need to look at the way in which the other aspects – Moon-Uranus and Moon-Pluto – combine with that Neptunian Moon if we want to understand McVeigh's dissociation. His Piscean propensities are part of who he was, and this Moon may have made him fear being engulfed by his emotional needs. It may also be connected to his messianic propensities: he identified with all those he felt to be, like himself, victims of a brutal government, and believed he was acting on their behalf. The sense of dependent helplessness, and the fear of being swallowed up in a sea of collective emotions, are important elements in McVeigh's psychology, and it is possible that the dissociating tendencies of Moon-Uranus were invoked as a defence against being engulfed.

The Moon and Uranus

Moon-Uranus does not "make" a person psychopathic. But it does suggest a tendency to disconnect when the feeling nature is put under extreme pressure. As I have said, the ability to disconnect can be extremely positive if it is conscious. People with Moon-Uranus who are hurt in early life look to a Uranian world to understand why they have been hurt. They want to disengage from personal feelings of injury and achieve a glimpse of a larger system in operation, so that they can put their own unhappiness in a context that makes the hurt not only bearable but also comprehensible. This is the creative potential of Moon-Uranus: to look for a universal system of ideas in order to stop pain from being overwhelming, and to acquire a larger or more inclusive world-view in which human suffering makes some kind of sense. A Moon-Uranus individual will try to place personal suffering within the context of a broader system.

At this end of the Moon-Uranus spectrum we find many sociologists, physicians, psychologists and astrologers, and also those involved in humanitarian causes. Although this expression of Moon-Uranus detaches, the dissociation is usually neither absolute nor permanent. At the other end of the spectrum, however, is the person who disconnects from any sense of empathy or emotional identification with others, yet who forever blames "the system" for its cold brutality. This is a form of projection, as McVeigh himself displayed the very qualities he hated about the government. Dissociation can become the primary means of self-defence in such a case, and it may be permanent and absolute. We cannot know from the chart alone whether Moon-Uranus will go in a creative direction or a destructive one, or a mixture of the two. Does the aspect describe someone who, when they are under extreme emotional pressure, simply must have breathing space and distancing in order to cope? That is common enough. But in Timothy McVeigh, the distancing seems to have been total and irrevocable.

The Moon and Pluto

Now, what does Moon-Pluto do when subjected to intolerable pressure and pain?

Audience: It destroys.

Liz: Everything is a survival struggle for Moon-Pluto people, and life is experienced as very dangerous even at the best of times. Moon-Pluto is acutely aware of death in the midst of life, and of inevitable endings as well as new beginnings. The emotional responses are intense, and it is quite impossible to react in a bland or superficial way to anything which is experienced as hurtful or a threat. That can be very creative if it is found in someone who can utilise this perception of the underworld of life through a creative medium. It can make a wonderful psychotherapist or healer, or a superb actor, artist or writer who brings depth, blood and passion into their creative work. That is the positive end of the Moon-Pluto spectrum.

Audience: My friend is doing a PhD on the psychology of prison inmates, and she has Moon conjunct Pluto on the Descendant. It works really well for her in that way.

Liz: Moon-Pluto is an instinctive psychologist. From the very beginning of life, there is a sensitivity to that which is not seen or spoken. The invisible world is first perceived within the family, and Moon-Pluto children are always aware of the unconscious dynamics in the family background. It is a great mistake for parents to try to deceive Moon-Pluto children about the real state of things, because lies are experienced as life-threatening betrayals. The negative extreme of Moon-Pluto is paranoia. Life is so full of danger that the only option is to strike first, before one is struck down. Grievances are accumulated and carefully nursed, and vengeance may seem the only way to release the pressure.

As with all aspects, we cannot tell from the chart alone whether Moon-Pluto aspects will be expressed positively, negatively, or both. But we can assume that this aspect gave McVeigh a particular aptitude, not only for sensing all the darkness going on in the world around him, but also for nursing his grievances and plotting revenge. But he also seems to have used the dissociating tendencies of Moon-Uranus to fend off feelings which threatened to overwhelm him, so he could experience neither compassion nor remorse. Uranus evidently offered a kind of salvation, allowing him to survive the overwhelming paranoia of Moon-Pluto and the overwhelming neediness of Moon-Neptune by simply not feeling them. Hopefully you will all have noticed that this chart does not lack water. But it does lack air; there are no planets in the airy signs. Without air, the capacity for objective thinking comes with difficulty. Ideas strike with the force of a thunderbolt, but they are collective ideas, not processed through an adapted thinking function. It is as though Uranus has risen up and taken over, offering salvation through blind adherence to an ideology, and completely cutting off the flow of feeling.

Audience: There is a Moon-Mars sextile.

Liz: Yes, the Moon is at 16° 35′ Pisces, and Mars is at 19° 13′ Taurus. And?

Audience: Mars is the only personal planet linked to the Moon, isn't it? The other aspects are all from outer planets.

Liz: Yes, the sextile to Mars is the Moon's only major personal planetary contact. And?

Audience: Moon sextile Mars is usually a very helpful aspect. It's physically strong, energetic and dynamic.

Liz: McVeigh was not lacking in physical energy and stamina. And the aspect was indeed helpful, but not in a way we would understand as positive. This energetic aspect seems to have enabled him to act out the outer planet energies in a direct physical way. But rather than serving the ego, Mars served McVeigh's destructiveness. Lots of people experience violent feelings, but they either cannot or will not turn such feelings into physical acts. McVeigh did.

Audience: If McVeigh's violence hadn't erupted in the way it did, and he had become, say, a powerful politician or a high-ranking soldier, would he have been considered a psychopath?

Liz: Probably not. But he may well have been one nevertheless.

Audience: Is it fair to pose that question?

Liz: Yes, it's fair to pose it. I touched on this issue at the beginning of the seminar. Different cultural norms and different periods in any culture reshape how we define psychopathy. During times of war, psychopathic behaviour is given licence, and gratuitous acts of rape, murder and cruelty often proliferate without censure. Such people may appear as heroes within the context of battle, and one could even say that special forces such as the SAS are full of socially sanctioned psychopaths who are given a useful job to do. There may also be such a thing as mass psychopathy. A whole collective can suddenly tip into behaviour which is utterly ruthless and devoid of remorse, and the psychopath can then appear to be the norm. It has been suggested that Hitler's *côterie* was just such a group, elevated to power and defining psychopathic behaviour as the new social norm.

Could McVeigh have become a high-ranking soldier? Probably not. His identification was not with the strong; it was with the weak, and he had a bit of a problem with authority figures. Now, if we were all Irish Republican sympathisers and McVeigh was a terrorist in the Real IRA, would we call him a psychopath? Of course not. He would be a hero. The politically correct term is "freedom fighter". If we were all Palestinians and he was a suicide bomber in Israel, we would see him as a great martyr. But if we were all Israelis, we would see him as a vicious psychopathic terrorist. How we judge him depends on our cultural background. But the fact remains that he murdered a lot of people, including children, who had no connection whatsoever with his life or his political ideals, and he felt no remorse at all. Whether he was socially or militarily sanctioned is irrelevant. He would still be a good candidate for psychopathy.

Audience: Do you know anything about his childhood?

Audience: He was bullied a lot as a child, and he finally tried to change from being a victim by joining the army. I suppose the Moon-Mars sextile came out there. He was very competitive and aggressive. But he couldn't take the discipline or the authority, and he was thrown out.

Liz: The need to excel is very strong in this chart, with all the planets in Aries and the rising Mars. It is exacerbated by Saturn and Chiron in Aries, because of the innate propensity to feel insecure about one's potency. The reason I am using this chart as a possible example of psychopathy is not that McVeigh did something lots of other people haven't done when it has been sanctioned in times of war. It's that he felt no remorse. There are individuals who feel that it is necessary to make this kind of social and political statement, but afterward they suffer inwardly for it. McVeigh didn't.

Lack of self

Audience: Is there any way to tell what would give him the sense of a real self at the centre?

Liz: This is a very important question. Why does someone fail to develop a sense of self, and is it possible to do anything to heal such damage? We can't look at the chart and say, "It's because he has Venus conjunct Saturn," or, "It must be due to his Moon-Uranus-Pluto configuration." McVeigh's lack of a sense of self may be connected with a certain kind of early environment, combined with aspects like the Venus-Saturn conjunction and the Moon-Uranus-Pluto configuration. It is not one or the other; it's a particular combination, a particular chemical mix. This is the case with every human being. Essential character – which may include hereditary factors – combines with environment to produce a unique individual. Those who believe in reincarnation might also throw the ingredient of past lives into the cooking pot, but we cannot be certain that this ingredient, if it does indeed exist, is in any way revealed in the birth chart. The ingredients connected with early environment might be amenable to therapeutic intervention. The ingredients connected with essential character, although they can be expressed in different ways and on different levels, cannot become anything other than what they are. But the chemical mix can mitigate against the wish, or the capacity, to change in any way. Usually narcissism is linked with severe disturbance in the early bonding with the mother, combined with a beleaguered Sun and Moon in the birth chart. It is these factors in combination which suggest difficulty in forming a strong enough ego-container.

Audience: I saw a television programme about McVeigh recently. He was being interviewed, and he told the interviewer he was depressed.

Liz: So are most of us, at one time or another. As I mentioned earlier, psychopaths can become very depressed if they are cornered and cannot manipulate their way out of the bind. Being in prison with an imminent death sentence does, I suppose, constitute being cornered.

Audience: The fact that he was victimised as a child must have contributed to what he became.

Liz: Being victimised and powerless to do anything about it is certainly an important environmental factor. So is being subjected to parental abuse, physically or emotionally. But these environmental factors are not stated explicitly in the chart. The chart describes whether McVeigh is likely to *feel* bullied, impotent and abused, and how he would respond to such treatment. Problematic lunar aspects usually reflect both the individual's emotional responses and an objective picture of the environment. But we don't know on what level that objective picture will be enacted. Moon-Pluto could reflect a strong, insightful mother who expressed intense feelings and passions in an honest way. It could reflect a manipulative, destructive mother who needed to maintain absolute power over her child. It could reflect a loving, affectionate mother who was deeply depressed because of family finances, chronic illness, the loss of a loved one or an unhappy marriage. We cannot tell from the chart alone. We only know that McVeigh would experience the archetypal patterns associated with Pluto through his mother, and respond to them in a Plutonian way. The same applies to Moon-Uranus and Moon-Neptune.

Audience: So even if he had a "good enough" mother, because of these aspects he would have felt engulfed and abandoned, and he would have harboured a grudge.

Liz: Probably. But he might not have become a psychopath. Lots of people have this kind of psychological picture, and they act it out within relatively stable and more or less loving relationships, through common or garden variety tantrums, manipulation, power battles, intense jealousy, and spiteful "punishing" tactics when they feel aggrieved. All that may be unattractive, but it's very human. I know it's sometimes difficult to see these distinctions, but it's important that we try. Moon-Pluto children are always sensitive to any unspoken threat in the environment, because they are receptive to all the deeper, darker levels of life. Because their own emotions are so frighteningly powerful, they often project them, and they easily feel engulfed by a possessive or emotionally demanding parent. But what is an "emotionally demanding" parent? And whose emotional demands are being described? The mother's or the child's? It's McVeigh's Moon-Pluto, after all, and not his mother's. He may have been sensitive to his mother's propensity for possessiveness because of his own possessiveness of her. He may have felt sexually invaded or abused because of his own precociously incestuous longings.

I have great respect for the psychological school of "object relations", to which people like Bowlby have contributed so much, because this approach can give us an excellent theoretical model for understanding severe borderline and psychopathic conditions.[6] But astrology is telling us something more. It tells us that the engulfing mother described by Moon-Pluto is also a quality within the child, perhaps shared with but not "caused" by the mother. Recognising this can help any individual to begin to take responsibility and make something more creative out of the usual Moon-Pluto cycle of resentment and depression. But if the actual mother – not the one portrayed in the chart – behaves like the worst form of Pluto, then environmental wounding exacerbates the fears of Moon-Pluto and fixes them in concrete. If the wounding is extreme, the results can be highly destructive.

If the parents cannot engage emotionally, the child with Venus-Saturn learns to devalue feelings, particularly his or her own. If the parents are liars, the child with Mercury-Jupiter or Mercury-Neptune learns to lie too, and devalues the importance of truth in human exchange. If the parents really couldn't care less, then why should the child with Moon-Uranus learn to care? What we internalise from the environment in early life glues itself to our chart configurations and puts flesh on their bones, and sometimes that flesh is corrupt, although the bones themselves are not. On this theme, I'd like to call your attention to a book called *People of the Lie,* by M. Scott Peck.[7] He does get heavily religious sometimes, which can be rather irritating, but if you ignore that side of it, I would recommend that you read this book. He is

---

[6] See John Bowlby, *Attachment,* Basic Books, 2000; *The Making and Breaking of Affectional Bonds,* Routledge, 1979; *Loss: Sadness and Depression,* Basic Books, 2000.
[7] M. Scott Peck, *People of the Lie*, Simon & Schuster, New York, 1983.

not addressing the issue of psychopathy *per se*; he is addressing the issue of evil, which may come to the same thing, and which is usually a taboo subject in psychiatric circles.

The dilemma of evil

Scott Peck's main thesis is that, in our efforts to be compassionate and fair in rehabilitating people who commit anti-social crimes or display psychopathic behaviour patterns, we have convinced ourselves that they are basically decent people who have been distorted by impersonal social forces such as poverty and oppression. Scott Peck is not interested in such sociological justifications, but talks about what he calls "the lie". He points straight at the family background, although he makes it clear that parents are the products of *their* parents and cannot be held responsible for the creation of a pattern which has existed in the family psyche for many generations. He is concerned with the subtle, unnoticed, incident-by-incident everyday refusals of mothers and fathers to deal with challenging life situations with genuine integrity. This gradually corrodes the inner integrity of the child and mobilises the child's own worst inherent characteristics. He cites examples of children who have been brought up by parents who fundamentally cheat with life. They inflict a bit of humiliation here or tell a bit of a lie there. They take the easy route – which may sometimes be the collectively sanctioned route – rather than struggling with their own conscience, their own inner values, their own ideals and their own emotional conflicts. It is like a slippery slope, and the child grows up without any solid image of goodness to internalise because the image always conveys a double message.

Here is the mother who tacitly says to her daughter, "I love you and want you to be happy, but I'm going to humiliate you because you're young and lovely and I'm getting old and undesirable. So I'll put the knife in." This may bounce off a Venus-Jupiter child, but it can have lifelong and devastating consequences in a child with Venus-Saturn. Here is the father who tacitly says to his son, "I love you, but you make me feel inadequate, so I'm going to cut you down to size." This may bounce off the Sun-Jupiter child, but it can deeply damage the child with Sun-Chiron. Here is the father who tells his son, "Never cheat with money!" while he is doing a bit of creative accounting at the office and nicking the odd five-pound note from his wife's handbag. This may bounce off most children, but it can seriously undermine the child with Sun-Neptune. Do any of you remember a film starring Donald Sutherland, called *Ordinary People*? It is an excellent example of subtle humilation inflicted on a child, not because the mother is "evil" in the grand, cosmic sense, but because she is mean-spirited and cowardly and won't face her own emotional conflicts. When this happens, the child is thrown into confusion. There is no sense of standards or limits, and no solid ground to internalise as an ego-model.

This kind of early environment, if someone has an inherently low frustration threshold as described by particular aspects to Mars, will breed trouble later. An ebullient Mars needs discipline. Mars-Jupiter and Mars-Uranus children need to be shown where their limits are. They will push at the limits all the time because they are very high-spirited. If the limits are like chocolate mousse and the boundaries keep shifting because the parents are too comfort-loving to put up with the odd tantrum, or the efforts at discipline alternate between sogginess and brutality, the child can never discover his or her own limits. At one moment the child gets beaten for doing something which, half an hour later, earns the reward of a plate of chips. How can he or she ever hope to develop a sense of self-control? Scott Peck unashamedly calls all these acts of parental cowardice evil, and all the little evils eventually coagulate, over a few generations, to produce some really big evils.

Audience: That's putting a lot of responsibility on parents. What about the inherent temperament?

Liz: Scott Peck's argument does not contradict the issue of inherent temperament. He is simply pointing out that parents also have an inherent temperament which they must deal with honestly. But he makes it clear that we have a very great responsibility if we elect to have children. How the parents develop their inherent temperament provides the model for how the child develops his or her inherent temperament. It is not a question of parents writing on a blank slate and "causing" psychopathy. It is a question of providing a model of how to live with integrity, which can help to offset even the most difficult of natal chart configurations. All parents make mistakes, and many are not very good at parenting even with the best of intentions. Some are truly awful. Not all these awful parents produce psychopaths. But psychopaths do tend to have truly awful parents – as Masterson points out, one or both parents are usually psychopaths themselves – and the child cannot find a way to cope with the destructive elements in his or her own nature.

Audience: I do believe there is a need in everyone, even the psychopath, to identify with something good.

Liz: I would also like to believe that there is something in each individual, somewhere deep inside, that seeks goodness. And I would like to believe that, given enough time and help, the most monstrous early wounds can be at least partially healed. But I am not sure whether this is possible in adulthood, if there is nothing good with which to identify in those formative early months and the chart configurations *in toto* are predisposed to a psychopathic pattern. Once the pattern has ossified, I don't know how much room there is to manoeuvre, especially when a deliberate choice has been made to refuse help. Sometimes real healing occurs. But we don't know whether such examples of genuine rehabilitation are psychopaths. We can all speculate on how different history might have been if Adolf Hitler had gone into therapy when he was twelve. We might like to believe that his childhood wounds could have been healed and he would have grown up to be a nice man who designed some attractive buildings. But are you sure? I'm not. I don't know whether Mars conjunct Venus in Taurus square Saturn in Leo at the MC, and Moon in Capricorn exactly opposite Chiron, and an unaspected Neptune-Pluto conjunction in the 8th house, and Uranus conjunct the Ascendant, all mixed together and subjected to the kind of early family environment and collective psychic and social pressures he experienced, could ever grow up to be a nice man.

Nor am I sure whether any amount of effort would have made Adolf stick to his therapy, or whether his father would have stopped beating him, or whether his mother, given her own inherent temperament, would have permitted her son to develop a relationship with anyone other than her. This is the fundamental question Scott Peck is addressing. Is there such a thing as human evil? If so, is it innate or is it formed by the environment, or by a chemical mix between the parental environment and the personality? Human evil is really what we are dealing with when we deal with psychopathy. I am not talking about evil in the theological sense. That is an entirely different and even more difficult question. But in our culture, it may be appropriate to call psychopathic behaviour evil because psychopaths destroy innocent people, physically or psychologically or both.

Audience: There is a writer called Neville Symington who has written on narcissism. He talks about the mother as "life-giver", and how our development as human beings depends on having a relationship with the life-giver. When this relationship doesn't happen, there is profound disturbance. When you have a creative emotional experience connected with mother, you get the mirroring you need. Sometimes it just doesn't happen, even if the mother seems to be "good enough". Symington says, "And we don't know why."

McVeigh's triggering transits

Liz: No, we don't know why. I would like to point out something interesting about McVeigh's Moon-Uranus-Pluto configuration. At the precise moment of the precise day on which the Oklahoma bomb went off, transiting Saturn was at 20° Pisces, in exact opposition to transiting Chiron at 20° Virgo. McVeigh's Uranus sits at 20° Virgo. Saturn and Chiron had, in fact, been banging about for quite a while over the Moon-Uranus-Pluto configuration. Chiron was retrograding at the time of the explosion, so it had already been over the Uranus-Pluto and opposed the Moon. Likewise, Saturn had already been over his Moon. It is not as if these transits arrived fresh and new for the very first time that very morning. They had been laying sticks of dynamite for some time. But on the morning when the transiting aspects were exact, the fuse was lit. McVeigh unleashed his destructiveness when the Moon-Uranus-Pluto was triggered. We might say that the bomb was an externalisation of this configuration. When any individual manifests behaviour of a violent kind, it is worth asking what is being activated in the chart. If we can find the natal configuration and the transit which triggers it, we can understand something about the meaning of that natal configuration. Not everyone acts out such a configuration with violence, but McVeigh can teach us a lot about the internal landscape of aspects like this.

Audience: I was thinking about all the times when I've hit back at someone who has hurt me and thought to myself, "I'm not sorry I did that." When John Prescott thumped somebody who threw an egg at him, the whole nation shouted, "Hurrah!"

Liz: I wouldn't say it was the whole nation. There was at least one exception: I thought Prescott richly deserved the egg. Be that as it may, I take your point, but when push comes to shove and someone actually sees a child dying or bleeding in front of them through their own action and feels nothing at all, that is rather a different thing.

Audience: But it might equate with what you feel has been done to you.

Liz: It certainly equates with what you feel has been done to you. But what you feel has been done, and what has actually been done, are not always the same thing. Moreover, many people feel terrible things have been done to them, but they don't act out their responses in the same way. Most child abusers have been abused in their own childhoods. That is not surprising. But why, out of all the people who have been abused in childhood, do only certain ones become abusers? It is a great mystery why one person who suffers abuse in childhood seeks healing and becomes a healer, another gets on with life and exhibits some fearful or aggressive responses in specific areas, and a third becomes a terrorist or a serial killer without remorse. As astrologers, we look at the birth chart and ask, "Is there something here that can give us a clue?" There are clues. The birth chart tells us as much about how we respond to our experiences as about what we innately are, since these two things are actually the same. But I don't know whether there are enough clues in the birth chart to answer the deeper questions.

Audience: I wonder about the huge public pressure put on McVeigh to show remorse. With all that Aries, and Jupiter in Leo, he was extremely proud, and the whole world was waiting for him to show remorse. Could that have pushed him to say to himself, "I will never show remorse"?

Liz: Possibly. Do you remember a film called *Dead Man Walking*? Only at the very last, before his execution, does the murderer show remorse, and only when he has been worked on in a one-to-one counselling situation in which he finally breaks down. It is an interesting film. There are a number of films which address the issue of psychopathy, but usually in a highly sensational way. This film is different. The character in *Dead Man Walking* might seem to be a psychopath, yet at the end he experiences remorse. Does that mean that the psychopathic personality can be rehabilitated? Or does it mean this man was severely damaged but not actually psychopathic? I don't know the answer.

Murder as a symbol: the head of "The Family"

Let's examine another example chart, very different from McVeigh's. Here there are no missing elements, although there is only one planet in the element of fire. This is a water-dominated chart, with four planets in Scorpio and one in Cancer. And look at that lovely Sun-Jupiter-Venus configuration in the 7th house. If you saw that configuration in the context of another seminar, it might seem a very attractive combination – perhaps a bit intense for some people's taste, but suggesting great sexual magnetism, insight and emotional empathy. It could be the perfect chart for a therapist, or perhaps a politician who handles the public in a particularly charismatic way. Let's consider the Moon first. It is in the 10th house, exactly on its own north Node in 4° Aquarius. What does that say to you?

Audience: Is Moon in Aquarius like Moon-Uranus?

Liz: Not really. Moon in Aquarius has some of the cool, impersonal flavour of Moon-Uranus, but not the erratic energy. But look at the aspects. The Moon is in a grand cross, involving an opposition to Pluto

and squares to Mercury and Uranus. We are going to see these lunar aspects to outer planets coming up a lot today. Charles Manson's Moon is also trine Chiron. McVeigh has no Moon-Chiron, but this aspect, as well as Moon-Uranus, is very important in terms of the disconnection associated with psychopathy. Keep in mind those two major fears: fear of engulfment and fear of abandonment. Both McVeigh and Manson have Moon-Uranus and Moon-Pluto. Here we see the Moon-Pluto opposition across the parental houses. What does this suggest?

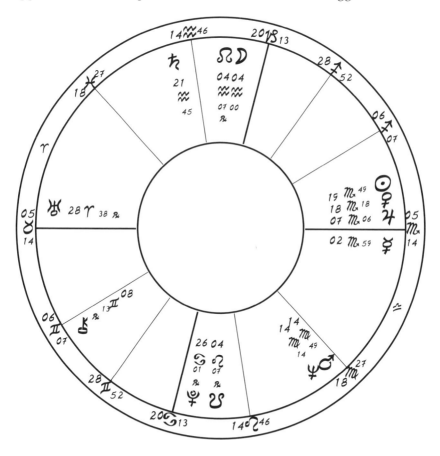

Charles Manson
12 November 1934, 4.40 pm, Cincinnati, Ohio

Audience: The Aquarian Moon is not exactly warm, but there is all the emotional power of Pluto working underneath. It is a bit similar to the other one, with Moon opposite both Uranus and Pluto.

Liz: Yes. The extreme polarity of Moon-Uranus and Moon-Pluto does seem to be a big problem: fear of engulfment and fear of abandonment, both at the same time. However, as I mentioned earlier, anyone born into the Uranus-Pluto generation group with the Moon in the mutable signs will have this "double whammy". It takes more than that to make a psychopath. How does the Moon in Aquarius feel with hard aspects to both Uranus and Pluto? How is it different from McVeigh's Moon in Pisces?

Audience: The Moon in Aquarius is quite detached. It would feel particularly threatened by Plutonian emotions. Moon-Uranus would be the easiest means of escaping all those frightening feelings. But I can't quite see how it would be different with a Pisces Moon.

Liz: Manson's Moon is in a Uranus-ruled sign and is also aspected by Uranus, emphasising the tendency to dissociate from overpowering emotions. McVeigh's Moon is watery by sign and house, and it is also trine Neptune. Both men cut themselves off from feeling. Perhaps the difference lies in how they expressed their destructive impulses. Manson worked with a group which he called "The Family", in a dreadful parody of the classic Aquarian tendency to enjoy doing things with friends. McVeigh, although he had a companion in the Oklahoma bombing, was essentially a solo performer, fulfilling some kind of compulsive messianic mission. Manson's chart, like McVeigh's, does not lack water. This is one of the reasons why these two men could manipulate others so well. The ability to utilise feelings as a means of adaptation is a water gift, but with most watery people it goes along with empathy. When there is an ability to use feelings consciously but without empathy, the result is a callous manipulator.

Audience: Is it possible that Manson is a "true" psychopath, but McVeigh was not?

Liz: Yes, it is possible. McVeigh may have felt intensely, but focused all his feelings in one gigantic fireball of consuming hatred which permitted no other emotional response. Manson is certainly more of a "classic" psychopath in the Hannibal the Cannibal mode. But even here, we cannot look at Manson's chart and say, "This is a psychopath." We can certainly say, "This is someone who is likely to have some very severe emotional conflicts." These conflicts clearly began in early life, because the Moon is in the 10th, which is the house of the mother, and Pluto is in the 4th, which is the house of the father, and they are in opposition. Uranus squares the Moon from the 12th, so the problem goes back further than the parents. The Moon is taking a heavy battering in this chart. Also, note the exact Mars-Neptune conjunction. This can reflect a deep sense of impotence and powerlessness. This sense of powerlessness appears in McVeigh's chart, too, where there is a Mars-Neptune opposition. There is a feeling that one is always being victimised, but one can't do anything about it. It can generate enormous rage, but the rage doesn't come out in a direct and honest way.

Mars-Neptune and cruelty

Audience: Is that from Mars-Neptune in particular?

Liz: It is a common characteristic of Mars-Neptune in someone who is very unconscious. It is difficult to act in a straight, self-assertive way because one is so identified with other people's feelings.

Audience: Can that be creative?

Liz: Of course it can. It is a common aspect in the charts of gifted actors and musicians, and it can give real magic to any performer because of the ability to "become" other people and intuit what they are feeling and yearning for. Like every other planetary aspect, it is double-edged. But we do need to look at the issue of potential cruelty in relation to Mars-Neptune. The aspect itself does not make people cruel, but one of the chief factors in cruelty is the need to transfer one's feelings of weakness and impotence onto someone else. Psychopathic behaviour is connected with cruelty. The psychopath takes pleasure in humiliating other people. There is delight in having power over others, and that is linked with unbearable inner feelings of powerlessness. If one feels powerless, one tries to rectify it by having power over someone else. One of the most unattractive extremes of this is the paedophile. This is because children are small and vulnerable, and if one feels like a victimised child oneself in a big, grown-up body, one way of feeling bigger and stronger, and of releasing decades of suppressed rage at the same time, is to abuse a child. It is a projection of one's own helplessness onto another person. If one can get rid of the feeling of helplessness in this way, one can puff up and feel strong. One of the roots of cruelty is the inner feeling of being a victimised child.

The statistical frequency of childhood abuse in psychopaths tells us clearly that early victimisation of one kind or another is a fundamental component of this personality structure. While we must remember that not everyone who has been abused becomes a psychopath, it is an important environmental factor. These people have usually been humiliated and subjected to cruelty at an extremely early age, and they carry these feelings around inside them. They do not heal, and they don't feel they have any power, so they must create the illusion of power in the most ruthless way. All it takes to trigger the rage and feelings of humiliation is a little frustration. Intolerance of frustration is, as we have seen, one of the chief characteristics of the psychopath. It is unbearably, globally humiliating if one has to apply for a job, and working under someone else's authority is equally humiliating because that awful sense of impotence is triggered again and again. Cruelty is an attempt to redress the balance. Of course Mars-Neptune can be a tremendously creative aspect, provided there is sufficient consciousness to recognise and contain the cyclical feelings of weakness, and sufficient commitment and discipline to express the energy through imaginative channels. But if the aspect combines with other factors such as an infantile personality structure and a propensity for emotional disconnection, it can become very cruel. In that form, Mars-Neptune can be either a victim or a perpetrator, but both spring from the same root. They are two sides of the same coin.

The Moon in the 10th house: identification with mother

Audience: Would it have been his mother who made him feel this way?

Liz: I am not sure it is as simple as the mother "making" him feel this way. It is, after all, his Mars-Neptune and not his mother's. Mars-Neptune feels victimised because it feels weak, not the other way around. A strong Mars, subjected to early abuse, would react in a different way. It is likely that the mother is involved, because of the Moon in the 10th. This suggests a powerful emotional identification with her. The father, or lack thereof, may be an equally powerful source of humiliation, because the Moon is opposite Pluto in the 4th. Manson may have perceived his mother humiliated by his father, and felt abused by them both. But remember that chart configurations describe how we respond to situations. Moon opposite Pluto easily feels humiliated because all emotional experiences are taken so very seriously and cut so very deeply. Every emotional encounter is a life-or-death experience.

Audience: There seems to be a need in Manson to be a big person to the outside world. How is that connected with the mother?

Liz: The need to be a big person in the outside world is related to the Moon in the 10th. Obviously this does not have to involve pathological inflation. Many people with Moon in the 10th feel they have an emotional bond with the collective, with "ordinary people", and they want to contribute in a way which nurtures or supports creative changes in the world. This is linked with mother because, at the beginning of life, mother *is* the world. Rather than describing the Moon in the 10th as the need to be a big person, I would say it is a need to belong, to feel part of society, to have one's feelings recognised and acknowledged by people "out there". Of course, identification with the mother, when mother is represented as Moon-Pluto, can prove a bit tricky. If the child feels what she is feeling, if he identifies with her emotions and her emotions are savage, he is both her victim and her surrogate lover/confessor. Then he is in trouble, because he has internalised something profoundly poisonous and threatening. Then the world "out there" also seems poisonous and threatening. Manson felt he "represented" an angry element in society, an underworld of people who were outcasts and whom he could champion through bringing destruction to the "enemy". In some respects he was right: with Moon in the 10th, he did connect emotionally with certain Plutonian elements of American society, and he did represent a dark alternative to the "American dream". Psychopaths are often the mediators for those enraged, destructive aspects of the collective which remain unintegrated and unconscious.

Charles Manson is still alive and kicking, albeit in prison, and he still exhibits no remorse. He holds court in his prison cell, gives interviews to the press and continues to display extraordinary arrogance. His message is, "You can't execute me. You can keep me in here for the rest of my life, but I have pulled one over on all of you." It is quite terrifying to see this man being interviewed, which happens at regular intervals. Journalists are freely allowed access to him, and he holds court like a potentate.

Audience: He could have been a really charismatic rock star.

Liz: Perhaps. The rock bands of the 1960s and 1970s certainly exhibited a lot of Plutonian qualities. We don't know why being a murderer seemed a more attractive alternative. Maybe being a Plutonian rock star was too respectable. Manson thought of himself as a black magician. And he was incredibly hypnotic. He surrounded himself with obedient accolytes who obligingly assisted him in his murders as part of a quasi-religious initiation rite.

Audience: People were afraid of Manson long before he began his reign of destruction. He could attract them, but then they backed away, which made him very angry and bitter. I found an amazing quote from him: "I am a mechanical toy. I am my mother's boy." Maybe he was sexually abused by his mother.

Liz: It's very likely that he was sexually abused. I have no factual basis for saying that. But there is something about all the Scorpio planets, combined with the Mars-Neptune, combined with the Moon in the 10th opposite Pluto, that makes me suspect that his bond to his mother was highly erotic. If there was no direct sexual abuse, there may have been erotic over-stimulation, as it is euphemistically called, by a mother who alternately swallowed him up and then abandoned him. Again, look at the basic temperament. McVeigh's Sun and Ascendant in Taurus and Moon in Pisces describe a gentle, affectionate nature: a child who felt easily victimised and overlooked, and identified himself with all society's victims. What kind of nature does Manson have, with Sun in Scorpio, Moon in Aquarius and Taurus rising?

Audience: Very fixed.

The symbolism of the crime

Liz: Yes, there is little flexibility in his nature. With all those planets in Scorpio, and Moon opposite Pluto, he would be quite unable to forgive early humiliation. His most famous and perhaps most vicious crime was the murder of Sharon Tate. He and his acolytes killed her when she was pregnant, and tore the baby out of her womb. The murder of Sharon Tate was a statement of overwhelming hatred, not only of his mother, but also of himself. We need to look at the symbolism of this act. Criminal investigators know that the manner in which serial murders are committed is highly personal: the psychopath invariably leaves a special "signature" on each crime which reflects something about his unique psychology. Because the people injured by psychopaths usually have nothing to do with them personally, the crimes are symbolic. They are different from a man murdering his wife because he's caught her in bed with his best friend. We can learn a lot about the psychopathic personality by looking at the symbolism of Sharon Tate's murder. Manson not only murdered a woman; he murdered a pregnant woman, so he was destroying an unborn child at the same time. What was he unconsciously saying about himself?

Audience: That he hated himself as a child. Or he felt he shouldn't have been born.

Liz: Yes. It is also likely that his mother felt he should never have been born. The self-hatred implicit in this act is extreme. Astrology, as well as the symbolism of the crime itself, can give us a glimpse of the emotions lying beneath this disconnected, cold personality. McVeigh's crime was also symbolic. His rage was directed against the perceived oppression of government authority, and he killed with explosives, from a distance. Manson's rage was directed against the feminine, and the method of killing was highly personal: he used a knife. The murder of Sharon Tate expresses ferocious self-loathing as well as loathing of a mother to whom he must have been desperately attached. This hints not at an intrinsic lack of feeling, but at some terrible and irrevocable distortion or crippling of feeling.

Manson's mother was a prostitute. When he was two years old, his progressed Sun moved into an exact square to natal Saturn. Progressed Venus was following right behind and just at the time Venus completed its exact square to Saturn, his mother went to prison and he was put into an orphanage. Given the nature of the progressed aspects, he may have experienced abuse there, or, at the least, intolerable loneliness. Progressed aspects, like natal ones, describe how we respond to experiences, as well as symbolising the nature of the experience. At around two to three years old – the age which Freud termed the Oedipal stage – the progressed aspects describe a collision between the developing individuality and an immovable obstacle, represented by Saturn in Aquarius in the 11th house. Perhaps the obstacle was a sense of society's condemnation and the impossibility of ever "belonging". At this point in Manson's life, something froze, and it seems never to have thawed.

Venus as chart ruler

Audience: In both these charts, there is a Venus-Saturn aspect. Might that be important?

Liz: It is undoubtedly one of the important ingredients, although, once again, I must remind you that one aspect does not make a psychopath. Venus makes several benign aspects in Manson's chart. It is sextile both

Mars and Neptune, trine Pluto and conjunct the Sun. But there is that Venus-Saturn square, echoing McVeigh's Venus-Saturn conjunction. In both charts, Venus is in the sign of its detriment, and it is also the chart ruler. What does the Ascendant ruler represent?

Audience: A mask.

Liz: I think it's rather more profound than that. The Ascendant ruler is a personification of the sign on the Ascendant. In mythic language, it is the god who presides over one's birth. In many fairy tales as well as myths, there is a deity or supernatural being present at birth, who bestows particular blessings on the child. But the child must grow up and seek those blessings consciously, or fight for them, or wait patiently for them until the time is right. The idea that a certain spirit, fairy or god presides over every child's birth is very old. It is one's tutelary deity, and this deity – which in astrology we call a planet – is the governor of the individual's path in the outer world. Both Manson and McVeigh have Venus as the Ascendant ruler. If Venus is the tutelary deity that presides over the birth of these individuals, what does that suggest? How many of you have Taurus or Libra rising? All of you who have raised your hands are ruled by Venus, and your journey through life is under the governance of this deity. Wherever you are and whatever you do, you will meet this deity in the outer world because it presides over your life path. What does it imply?

Audience: We want to be admired and attractive. With Venus in Scorpio, the admiration needs to be sexual, and it needs to be intense.

Liz: Anyone with a Venus-ruled sign on the Ascendant craves beauty, pleasure, and contact with others. Venus-ruled people long to be liked. They are social creatures, whether Taurus or Libra is on the Ascendant. They want life to be easy and lovely. The definitions of beauty, and the levels on which beauty is sought, differ between Taurus and Libra, but the ideal is still beauty. This is the world Venusian people expect when they are born. In Manson's chart, Venus is in its own natural house, the 7th. Relationships are critical for this child. His emotional needs are very powerful, and he longs to experience beauty through intense contact with others. What does he get instead? A mother who is a prostitute, an enforced separation from her at the age of three, and abandonment in an orphanage. This Venusian child came into a world which was his definition of hell.

The loneliness of Saturn in the 11th house

The ruler of the chart in square to Saturn suggests that there is something within Manson that conflicts with this need for beauty and ease: something with which he must come to terms. There is a limitation which must be accepted and integrated if he is to develop into a whole person. What is the limitation, with Saturn in Aquarius in the 11th?

Audience: The reality of loneliness. The impossibility of ever being fully accepted by the group.

Liz: Yes. He doesn't "belong", and his early experiences confirmed this. But he could never come to terms with it. A Venus-ruled person with Venus in the 7th is eager for contact. But Saturn in the 11th says, "You will never be one of them. You are different." Wherever Saturn is placed in the birth chart, we never feel we are getting what we need. The house and sign in which Saturn is placed describe qualities and experiences which matter deeply to us. These things make us feel secure and strong in the world. They form the basis of our sense of incarnate reality. Saturn in the 11th seeks embodiment through the group, but somehow the group never feels welcoming. Part of the reason for this is that Saturn's expectations cannot be fulfilled by other people. Being liked by everybody is not a path which this Saturn allows. "The group" needs to be something deeper than a superficial social milieu. Manson always wanted to be part of a group, but the nature of his early experiences ensured that this could never be. Had he been capable of accepting his loneliness, understanding and forgiving the conventional thinking that made people reject him, and forming genuine emotional bonds with a few real friends, he might have been difficult and rebellious, but not a murderer. But he built up enormous hatred toward a society which he perceived as cold, cruel and rejecting. In the end, he did form bonds with people who shared his vision, but the bonds were corrupt and the vision was one of destruction.

In order to tap the creative potential of Saturn in the 11th, the child needs to understand that the kind of friendship they seek will not be found on the school playground. They are going to have to build it, slowly and patiently, with people who may enter their lives only when they are older. People with Saturn in the 11th need a depth of contact which only comes with maturity. They need to learn to be more self-sufficient, and to value those with whom they can truly communicate, rather than merely wanting to be popular. In some cultures, this is made very difficult because of collective values. An American child with an 11th house Saturn may suffer more than a European child with the same placement, because extraversion is deemed to be the norm in American culture. A child is perceived as maladjusted or troubled if they haven't got hundreds of friends. In Europe a child can be introverted, introspective and solitary, yet not be labelled abnormal. Here is an example of outer environment and inner nature creating a difficult chemical mix.

We can only speculate about when Manson's emotional disturbance took root. The Moon-Pluto opposition is a separating aspect, and by progressed motion it would have been exact eight months before he was born. That is virtually the beginning of his mother's pregnancy. It is possible that his mother became pregnant unwillingly, and was deeply depressed because of it. She may have wished him dead. I believe children feel such ill-will if it is very intense, even in the womb. Being a prostitute, she may even have been raped. When she found out that she was pregnant, she may have been horrified or enraged. She may have tried to abort him. The chart, of course, cannot give us such information. Manson's Moon-Pluto does not tell us any of these things. It tells us that his first encounters with life felt fraught with danger. But we can speculate on the kinds of things that might have disturbed the primal bonding with his mother, based on what knowledge we have of his early circumstances. The Moon-Uranus square was exact by progressed motion six months before he was born, and the Moon-Mercury square was exact around a month and a half before his birth. All these difficult lunar aspects are separating aspects. It seems that Manson came into the world already feeling unwelcome, misunderstood and life-threatened. If we want to explore the deeper roots of psychopathy, we may have to go back even before birth.

The suffering of the soul

The Moon and Chiron

As you are all well aware, I am not a statistician. I don't have the temperament for that kind of astrological research. Nevertheless, out of curiosity I had a look at a database of violent criminals. The database wasn't large – only a hundred charts – but that is comprehensive enough to yield an interesting pattern, although not big enough to convince a sceptic. I excluded the individuals who had obviously committed "crimes of passion", because the term psychopath is inappropriate for people who relate to others quite well and then suddenly blow up and commit a murder because something emotionally devastating happens to them. Any of us could be in that position, and usually these people suffer terribly from remorse afterward. It was the cold, calculating serial killers whose charts proved most fruitful, because their character portraits seemed to fit the psychopathic profile. This group comprised forty-seven charts.

Here are some interesting results. What I found was that 80% of them had major Moon-Saturn or Moon-Chiron aspects, and the trines outnumbered the hard aspects. In Manson's chart there is a Moon-Chiron trine. The percentage of charts that had Moon trine Chiron was 30%. A statistician would tear such an assessment to pieces because there is no neutral control group, and forty-seven charts, like one swallow, don't make a summer. Nevertheless, that is a high percentage, and I find it curious. We might expect to find Moon-Pluto or Moon-Uranus aspects. But these aspects, although both McVeigh and Manson have them, were actually not all that common in the group of charts I examined. Chiron is concerned with a sense of irrevocable wounding, a feeling of damage that comes through the collective but which we feel personally. We might not be surprised by Moon-Chiron squares, conjunctions, or oppositions, such as we find in Hitler's chart. But what is it about Moon-Chiron trines that could reflect something in the psychopathic personality?

Audience: With a trine, you might not feel it's a wound.

Liz: The trine suggests that it may be easier to disconnect from the pain of the feelings, leaving only a cold cynicism. One might also identify in a passive way with the victim's role: "I am damaged and there's nothing I can do about it." Chiron experiences, like those of all the planets, involve a developmental process and have the potential to pass through several stages. There is an initial rage-and-blame stage: the feeling of being unfairly victimised, damaged or maimed, and filled with black bitterness because of it. With greater consciousness, this stage may transform into an experience of suffering without rage, and ultimately one can arrive at a place of profound compassion and philosophical acceptance. A lot of people get stuck in the rage-and-blame stage and, with a trine, they may be quite unconscious of it.

Chiron can be very destructive if one hasn't relinquished the ideal against which one's wounding is measured. In myth, Chiron is half god and half animal. The divine side, which reflects the teacher and healer, carries a vision of a perfect world, an ideal of human evolution and eventual wisdom. The horse side, which provides the energy and life-force, is instinctual and vulnerable. It is here that Chiron is wounded and poisoned by the Hydra's blood. The Hydra symbolises the darkest, most destructive dimensions of the human psyche, and Chiron's suffering is connected with the apparently unbridgeable gap between what human beings are like in reality, and that beautiful, noble vision of human civilisation governed by divine reason. The wound reflects our despair in the face of this irreconcilable conflict between what we hope for and believe in, and what we experience in life through the blindness of human nature.

To have a trine between Moon and Chiron can mean that the poison remains in the system, and there is no impetus to struggle against it. A good parallel can be seen in the way the human body deals with infection. Abcesses are the body's way of throwing off infection. They are extremely painful, but they are a sign that the infection has now localised, the pus can be released, and healing can take place. But sometimes an infection remains hidden in the system, causing debilitating low-grade fever but never causing enough discomfort to make the person seek treatment. It doesn't hurt, but the life-force is constantly drained away. If you think of this analogy on a psychological level, you can see that a Moon-Chiron trine can operate like a chronic low-grade psychic infection. There is great bitterness hidden in the soul, and it drains away all joy and hope, but the bitterness never shows itself in an obvious way. It leads to cynicism and disconnection, rather than the kind of suffering which might lead to compassion and release. Of course this does not mean that every person with a Moon-Chiron trine or sextile goes around in this state. Nor does it mean that the hard aspects automatically generate consciousness. Both hard and soft aspects can lead to an ability to understand and empathise with suffering. But if the passive bitterness of the harmonious aspect gets mixed up with more destructive chart factors and the individual is unconscious of both, the result may comprise an important part of the psychopath's inner dynamic. This may be why Moon-Chiron aspects appear so frequently in the charts of serial killers.

The Moon and Saturn

Why should Moon-Saturn contacts be so frequent in the charts of psychopathic killers? This is an aspect which can reflect a strong sense of responsibility and a capacity to cope with considerable frustration. Yet on our clinical list, failure to accept responsibility and inability to cope with frustration are important characteristics of the psychopathic personality. What do you make of this contradiction?

Audience: There's often a problem with emotional nurturing in childhood. The self-sufficiency of Moon-Saturn is a defence. If you have never felt emotionally nurtured, frustrations will build up against the world.

Liz: Yes, I agree. Moon-Saturn people can sometimes feel deeply isolated. Because they did not feel emotionally nurtured early in life, they expect no generosity from others, and therefore find it very difficult to ask for help or express vulnerable feelings. That can lead to resentment and feelings of being unappreciated or badly treated by the world. Self-pity can be a big problem with Moon-Saturn, although, as you say, it is often hidden behind a very self-sufficient manner.

Audience: But Moon-Saturn people can have very good boundaries.

Liz: Yes, Moon-Saturn can sometimes be very strong and self-sufficient, and very well-defended against exploitation. In many people it works in an extremely positive way, if it is integrated. These people contain their emotions and deal with their own problems. They don't expect free lunches and they are realistic about their own and other people's limits. But, like Moon-Chiron, it can generate a feeling of victimisation. If the aspect is not integrated and Saturn is projected onto others, it can be a real whiner: "Nobody ever helps me. I always have to do everything myself. Other people are selfish and cold. Life has treated me harshly." Like Moon-Chiron, Moon-Saturn describes a process and can move across a wide spectrum, from infantile resentment to deep worldly wisdom and strength. As with all planetary configurations, most people exhibit a mixture of the two, and we don't know from the chart alone what a person will make out of the aspect.

Moon-Saturn can feel terribly exploited and vulnerable, because there is difficulty in internalising a positive mother-image. Mother may have seemed cold or inaccessible. The person may have been the eldest child, burdened with the task of looking after other children, or an "only" child with no siblings to communicate with. There is often great loneliness in childhood, and no real chance to be irresponsible and joyful. Sometimes Moon-Saturn describes a child who is literally abandoned, but even if the parents are present, the internal landscape is often that of an orphan. If the hurt is great enough, Saturn can stifle the lunar need to reach out to other people. Saturn says to the Moon, "Don't even think of asking anyone for anything. You'll just get rejected again." Moon-Saturn can be terrifically proud, and isolation can become entrenched as a way of life. Try to imagine a child with Moon-Saturn who has been subjected to abuse. How is this different from a child with Moon-Jupiter, who has been subjected to the same abuse? How will they feel? Remember what I said earlier about the Moon responding to extreme stress and hurt according to its natal house, sign and aspects. If a Moon-Saturn person is deeply injured, what might be a characteristic response?

Audience: It would confirm their cynical view of other people. They would never trust anyone again.

Liz: Yes, the mistrust and resentment are set in concrete. Moon-Saturn then says, "I will never need anyone again. I will never let anyone close to me. I will never become dependent on anyone again. No one will ever have the power to control me."

Audience: Moon-Saturn makes a person very defensive. I can sense this aspect immediately when I meet people who have it, because they always make me feel unwanted. They are so cold. They give the message, "I don't want to have anything to do with you."

Liz: Yes, Moon-Saturn can be extremely defensive. The defences against vulnerability, in extreme cases, can lead to total dissociation from feelings.

Audience: So they reject because they are so afraid of rejection?

Liz: Yes. That is the potential tragedy of the aspect. Moon-Saturn people often unwittingly create the thing they fear the most, and don't realise that they have architected their own isolation. They are so frightened of rejection and humiliation that they wall out other people, or demand so many guarantees of love that others are put off. The mistrust of a Moon-Saturn person can feel very hurtful. Every effort to offer them warmth and support results in criticism or the implied accusation that one has not offered enough, and eventually one gives up trying. Moon-Saturn people often create their own problems in relationship. An ordinary garden variety Moon-Saturn, as opposed to a psychopathic Moon-Saturn, can still fear showing emotional needs, and partners and friends start feeling unwelcome and unnecessary. Neither McVeigh nor Manson has a Moon-Saturn contact, although Manson's Moon is in a Saturn-ruled sign in Saturn's natural house. But you can see how this aspect can contribute to the building up of a psychopathic profile, if other factors collude. Underneath the disconnection, there is the most terrible loneliness and isolation. But a psychopathic personality with Moon-Saturn prefers to keep things that way, and this splendid isolation becomes part of the grandiose feeling of being special and superior to other beings with their pathetic emotional needs. Others can be manipulated through their needs, but the psychopath is determined never to be vulnerable in that way.

How very strange: no one has offered me an example chart for discussion in the group yet. Two people have handed me their charts, but they are not on a transparency. As you all know perfectly well that I can't put a chart on the overhead projector unless it is on a transparency, this seems to be saying something.

John: I have mine on a transparency.

Liz: Thanks, John. Before we look at it, are there any other questions or comments?

The psychopath in myth

Audience: Does the figure of the psychopath exist in myth?

Liz: There are certainly evil creatures in myth who do nothing but kill, or who are cold and cruel. In that sense, the image is there. But they have neither charm nor a grandiose sense of self. They are simply killing machines, like Jaws. Fairy tales have much better images of psychopathic behaviour.

Audience: Like Bluebeard?

Liz: Yes, we could probably call Bluebeard a psychopath. The character is said to be based on the 15th century French soldier, Gilles de Rais, who was one of Jeanne d'Arc's captains. Gilles was a brave fighter, but he had an unpleasant habit of raping and murdering young boys, and burying their remains in various chambers in his castle. Gilles de Rais would certainly qualify as a psychopath.

Audience: How about Loki in Norse myth?

Liz: Loki is not a psychopathic character. He is a trickster, like his Greek equivalent, Hermes. He can be pretty nasty at times, and he is certainly a liar when circumstances require it, but he always lies for a reason, and he is not dissociated. The gods in all mythologies have a cruel side, but it is integrated into the whole deity. They can exhibit goodness and generosity as well. Artemis, for example, is extremely spiteful in the way she strikes down those who offend her. They do very little, but end up with horrific punishments, like Aktaion, whom she turns into a stag so that his own dogs can tear him apart. Aktaion, although he is a boaster and accidentally sees the goddess naked, doesn't merit this. It isn't as if he was working for *The Sun* with a pair of binoculars and a digital camcorder. The same over-the-top spitefulness can be seen in the character of Dionysus in Euripides' *Bacchai*. For that matter, we could also consider Yahveh's behaviour toward Job as psychopathic. The gods can exhibit cruelty, cold-bloodedness and lack of remorse, but they can also be supportive, loving and benign. What we might call the psychopathic component is an integral part of the whole.

Myth may be telling us something profound about the problem of psychopathy. Modern Western culture splits good and evil in a very stark way, and there is absolutely no relationship between the two – only an eternal struggle. This may arise from the dualistic world-view which is part of our Judeo-Christian heritage. We seem to have split off the psychopathic element in ourselves, and it gets enacted by individuals who are entirely psychopathic rather than having a mixture of light and dark elements. Of course we could easily idealise ancient society, and say it was much healthier because crimes could be perpetrated and forgiveness or punishment offered without the concept of sin so characteristic of the Judaeo-Christian world-view. On the other hand, as has often been said, life in ancient times was nasty, brutish and short, and an individual life had little value.

Perhaps it is wiser not to view the ancient world as a time when psychopathy did not exist, but rather, to take the model offered by myth and try to see where it might offer us insights applicable to the individual. The more socially conscious we become, the more we split off from our destructive feelings. The more we recoil in horror from any kind of violent crime, whether on an individual or a collective level, the more psychopathic individuals seem to act out something for us. I am not suggesting that we should not feel deeply disturbed by violence, gratuitous cruelty and lack of remorse. But we may need to be more honest about these elements in ourselves. We have reached such extremes of political correctness now that the proliferation of peculiarly brutish crimes reported in the papers may be the shadow we are trailing behind us. Both McVeigh and Manson have the Moon configured with outer planets, and this suggests that these men carry something for the collective.

R. D. Laing hypothesised that schizophrenics are society's mouthpieces: they enact our madness for us while we perpetuate the illusion that we are sane.[8] In certain approaches to family therapy, it is recognised that within a disturbed or dysfunctional family there is often an "identified patient" who acts out the conflicts present in the family psyche. The "identified patient" is then carted off for treatment, while everyone else congratulates themselves on being normal. Laing believed that schizophrenia is not just a family issue, but involves society as a whole, because on the collective unconscious level we are a unity. It is possible that the psychopath, who is not deemed mad like the schizophrenic, nevertheless serves the same function on the collective level, and enacts something that we have disowned and cannot bear to face. Psychopaths are survivors. They have adapted to life's more brutish face in a way that allows them to disengage emotionally. Their method of survival appears to us as horribly cold and cruel. Yet we may have a closer link with them than we can bear to acknowledge, and this may be reflected in our fascination with films and novels dealing with this theme. It is like looking into a dreadfully distorted mirror and seeing our own faces reflected back to us. The issue of whether psychopaths are born or made is, in a sense, irrelevant, because we are involved either way. This becomes apparent when we look at their

---

[8] See R. D. Laing, *The Divided Self,* Viking, 1991; *Wisdom, Madness and Folly,* Canongate Publishing, 1999; *The Politics of Experience,* Random House, 1983.

charts, and see the prominence of outer planets as well as configurations which reflect personal suffering and dissociation.

The psychopath as leader

A great many dictators fit the clinical description of a psychopath. Some psychopathic personalities become mouthpieces for the collective in a big way, because their particular collective is itself in a state of psychic disintegration and identifies with the psychopathic individual as a redeemer. We cannot understand such individuals on the basis of their personal history alone.[9]

Slobodan Milosevic and the Chiron-Pluto cycle

Slobodan Milosevic is very much like Hitler and Stalin: a product of and a mouthpiece for the collective. When we look at Milosevic's chart, we can see the extent to which he carries and identifies with the aspirations, suffering and mythology of his nation. In the 4th house of the chart we find the Moon in Leo, sitting close to the Chiron-Pluto conjunction which occurred in 1941. Cyclical configurations involving two outer planets, or Saturn or Chiron with an outer planet, are extremely important on a collective level because they reflect crises or turning points in the collective psyche. Those who are born under such configurations often embody the tension and conflict being enacted in the world around them at birth. Charles Manson was born under Uranus square Pluto, with the Moon square Uranus and opposition Pluto. Timothy McVeigh was born under Uranus conjunct Pluto, both opposition the Moon. Hitler was born under Neptune conjunct Pluto, with the Moon quincunx Pluto as well as in exact opposition to Chiron. Stalin was born under a Mars-Chiron-Neptune

---

[9] For an in-depth exploration of the links between the charts of leaders such as Hitler and the charts of their national collective, see Charles Harvey, *Anima Mundi: The Astrology of the Individual and the Collective*, CPA Press, 2002.

conjunction in Taurus; the Moon conjuncts Uranus in Virgo and forms a grand earth trine with this Mars-Chiron-Neptune and the Sun in Capricorn. Milosevic was born under a Saturn-Uranus conjunction, which squares his Sun, and a Chiron-Pluto conjunction sitting on his Moon.

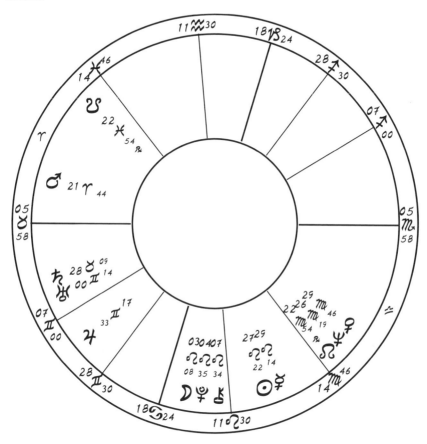

Slobodan Milosevic
20 August 1941, 10.00 am, Posarevac, Yugoslavia

Milosevic's emotional life and individual aspirations are thus plugged into the convulsions of the collective in 1941. I would not hesitate to call this man a psychopath. Both his parents committed suicide, and that is tragic, but early tragedies do not create psychopaths unless they interact with an innate predisposition to produce a particular set of responses. When he was a baby, his country was torn apart by war. But war does not create psychopaths. It merely provides them with the opportunity to justify their actions.

Chiron-Pluto conjunctions have a sixty-year cycle. I did some work on this cycle, and found that an outbreak of collective scapegoating occurs every time the conjunction comes around.[10] When the Plutonian collective survival instinct gets mixed up with Chiron's sense of irrevocable wounding, a defence mechanism seems to erupt in the collective: purge the scapegoat. This mechanism, in individuals and collectives, is a way of trying to get rid of Chiron's sense of inferiority by projecting it onto, and then destroying, those who, through race, culture or religious background, are perceived as "different". The mythic background of the scapegoat ritual tells us that, as a symbol, the scapegoat carries society's sins. If the scapegoat is purged, society is cleansed and made whole again. Chiron-Pluto conjunctions are linked with historical episodes where the collective is seized by a compulsion to purge itself, localised according to which national charts are triggered by the particular conjunction. Processed through the mentality of a psychopathic leader, such a collective compulsion can lead to genocide. It can also be a configuration of the most profound transformation. But this potential is more easily reached by conscious individuals, and not by collectives which have allowed a psychopath to take power.

When the Chiron-Pluto conjunction erupted in 1941, two things happened. The first was the inauguration of the death camps. While the conjunction was building up, the Jews were incarcerated in prison camps. But when the conjunction became exact, the Nazis began filling the gas chambers. The second thing that happened was that Hitler invaded Yugoslavia. Milosevic was born in the midst of this. His Moon-Chiron-Pluto, because it is in the 4th, connects him not only with the fate of his country at the time of his birth, but also with his country's longer history. His emotional life is rooted in the past, and in an inheritance

---

[10] See Part Three of this volume, "The Scapegoat", for an in-depth exploration of the scapegoat pattern in individual psychology and astrology. Milosevic is used as an example in this seminar as well. Also see my article, "The Good, the Bad and the Ugly: the Chiron-Pluto Conjunction", first published in *Apollon,* Issue 6, January 2001, now posted on www.astro.com.

that comes down through the father's line. His father's suicide is only the top layer of a much deeper and older issue. The Serbs were invaded in 1389 by the Muslim Ottoman Turks led by Bayezid I, and were subjected to terrible atrocities. Despite a fierce and desperate revolt in 1804, they remained vassals of the Ottoman Empire until 1878, when they finally achieved the status of an independent kingdom. That is nearly half a millennium of servitude to an Islamic conqueror, and collectives do not forget such experiences. Milosevic's Moon-Chiron-Pluto in the 4th suggests that he has inherited this "racial memory" of humiliation and persecution. He has two collective issues to contend with. He was born at a juncture of history when an appalling holocaust was exploding around him. And he has also inherited a powerful racial memory, for which the German invasion of 1941 acted as a trigger.

The first thing Milosevic did when he took power was to remind the Serbs of what had been done to them by the Muslims five hundred years before. He worked on his collective to stir up an ancient hatred and, like Hitler before him, he told his people exactly what they wanted to hear, even if they didn't realise it themselves. He was their mouthpiece. He didn't make them hate. He shared their hatred with them, and gave it a voice and a focus. He was the medium of his time, as Hitler was the medium of a Germany which had been beaten to its knees after the First World War. The Germans wanted a messiah who would tell them exactly what Hitler told them. The Serbs wanted a messiah who would tell them exactly what Milosevic told them. Undoubtedly he is a psychopath, and it is obvious that he experiences no remorse. But the manner of his rise and fall suggests that psychopaths express a split-off aspect of their collective. Milosevic's collective was under the threat of total destruction when the Germans invaded under the Chiron-Pluto conjunction of 1941, and the sense of threat was reawakened when Chiron conjuncted Pluto in Sagittarius and Milosevic began his full-scale persecution of the Muslims.

Milosevic encompassed a complete sixty-year Chiron-Pluto cycle from his birth to his downfall. Psychopathic dictators like Stalin, Hitler and Milosevic achieve political power when their country is in need of them. When does a country need a psychopathic ruler? Perhaps these people take control of government when the collective feels humiliated and impotent, and believes its survival is threatened. This is the position of an abused child. Even if the humiliation and the threat are not objectively real, it is the subjective feeling that matters. When psychopaths murder, they are not threatened by their victims. But their inner necessity dictates that everyone is an enemy, and they strike before they are struck down. A nation, like an individual, can respond to real or imagined abuse in the same way, and may, for a time, exhibit great hatred and destructiveness and feel no remorse afterward. This has occurred throughout history, and even today many nations – including Britain and America, who so love to claim the "high moral ground" – find it difficult to acknowledge and show remorse for their past atrocities. Psychopathic leaders like Milosevic step in at the critical moment and fulfil a collective need, unless there are enough conscious individuals to recognise what is happening and process their own destructiveness on an inner, individual level.

The healer as destroyer

Just to cheer you up further, why don't we have a quick look at Josef Mengele's chart? Dr. Mengele wasn't just an ordinary garden-variety Nazi who followed orders. He was quite creative with his orders, and he earns the diagnosis of psychopathy independent of his attachment to Hitler. The chart is worth looking at briefly in the context of today's theme.

Dr. Mengele

We are in the watery realm again. The Sun is in Pisces, which we usually think of as sensitive and compassionate. Charts like this one baffle us because they challenge our traditional interpretations of astrological signatures. Cancer is rising, and both the Sun and Mercury are trine to Neptune on the Ascendant. Remember our clinical list? The first characteristic is charm: the ability to manipulate through easy identification with the feelings of other people.

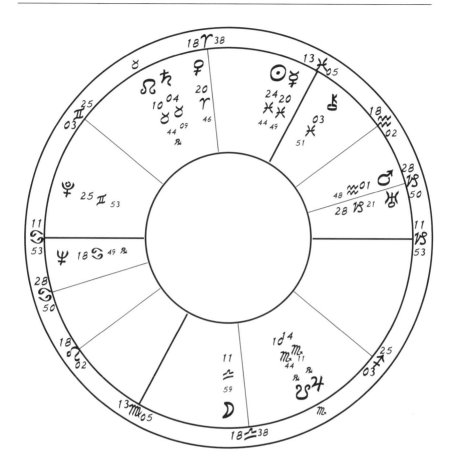

Josef Mengele
16 March 1911, 11.45 am, Gunzburg, Germany

Mengele has neither a Moon-Chiron nor a Moon-Saturn contact, nor does the Moon aspect Uranus or Pluto. However, the Moon is the chart ruler, placed in Libra in the 4th house, opposite Venus and square Neptune and forming a T-cross with them. The Moon is also exactly square the Ascendant. It doesn't quite manage a trine to Mars, as the orb is too wide. Mars, in turn, is in the 8th house in early Aquarius, conjunct Uranus on the cusp of the 8th in late Capricorn. Mars is also square Saturn. The question we need to ask about Mengele is, "Can we see cruelty in this chart?" Like so many people who occupied prominent positions in the Nazi hierarchy, Mengele was a participant in a collective episode of psychopathy, so the absence of personal signatures like Moon-Chiron is not that strange. A great many people behaved in a psychopathic fashion in Germany in the 1930s and 1940s, and it was deemed the norm at the time. But we do need to ask why Mengele was so particularly cruel and sadistic, because cruelty and the need to humiliate others are an important component of psychopathic behaviour. Can we see this in his chart?

Mars-Saturn and humiliation

Audience: Could it have to do with Mars-Uranus in the 8th?

Audience: And Mars square Saturn. I think that can be cruel.

Liz: Saturn is square both Mars and Uranus. But a great many people are born with these contacts, and most of them are not cruel. Is this innate cruelty, or is it the way the aspect is being dealt with?

Audience: Mars-Uranus likes to experiment. It is very independent and self-willed. If it is put together with other things, like dissociation, then the experimenting is done without any feeling.

Liz: That is a good point. There is an experimental quality to Mars-Uranus which, ordinarily, we would see as highly creative. Mars-Uranus people can be very inventive. They like trying new things, and they love to take on challenges which force them to discover new resources. But if this inventive quality is disconnected from the capacity to empathise, then it is a bit like pulling the wings off an insect just to see what happens. Mars-Uranus is not a signature of psychopathy in itself, nor is it innately cruel. But if it is present in the chart of a psychopath, it can be expressed in the way Mengele expressed it: sadistic experimentation without remorse.

Audience: It's interesting that both Mengele and Hitler were dark, ugly men, when everyone at the time idealised the blonde Aryan dream.

Liz: Yes, the question of racial purity must have irked Dr. Mengele, as it did Hitler, every time he looked in the mirror. Both these men had Mars square Saturn, which even at its best is not especially confident and self-assured. The prevailing collective fantasy of masculine perfection – tall, strong, fair-haired and blue-eyed – must have been painful for our good doctor when he was growing up. Progressed Venus would have conjuncted natal Saturn, which, like Manson's, is in the 11th, around the time he was going through puberty.

Audience: He trained as a doctor. So the caring qualities of Pisces and Cancer must have been there somewhere when he was younger.

Liz: In theory, yes, although many people become doctors for reasons other than the desire to heal.

Audience: If the desire to heal ever had been there, it got lost or terribly twisted. Did he practice medicine before the Nazis took power?

The irreconcilable split

Liz: Hitler took power in 1933. Mengele was born in 1911, so he was only twenty-two years old at the time. He was probably still in medical school. His movement into adulthood and into society occurred at the very moment when the Nazi regime was beginning to take control of his world. He was only seven years old when the First World War ended in 1918 and the Versailles treaty was signed condemning Germany to defeat and humiliation. What he saw, all through his childhood and adolescence, was a collapsing economy, galloping inflation and social chaos as his country disintegrated around him. His Neptunian nature made him particularly receptive to all of it. In this chart, there is an extreme split between the side of his nature represented by Mars-Uranus square Saturn and the side represented by Neptune rising in Cancer trine the Sun in Pisces. We might bear Timothy McVeigh in mind here, with his natal Moon in Pisces trine Neptune. Mengele must have identified very strongly with his suffering collective.

Audience: That is part of the split, isn't it? He identified with his collective, and felt compassion for his fellow countrymen. Everyone outside that collective, especially the Jews, was considered non-human, and therefore he could do whatever he liked to them.

Liz: Yes, that is part of the split. Mengele's chart doesn't convey the same bubbling, oozing darkness as Manson's. That chart hits us between the eyes, because it is so palpably full of agony and rage. We can see how the brutality of his background mixed with and twisted his basic nature, so he became what he became. Mengele's chart also lacks the fierce pride and grandiosity of Milosevic's. We can see how the brutality of *his* background mixed with and twisted his basic nature. Mengele is harder to fathom, unless we look at his Neptunian porousness and think of him as a kind of vessel filled with the despair and hatred of his collective.

Audience: There is a parallel with the Grand Inquisitor. He believes that he is right, and that what he does will be good for the other person, even if it means torturing them. It is a mistaken belief system.

Liz: The word "mistaken" may be somewhat inappropriate. And I would hardly say that Mengele had the good of the Jews in mind. They were simply objects for highly sadistic experiments. If he believed in anything, he believed that it was good for the Germans.

Audience: But he believed that what he was doing was good.

Liz: I'm not convinced of that either. Certainly there is a sense of mission, suggested by the Sun in the 10th trine the rising Neptune, and a sense of mission is an important component of the psychopathic personality. Aspirations toward goodness are another matter. McVeigh also had a sense of mission, as did Manson and Milosevic. All the individuals we have looked at were driven by beliefs which conferred on them the status of a messiah or instrument of collective salvation. But power rather than goodness seems to be the prime mover.

The Moon in the 4th: identification with the homeland

Audience: I'm struck by the Moon in the 4th house. Does that mean his feelings were bound up with his family and roots?

Liz: Yes. As with Milosevic, this can reflect a powerful identification with one's homeland. When the Moon is in the 4th, there is a deep taproot into the national collective, and a strong connection with the place of one's roots. It is not only the personal father who is a hook for this identification. It is the land itself. People with the Moon in the 4th often suffer deeply if they are uprooted, although this may be a necessary experience in order to become a conscious and separate individual. How many of you have a 4th house Moon? Do you have a strong sense of connection to the place of your roots?

Audience: Absolutely. I don't live there any more, but whenever I go back, I feel a very strong connection. It also makes me uncomfortable. I feel I become a more collective person. I sometimes feel overwhelmed. I hate nationalism, but when I go there I do feel my national identity much more strongly.

Liz: Why do you hate nationalism?

Audience: Because of what it can do. There have been some terrible examples in history, like Nazi Germany.

Liz: There is a difference between xenophobia, nationalism as an ideology, and a feeling for the spirit of the land. The destructive face of nationalism as expressed by Milosevic and Mengele is not "caused" by a 4th house Moon, but is a combination of many ingredients resulting in a nasty chemical mix. Xenophobia is a form of projection rooted in fear and ignorance, and it can occur whether or not one is genuinely attached to one's homeland. Nationalism as a political ideology is usually trotted out as a justification for aggression against another nation, and has little to do with the Moon. A feeling for the spirit of the land, the "folk soul", is much more a lunar experience. It is an instinctive feeling of identity which, in the hands of a conscious individual, can bring profound and immensely creative insights. When Goethe, who had the Moon in Pisces in the 4th house, created the figure of Faust, he encapsulated the deepest archetypal themes of his nation, and Faust continues to stand as the great symbol of both the noblest and the darkest aspirations of the spirit of Germany.

This is not nationalism in a political sense, and it doesn't involve demeaning other nationalities. It is a feeling for the *deus loci*, the god of the place. 4th house Moon people feel their land very deeply. Of course this can easily get mixed up with political nationalism, as well as with personal wounds of the kind described by Milosevic's Moon-Chiron-Pluto conjunction or Mengele's Mars-Saturn square. One's inner sense of victimisation then fuels the belief that one's homeland is the passive victim of other nations' aggression. Mengele's 4th house Moon is particularly important because it is his chart ruler. As Venus presided over McVeigh's and Manson's entry into life, the Moon presided over Mengele's. His whole being is identified with *den deutsches Volk*, the German "folk soul". In combination with other factors, this helped to make him particularly amenable to Hitler's propaganda.

Audience: Mengele experimented on children, but the day before he was going to experiment on them, he would take them out in his car and give them a good time. Then, the next day, he would torture them.

Liz: Psychopathic behaviour often displays this kind of terrifying contradiction. The charm and shallow sentimentality are evident one moment, and the sadism the next moment. Mengele probably took pleasure in "fooling" the children while knowing that he had absolute power over them. It's rather like playing God: dispensing joy one moment and horror the next. If he truly felt what he was about to do, how could he enjoy the ride with the child?

Pluto in the 12th: the ancestral survival instinct

Audience: Did Mengele have a strong sense of survival, with Pluto in the 12th?

Liz: He certainly proved to be a survivor. Unlike his mates, he was never caught or driven to suicide. He managed to escape to South America, and simply vanished. The 12th house Pluto in Gemini squares the Sun and Mercury. The 12th is the house of the ancestors. What is coming down through the family from the ancestral past?

Audience: Maybe he needed to seek revenge for the past.

Liz: This Pluto has something to do with an obsessive survival instinct, operating beneath the threshold of the family psyche. With Pluto in Gemini, the group survives through knowledge: knowledge is power, and power is survival. The sign of one's Pluto generation group tells us something about what that group calls upon to survive. For the Pluto in Gemini generation, survival means knowing as much as possible. Survival is also mobility: the capacity to escape, to shape-shift, to out-think others. Linked with the Sun and Mercury, it gives a ruthless quality to his nature. Mengele was a true Plutonian. He and his nation were going to survive, no matter what. There are many factors we can look at in this chart which might contribute to what Mengele became. Saturn in Taurus is also a relevant factor. Remember what I said earlier: Saturn's sign represents something that is immensely valuable to the person, something they want quite desperately, yet they feel they never received it in childhood and possibly never will. They feel deprived of something very precious. What does Taurus want badly?

Audience: Money.

Audience: Security.

Liz: Both are certainly important. How about physical beauty?

Audience: So we're back to the blue-eyed blonde.

Liz: Never underestimate the power of the archetypal Aryan superman on the German collective psyche in the first half of the 20th century. Like Hitler, Mengele had black hair and was rather ugly. He was an utter failure from the point of view of the "ideal" Aryan image. He may have suffered from feelings of sexual inadequacy, linked with Mars in the 8th square Saturn. We know that Hitler, with Mars and Venus in Taurus square Saturn in Leo, had many sexual problems. Mengele, like Manson, was the lonely child whom other children don't like: the one who looks "different", or just doesn't fit. We can see in this troubled Mars-Saturn configuration a hint of the sense of personal injury and inferiority that got linked up with all that collective suffering. Psychopathy invariably involves an overwhelming sense of personal inferiority. That is what fuels the mythic self-aggrandisement.

In the charts of both Manson and McVeigh, the Moon is under great stress. Mars is under stress as well, and it seems to be linked in the charts of many psychopaths with either Saturn, Chiron, Neptune or Pluto, or a combination of two or more of these planets. Such contacts can reflect immense frustration, a sense of impotence and weakness, feelings of inferiority as a man, and the belief that one has no power to shape one's own life. A stressed Mars is common to all these charts, reflecting a profound feeling of ineffectuality that can only be alleviated by becoming super-powerful. Hitler, who had Mars square Saturn, collected around him a *côterie* of damaged people, all of whom had grievances against life because they were all suffering from feelings of inferiority for which they were going to make other people pay. Nazi Germany was a playground for psychopaths. In more stable times, these people would be setting fire to vagrants, torturing cats, and raping and murdering children. They might get arrested, but they would not have the power to run a country and start a global war. One of the great attractions of the Nazi regime to these men was that, at last, the inferior people could rule and take revenge on those they envied and feared. Now I think we should leave the good doctor behind and move on.

Audience: All these names all start with M. McVeigh, Manson, Milosevic and Mengele.

Liz: I will try to find an example that doesn't start with M. Perhaps there is a numerological explanation.

Audience: What happened to Mengele in the end?

Liz: Well, if you believe *The Boys from Brazil,* he got his comeuppance at the hands of a Nazi-hunter. Unfortunately, *The Boys from Brazil* was a work of fiction. Mengele managed to escape to Paraguay, and lived out his days there. Recently his remains were found. He left no diary to let us know whether he ever felt any remorse. But it is highly unlikely.

The Moors Murderess

Let's examine one more of these charming examples, and then we can look at the chart that John kindly offered earlier. If you have second thoughts about the company you're keeping, John, you can retract your offer. Here is a person whose surname doesn't start with M, although the Christian name does. And this is a woman's chart. And we have yet more water. The odd one out in this delightful group is, of course, Hitler, who had only Chiron in a water sign and whose name has no M in it. But once again I would remind you that lack of water does not indicate lack of feeling. If there is a lot of water and the feelings are dissociated, the charm and subtlety of water are utilised for manipulative purposes. It is a salutary lesson in not making simplistic astrological assumptions.

Here the Sun is at the end of Cancer, conjunct Pluto at the beginning of Leo, and Pluto is just a degree away from the IC. The Moon is in Scorpio, which is Pluto's sign. This chart is strongly Plutonian. There is also a 12th house Saturn-Uranus conjunction in Gemini, with Saturn within orb of conjunction of the Ascendant. There is a Mars-Chiron conjunction in the 4th house, which squares the Moon in the 6th. Here is another stressed Mars, with its inevitable sense of impotence and inadequacy. Interestingly, the Sun and Moon are trine. Benign Sun-Moon aspects, particularly the conjunction, turn up frequently in criminal charts. We need to look at this more carefully later. Now, does anything here leap out and strike you?

Audience: It is quite a serious, interior chart. There seems to be a lot of repressed energy.

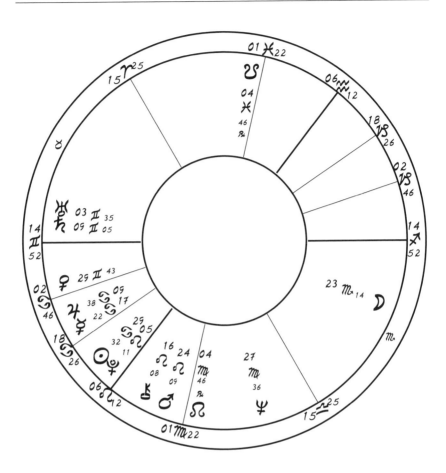

Myra Hindley
23 July 1942, 2.45 am, Lancaster

Liz: Let's look at the Moon's aspects. The Moon-Chiron square is a separating aspect. By progressed motion it would have been exact between six and seven months before her birth. The Moon-Mars square is applying, and by progressed motion would have been exact in the first month of life. Here are clear statements about disturbances in the family background before and just after birth. What does this Moon feel like, with squares to Mars and Chiron, yet with an applying trine to the Sun in Cancer, the Moon's own sign?

Audience: A sick child?

Audience: I get a feeling of potential healing skills which have gone badly wrong and have become destroying skills.

Liz: Both of you are presumably focusing on the Moon's placement in the 6th, since both illness and healing are associated with that house. The Moon in the 6th needs a sense of order and structure in everyday life to feel emotionally secure, and the Moon in Scorpio needs a great deal of emotional closeness of a particularly intense kind. This is a Cancerian with the Moon in Scorpio and Gemini rising. What is the basic temperament?

Audience: Very sensitive.

Liz: Yes, very sensitive and emotionally intense, with a longing for order and stability in her environment. There is also a great need to communicate. The Sun is in the 3rd house and Gemini is rising. As a child she needed not only emotional contact, but also plenty of verbal exchange with the people around her. Mercury is conjunct Jupiter, and these people are often great talkers. Do you think her needs were met?

Audience: No. The Sun is with Pluto, which is on the 4th house cusp, so she probably felt that her father crushed her individuality in some way. Maybe her mother did as well. Or maybe the mother was so angry and wounded that she couldn't listen to her child or respond to her. Or possibly the mother was very sick and couldn't nurse her or hold her.

Liz: Any of these situations is a likely possibility. Now we are back to our original question: is the psychopathic character innate, or is it created by the early environment, or is it both? And what astrological signatures might suggest this kind of innate predisposition? There is no aspect in this chart that, by itself, would suggest psychopathy. Lots of people have hard Sun-Pluto contacts. Once every year the Sun conjuncts Pluto, once a year it opposes Pluto, and twice a year it squares Pluto. Fortunately, not all these people are psychopaths. The same applies to Moon-Chiron. Twice a month the Moon squares Chiron, and twice a month it trines Chiron. The conjunction and opposition each occur once a month. In itself, Moon-Chiron is a common enough aspect. Yet it figures prominently in the charts of psychopathic personalities.

Audience: The 10th house is empty, but the rulers are Uranus and Saturn in the 12th, so the mother is experienced as cold or unavailable. Yet the Moon is in Scorpio and square Mars, which may be too hot and intense a mother. I wonder whether this is a mother who alternatively rejects and suffocates. It's like McVeigh's Moon opposite both Pluto and Uranus.

Mars-Chiron-Pluto in the 4th: father as destroyer

Liz: You may be right about a mother who swings between intense attachment and cold distance. The Moon square Mars-Chiron also suggests violence, emotional or physical, connected with the mother. But here we are also looking at something to do with father. The Sun is with Pluto, which is right at the IC, and Mars and Chiron are in the 4th. There is a whiff of something quite sulphurous in the paternal relationship and inheritance. This could be a sexually abusive father, or there might have been violence from or between the parents. The Chiron-Mars-Pluto father is a masculine image which this woman has internalised. If a woman internalises such a father-image, what might the consequences be?

Audience: She might be attracted to violent men.

Liz: Yes, such aspects are often projected. But the real violence is done internally, to her sense of herself as a woman. Childhood abuse from the father, emotional or physical, is internalised as a source of inner humiliation and shame. One feels perpetually demeaned, violated, humiliated and worthless, and that generates violent rage.

Audience: The father is a destroyer.

Liz: Yes, he is an archetypal destroyer, and he lives inside her. He is an aspect of her own psyche, whether she acts it out herself or finds a violent man to enact it for her. The Greeks didn't really have a figure like this, but in Hindu myth it is a kind of male version of Kali. It is a very dark, destructive energy. One way of expressing it is to marry a psychopath, or find one to join forces with.

Audience: Like Myra Hindley.

Liz: Actually, it's not *like* Myra Hindley. It *is* Myra Hindley. Psychopaths don't usually run in pairs, but Myra needed a male figure to carry her Mars-Chiron-Moon and Sun-Pluto. Are they both psychopaths? Is Myra the psychopath? Or was she manipulated by a psychopathic partner?

Audience: For years she has been trying to appeal against her life sentence.[11] She blames everything on her partner, who is also still in prison.

Audience: I met a prison warden who dealt with both of them. He said that her lover was criminally insane, rather than psychopathic.

Liz: Perhaps Myra is the psychopathic side of the couple. But evidently she needed Ian Brady to help her sexually abuse, torture and murder five children.

Audience: She was definitely the stronger person in the relationship.

Liz: Let's consider the crime as a symbol. Charles Manson's victims were primarily women, and his murder of the pregnant Sharon Tate tells us a lot about the source of his inner rage. Timothy McVeigh's victims were all the people who happened to be nearby when the bomb exploded, but his real target was the perceived tyranny of the American

---

[11] Myra Hindley died sixteen months after this seminar was given, of a chest infection following a heart attack. Her death occurred at 4.58 pm GMT on 15 November 2002, in Bury St. Edmunds, Suffolk.

government and American society. That tells us a lot about the source of *his* inner rage. Milosevic's victims were Muslims, and Mengele's were Jews: collectives which symbolised something for these two men. Myra Hindley's victims were children. What kind of statement is this for a Cancerian woman? This is the sign of the zodiac which is associated with mothering and nurturing.

Audience: She is Kali.

Liz: What is she murdering, if not her own child-self? There is something here about transferring her own experience of childhood onto a child, and subjecting that child to what she herself suffered.

Audience: Could it have something to do with siblings as well?

Liz: Possibly, since the Sun is in the 3rd house. Myra has a sister, who testified against her in court. It really upset her that her sister was the one who rang the police with evidence. I am not sure this indicates any particular viciousness on the part of the sister. Many people might do this, however much they loved a sibling, if they knew the sibling was out murdering children in her spare time. Given Myra's 3rd house Sun, she may have loved and looked up to this sister, but given her Moon in Scorpio square Mars, there was probably intense rivalry between them.

Benign Sun-Moon aspects

Audience: How would easy Sun-Moon aspects contribute to her violence?

Liz: A Sun-Moon trine does not contribute to violence. But it may have contributed to the split in Myra Hindley's nature, and exacerbated her tendency to dissociate. Sun trine Moon is what I call the "and they lived happily ever after" aspect. It is very benign, but there is sometimes too much complacency and even a certain smugness, and a refusal to look at the nastier side of life. Sun trine Moon describes equanimity between one's sense of individual purpose and one's emotional needs. They work together in harmony. The person with a trine or sextile between the luminaries generally believes that life is, and ought to be, harmonious. The gift of the aspect is that these people often have the power to generate harmony around them. But they expect harmony and want to see it everywhere, and they are often dreadfully shocked when they are confronted with a less harmonious reality. In fact, they may avoid facing reality for many years, speaking of a violent or abusive parent as "wonderful" and wilfully editing out their own suffering and humiliation. It is a lovely aspect, unless one has parents from hell. Then it can be dangerously blind, and may contribute to a deep split between a fantasy of life as Disneyland and the horror of one's actual experience.

The Sun and Moon are parental significators, and with the trine, sextile or conjunction, the parents are often perceived as working to preserve a "normal" appearance. But behind this façade, absolutely anything could be happening, including sexual abuse of the children. There is often a deep-rooted belief in "happy families", in the parents as well as the child. In itself, this is not negative. But if a Sun trine Moon person is born into a severely dysfunctional family, the parents may be saying one thing and feeling or doing another, yet the child cannot believe that anything could be seriously wrong. They go into what is known in psychological jargon as a state of denial.

The person with Sun square or opposition Moon says, "Here they go, fighting again. Relationships are always a battleground." There is an innate assumption that relationships require struggle. Internally there is always a conflict between goals and feelings, and this is often echoed in the parental marriage. There is an acceptance of the fact that one must work hard to get even a moment's real peace and harmony. But when the Sun and Moon are in trine, sextile or conjunction, there is an assumption that everything will always come out "right" in the end. Mother and father should live happily together and the world should be a wonderful place. The Sun trine Moon nature is often extremely likeable, because these are essentially optimistic people who want other people to be happy. But Myra is a Sun trine Moon person with Moon in Scorpio emotions, born into a Mars-Chiron-Pluto environment. She must have withdrawn into an alternative fantasy world very early – the applying trine would have been exact at around five to six months old –

and so her real feelings became completely dissociated, and erupted later as terrible cruelty and violence.

There is a disturbing dichotomy in Myra Hindley's chart. She has Sun trine Moon, and both Sun and Moon are sextile Neptune. But at the nadir of the chart, Mars, Chiron and Pluto are bubbling away, with Mars-Chiron square the Moon and Pluto conjunct the Sun. Two completely separate realities are portrayed here: a sensitive, caring, communicative child with very deep feelings and a receptive Neptunian nature, born into a world which was not only brutal but which mobilised her own latent brutality.

Audience: So there is a lot of collective receptivity in this chart as well.

Liz: Yes. I would always expect this in the charts of psychopaths, because they do carry something for the rest of us. Here also is the generational Saturn-Uranus conjunction. Like Milosevic, she was a "war baby" who entered a world which had fallen into chaos. What was happening in Britain in the summer of 1942?

Audience: The Blitz.

Liz: Yes, Britain was being bombed to pieces. Myra entered that world of chaos and destruction with Sun trine Moon and both Sun and Moon sextile Neptune. Her essential nature was not equipped to cope with this collective horror, let alone dysfunctional parenting. What inner resources could she muster to deal with such an environment? She had to mobilise the most ruthless and destructive aspects of her character – Mars-Chiron square Moon, and Sun conjunct Pluto – in order to survive psychologically. Her crimes were a compulsive re-enactment of the personal and collective savagery of her childhood. First she had to find a male who could carry these destructive energies for her, in much the same way Manson needed female acolytes to carry his Moon-Pluto and help him with his murders. Then she performed acts which were both a symbolic destruction of herself and an expression of the rage she had accrued by constantly living under the threat of being destroyed.

Audience: She was very charming as well. I suppose that would fit Venus in the 1st in Gemini.

Liz: Yes, the charm is there. What about the propensity to dissociate?

Audience: Could it be the combination of Gemini rising with all the Plutonian qualities? They really don't mix. Gemini is good at disconnecting. She recorded all the deaths on a tape recorder.

Liz: I would look at Moon-Chiron rather than Gemini for a propensity to dissociate from painful feelings. Like Moon-Uranus and Moon-Saturn, Moon-Chiron has the ability to disconnect. Sometimes this seems justified by the sense of being scapegoated: "Why should I feel anything for these people after what they have done to me?"

Audience: It's a sort of "avenging angel" attitude. A mission.

Liz: That is part of the psychopathic profile. If you think about our list, you will see that Myra Hindley fits every characteristic.

Audience: Do you believe she really has changed, and feels sorry for what she did?

Liz: I don't know. If she is sorry about what she has done, and is capable of changing, was she ever a "real" psychopath? I don't have an answers to these questions, and I don't know if she genuinely feels remorse.

Audience: Is the psychopathic personality capable of change?

Liz: Since everything in life is capable of change, psychopathic tendencies should, theoretically, also be able to change. The problem is that there is no evidence of it, despite the help which is offered.

Audience: Myra Hindley now says that if she had never met Ian Brady, she would never have committed the crimes.

Liz: Well, she would say that, wouldn't she? Holloway isn't an especially nice place to spend one's life. This claim might also be part of the psychopathic profile. Psychopathic behaviour is always someone else's fault in the eyes of the psychopath, so naturally the murders were Ian Brady's fault. I may be doing her a dreadful injustice, but my gut feeling is that Myra Hindley has not changed at all. She is still not taking responsibility for what she did.

Audience: What she did is so enormous.

Liz: Her crimes are no more enormous than that of Jamie Bulger's killers. For that matter, her crimes are no more enormous than a terrorist's bomb, which blows up dozens or even hundreds of innocent men, women and children.

Audience: There is a big political element in whether she is released. There would be too much of an outcry against the government if she were set free.

Liz: I am sure you are right. The government has released many IRA bombers who have murdered far more people than Myra Hindley because it is politically expedient. Releasing Myra would not win votes. As a society, we do not know what to do with psychopaths. Should we have compassion for them, execute them, lock them away or believe their claims of rehabilitation and forgive them? I cannot answer this question. What I am trying to do today is get beneath the psychopath's behavioural patterns to the emotional dynamics which generate the behaviour. These dynamics are not very far away from so-called ordinary people's inner lives. The difference lies in the degree of dissociation, which in the case of the psychopath is complete.

Sun-Moon conjunctions

Audience: Could you say more about a Sun-Moon conjunction? That's an eclipse. In mediaeval astrology eclipses were considered ominous.

Liz: Eclipses are triggers which release energy, and they are ominous only when ominous planetary configurations are involved with the eclipse. And not all Sun-Moon conjunctions are eclipses. Solar eclipses occur twice a year, when the new Moon is lined up on each end of the Moon's nodal axis. But there is a Sun-Moon conjunction every month. There is nothing intrinsically sinister about it.

Our perceptions of and responses to life are based on our Sun-Moon dyad, which describes what we aspire to become as individuals and what we need in order to feel related to others. We look out at life through these two lenses – self-development and relatedness – and in ancient astrology this was understood literally. It was believed the right eye was ruled by the Sun and the left eye by the Moon. If the Sun and Moon are not in aspect, these two inner motivations function differently, but do not interfere with or block each other. If they are in harmony, we believe life is harmonious because we suffer no inner conflict. What we want and what we need are in accord. If the Sun and Moon conjunct, our aspirations and needs are not just harmonious; they are the same thing. New Moon people are very powerful, because their goals and emotional needs function as a unit. This conjunction can be immensely creative because the person is so focused and one-pointed. There is no hesitancy, no inner tension or conflict.

Of course other natal aspects can reflect stress and suffering, but on the most fundamental level the individual does not question his or her rightness, and life is expected to reflect this. At the time of a Sun-Moon conjunction, the Moon is obscured – the "dark of the Moon" – which symbolically suggests that one's emotional sensitivity to others is obscured by the intensity of one's drive toward self-development. That is why new Moon people often get into trouble. They assume everything should fit into their unified vision. When other people say, "Excuse me, but I have an opinion, too, and it isn't the same as yours," these people are often baffled and upset. It is a surprise to discover that other people are truly other, and that life might not always fit one's expectations. This is not innately negative, although it can sometimes be insensitive and inflexible. But we must always think in terms of the chemical mix between such one-pointedness and the early environment.

What makes the difference?

We need some relief from this relentless parade of dreadful people, so we can now look at John's chart and, if there is time, perhaps another chart from the group. If I am correct in my basic hypothesis, this exercise will reveal aspects which are identical to those in the charts of psychopaths but are being expressed in other ways. What is the difference between a Moon-Uranus that dissociates completely and a Moon-Uranus that detaches in a creative way? What is the difference between a Moon-Saturn that is utterly isolated and a Moon Saturn that is contained and self-sufficient but nevertheless related? What is the difference between a Mars-Chiron which exhibits cruelty and a Mars-Chiron which works patiently and with integrity toward a positive goal? The aspects themselves may be identical. But there *is* something different. It might be a subtle disparity in the arrangement of the ingredients, or there might be an extra ingredient which changes the whole picture. Or there might be a difference in the family background, or in the individual's attitude or level of consciousness. We don't know yet, and we might not find out. But we need to ask this question, because that is where we have something to offer as astrologers. We can't do anything about Myra Hindley or Charles Manson or Slobodan Milosevic. But we might be able to offer something to our clients, particularly those who come with their children's charts and want to know how to work with difficult configurations such as the ones we have been examining.

Why did you offer us your chart, John? We can safely assume that you are not psychopathic.

John: There are a few reasons. Firstly, as you were saying, there are so many similarities, but it is my chart you have put up there, not a psychopath's. Secondly, I went through a big phase in my twenties when I was very interested in psychopaths. I was into Manson and the Moors murders. I was attracting people with those tendencies. I was attracting women who had strange ideas. Thirdly, I wrote a novel a few years ago about serial killers, and it was rejected because I was too sympathetic toward the main serial killer.

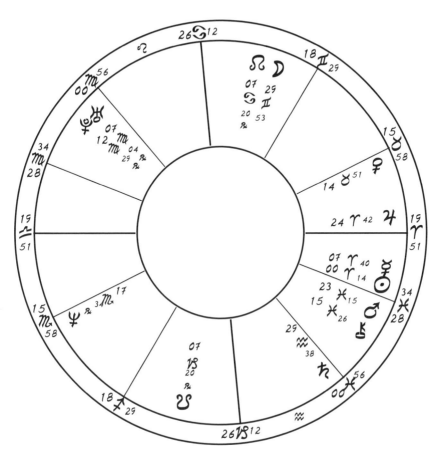

John
Birth data withheld for purposes of confidentiality

Liz: It's very helpful that you are being so open about it. Yes, there are similar configurations. Libra is rising, so Venus is the chart ruler. The Moon and Saturn are in exact trine. If we had seen this aspect in one of the earlier charts, we could have made a meal of that Moon-Saturn, because it is so common in the charts of violent criminals. There is also a Mars-Chiron conjunction, which we have been bumping into a lot. Here is the Uranus-Pluto conjunction again, which we saw in Timothy McVeigh's chart, and Chiron is in opposition to them. But they do not aspect the Moon. Apart from the trine to Saturn, the Moon makes a sextile to Jupiter and squares to the Sun, Mercury and Mars. It makes no aspects to any outer planets, unless we consider it sesquiquadrate Neptune with an orb of 3°. Given the Moon's critical importance in all very early psychic disturbances, it may be significant that John's Moon makes no strong contact to the outer planets. But let's look first at the Mars-Chiron conjunction in Pisces in the 5th house. It is interesting that you wrote a novel about serial killers, John. Why were you able to express the darkest elements of that aspect through creative work, rather than acting it out? What do you think makes the difference?

A creative Mars-Chiron

John: I think it's what you decide to do with it. To me, Mars-Chiron is about not having been able to express very Martial things in early life. It is about not being able to play when I was a child. I was born with a heart condition, so they said I couldn't do sport, games, swimming – I couldn't just play along with everyone else. It took me a while to get used to that, being an Aries. That was quite hard, the fact that I couldn't use my Mars. I think it is about finding other outlets for it, showing my strength in a different area. At school I tried to do that academically, and creatively I tried to do it with writing.

Liz: Did your heart condition make you feel humiliated in any way?

John: No. I wasn't bullied at school. It actually had the reverse effect. Because I couldn't do games, I used to have to sit in other classes, and it meant I got to meet a lot more of the school. The people who would have bullied me got to know me and became friends rather than trying to do anything unpleasant. So that helped. It was an advantage. If anybody picked on me, other people would say, "Oh leave him alone, he's all right."

Liz: You have said two things which are very important. Firstly, about the Mars-Chiron conjunction, you said, "It's what you do with it." You made a conscious choice to try to express it, rather than suppressing it, reaching boiling point, blowing and acting it out destructively. You seem to have accepted the fact that this was how it was, and you tried to find another outlet. This ability to accept limits seems to be a critical factor. The Mars-Chiron people we have been looking at, such as Myra Hindley, couldn't accept frustration. Your perspective implies the early development of an ego which could contain frustration. An infant cannot tolerate frustration, but a reasonably formed ego can, however painful it might be.

Secondly, you have told us that you were not subjected to abuse or humiliation. You were denied the normal athletic expression of other boys, but you were not made to feel devalued or demeaned because of it. Mars-Chiron always suffers frustration, but the environment can add to that frustration in an unbearable way. Mars-Chiron in a birth chart doesn't say, "You were abused by your parents and your peers." All it says is, "There is a sense of frustration around the expression of Mars, due to factors which are not personal, are not linked with any individual culpability, and may seem very unfair." But if there is a violently abusive parent, a whole range of psychological patterns and responses may be linked to Mars-Chiron which would not develop with a different experience of early life. The ability to make the kind of choice you made may be partly due to something innate which is not portrayed in the chart. People are not born the same, and a greater degree of intelligence or consciousness may provide the "X-factor" which we cannot see in the planetary configurations. More esoterically minded people might talk about the soul in this context. But the way the environment has interacted with your Mars-Chiron is important. The environment did not place unbearable pressure on you. Elements of violence and cruelty are obviously there, or you would not have become fascinated with psychopathy, nor written a novel about it. But we all have dark elements in us, and yours were contained and expressed in a way which was creative rather than destructive.

Also, the conjunction is not in a fixed sign. It is in Pisces, and the mutable signs tend to be able to adapt and let go more easily than the fixed signs. Your Mars-Chiron in Pisces doesn't nurse grievances in quite same way that Myra Hindley's Mars-Chiron in Leo did. One of the common denominators about all the examples we have looked at today is that they are all so fixed. Fixed signs really dominate these charts. But yours is more a mix of cardinal and mutable signs. There are three planets in fixed signs: Saturn in Aquarius, Neptune in Scorpio and

Venus in Taurus. You have enough fixity for staying power and stability, but you are flexible enough to let go and move on. How much is choice, how much is the chart, and how much is the environment? Or is it all three? The world of psychopathy fascinated you, perhaps partly because of Mars-Chiron, but being fascinated by psychopaths is not the same as being one.

John: I think there was always an understanding of the sense of frustration, an understanding of wanting to change the world. Yes, I wanted the world to be beautiful and perfect and harmonious, but I always knew that it isn't. I think I have been lucky to express that frustration through a creative outlet, to express it to other people through writing and the imagination to work through it.

Liz: Another thing that may affect the way you have handled the difficult aspects in your chart is the Sun-Moon square. You don't deny the disharmony of life, although it is offensive to a Libran Ascendant, because you live with it internally all the time. In Myra Hindley's chart there in a Sun-Moon trine, and this says something about an inability to cope with disharmony and conflict. The gap was too great between her perception of life and what life presented her with. These are very subtle differences, but it is interesting how important they seem to be.

The Venus factor

John: Is there an issue with self-esteem as well? I wasn't frightened of other children. I didn't automatically think they might bully me. I just thought, "Cool, I am going to experience another class." It is a different attitude. I expected to be liked.

Liz: Yes, the issue of self-esteem is a very important difference. It may be relevant that your Venus, although it is involved with outer planets, is in its own sign and is therefore solid and strong.

Audience: It's on the cusp of the 8th, trine Pluto. That's pretty dark.

Liz: Yes, it reflects a certain taste for the dark side of life. But it is still a strong Venus. McVeigh had Venus in Aries, the sign of its detriment, exactly conjunct Saturn in the sign of its fall. That's what used to be called a debilitated Venus. Manson's Venus is also "debilitated", as it is in Scorpio, the other sign of its detriment, and is square Saturn. I am not making the case that psychopathy is attributable to the chart, nor am I suggesting that Venus in detriment is a sign of psychopathy. Hitler, after all, had it in Taurus. But we are really looking at how individuals cope with the hurts and disappointments life throws at them. A strong Venus copes better than a weak one because the sense of self-esteem holds up better under battering. The aspects which tend to undermine even a strong Venus are squares, conjunctions or oppositions from Chiron and Saturn. Hitler's Taurean Venus is square Saturn. John has no contact between Venus and Saturn, and between Venus and Chiron there is a sextile.

Tight aspects

Another relevant factor may be the tightness of the difficult aspects to personal planets in the charts of psychopaths. In McVeigh's chart, there is no room for Venus to manoeuvre because Saturn was sitting exactly on it at birth. There are very tight aspects in all the charts we have looked at. In Manson's chart, Mars and Neptune are exactly conjunct. There is no room for Mars to manoeuvre. Myra Hindley has a virtually exact Mars-Moon square, within 1° of orb. Of course tight aspects alone do not create psychopathic propensities. But they make it very difficult for personal planets to get breathing space or find flexible ways of expression when they are beleaguered.

Audience: Do you mean that the transpersonal planets squash the expression of the personal planets?

Liz: The squashing is not always transpersonal. In Myra Hindley's chart, it is a Moon-Mars square. The Moon cannot express itself without feeling angry. In McVeigh's chart, it is Venus-Saturn. Venus cannot express itself without feeling restricted and isolated. When the orb is wider, there is greater flexibility, and Venus can sometimes come out to play without Saturn constantly in tow. With Mars sitting under Neptune in Manson's chart, the sense of being engulfed is extremely powerful, because the aspect is exact. Mars cannot express itself without feeling weak. All planetary conjunctions link planets together for the duration of one's life, but with a wide orb there is a long cord. When the aspect is exact, they are manacled together by the wrists and ankles. This, too, can be positive, but it takes a strong ego to create the right vessel for such intensity.

Audience: And the fixity doesn't help.

Liz: No, the fixity doesn't help, because there is a deep resistance to changing internal patterns. McVeigh's Venus-Saturn is in a cardinal sign, but his Sun and Ascendant are fixed, and his fundamental attitudes are very set. There is something uncomfortable about the combination of fixity and very tight difficult aspects.

Audience: So the tendency is to give into any impulse that comes?

Liz: It is more an experience of being overwhelmed by patterns which one cannot break – a sense of being helpless in the face of compulsions which *must* be acted out. I agree with what you said earlier, John. I do think there is a choice involved. But the environmental factor is also important. Whatever failings your parents might have had, they clearly loved you, and they did not brutalise you.

John: That's true.

Accepting limits

Liz: Although the Sun and Moon are in square, any disharmony between your parents did not drive them to abuse you in early life. Although so much depends on individual character, the early environment has an enormous influence on how a person deals with a natal aspect. For example, some Mars-Chiron children – especially when

Mars is in a fixed sign – can be infuriating and provocative, and they often refuse to respond to discipline. They have an overwhelming need to prove that they are potent because they experience a constant sense of frustration. So they may push against authority in little or big ways. If the parents react to this with violence because their own frustration has built up over a lifetime of being thwarted, then a potentially creative Mars-Chiron may turn brutal.

Hard aspects between Mars and Chiron frequently appear in the charts of violent criminals. Yet many of us here today have such contacts. What makes the difference? The sign and house in which these planets fall is clearly important, as is the way the aspect "sits" in relation to the rest of the chart. But we also need to ask how the childhood environment interacted with the aspect. Parents provide us with models, and if the model is too destructive too early, we grow up with no other perception of how to express what we are. Children who display what are euphemistically called "antisocial propensities" often have parents who are themselves children. Such parents do not know how to contain their child because they received no containment themselves in childhood. They swing between helplessness and violence, but cannot set consistent limits. In Britain it is now illegal to slap one's child. Political correctness dictates that the application of any physical discipline whatsoever is unacceptable. Like many solutions borne out of ideology rather than genuine human understanding, this may turn out to be a future disaster. Difficult Mars aspects often need physical boundaries, and there is a big difference between a carefully administered slap and a violent beating. Where can these children learn about boundaries and limits? Teachers too are no longer allowed to impose any kind of physical discipline. They must never touch the child, and therefore cannot remove a violently disruptive child from the classroom.

Audience: As a teacher, I can say that the only way to deal with children who are misbehaving is to help them understand that, first, they are responsible for their actions, and second, there is a difference between "Yes" and "No". If you can get that from a child, you can work with them. If you don't get it, you can't work with them. Children who can't grasp these things are usually from a home where no one said "No", and they didn't have to face the consequences of what they did.

Liz: Were you punished as a child?

John: No, I wasn't punished. Hardly ever.

Liz: So you were well-behaved?

John: Fairly, yes. I tended to get a better result by manipulation.

Liz: It must have been a Libran who said that discretion is the better part of valour. There also seems to be no major conflict with authority reflected in your chart. The Sun is not hampered in its expression. It is conjunct Mars, so you can be very self-willed, and the Sun-Moon square can generate tension, restlessness and a tendency to see life as a battleground. But that doesn't worry an Aries. There is no blockage of the Sun from Saturn, Chiron or the outer planets. The Sun's development is encouraged by being in the sign of its exaltation and conjunct Mars in the sign of its dignity. Despite having Mars conjunct Chiron, it seems you have never felt internally beaten down or humiliated by authority.

John: No. I tend to deal with authority by avoiding it, or by going along to a certain extent and then backing away.

Liz: The psychopath is usually on a lone campaign against authority. This is linked with their anti-social and often criminal behaviour. Although you belong to the Uranus-Pluto generation group, conflict with authority is not a dominant theme in your chart. As we have seen, authority is experienced as humiliating to the psychopath. You may also benefit from the realism reflected by your Sun and Mercury in the 6th house. It is interesting that, given the 6th house association with health, you have had to struggle with a health problem and, in doing so, you have learned to inhabit the real world and accept its limits.

The isolation of Moon-Saturn

What about the Moon-Saturn trine? Do you dissociate, or do you detach and then engage again?

John: I tend to detach, but not all the time. It depends on the circumstances. I am sometimes very isolated.

Liz: Is the isolation absolute, or is it something you feel you can move out of?

John: Again, different periods in my life have been different. There have been times when the isolation has been pretty complete. But I have always been able to feel depressed when I am isolated. I don't cut off from it.

Liz: One of the characteristics of the psychopathic personality is that depression only occurs when they are cornered. They are not depressed about their loneliness, because there is such complete dissocation that they do not feel it. They will often abuse substances such as drugs or drink, but they don't *feel* depressed. The ability to feel the pain of isolation seems to be very important. To feel it means one is no longer isolated, because one is connected to one's own feelings. Psychopaths cannot feel their isolation.

Audience: It is a complete lack of awareness.

Liz: One author calls it "emotional blindness". There is no consciousness of feelings. The only feelings that are recognisable are anger and frustration. One of the most creative ways to work with Moon-Saturn is to allow oneself to be depressed, isolated and lonely. To disconnect from such feelings is not a good idea. It may be inevitable that one does disconnect from time to time. Dissociation is something we all do occasionally. But it is not permanently built into the personality structure. And we must dissociate at times, because if we didn't, we would all go off and kill ourselves in the face of life's misery and unfairness. We have to disconnect, but we come back again. The psychopath does not.

Audience: I think I remember hearing you say once that the shadow side of water signs is the ability to be very sensitive to their own feelings but not the feelings of others. Maybe that has to do with the lack of empathy.

Liz: All the charts we have looked at should, in theory, be empathetic. They are all people with lots of planets in water. These flagrantly empathetic qualities are not so flagrant in John's chart. That may be worth noting, because having that much empathy means that one can easily feel engulfed. Given a reasonable early environment, this may cause relationship difficulties later in life, but it may also contribute to a creative imagination and an open, compassionate heart. In the psychopathic personality, alongside the black, bitter rage, there is an intolerable fear of being engulfed or overwhelmed, by other people's feelings as well as one's own. I've mentioned this already several times. This fear of engulfment is reflected in the Plutonian and Neptunian components in the charts we have been examining. Now, you have a reasonably engulfing Neptune, John, but it's not the Creature from the Black Lagoon variety.

John: Yes, I can appreciate that one.

Liz: There is plenty of empathy and emotional receptivity described in the chart, with Neptune in Scorpio opposite Venus, the chart ruler, and trine Mars-Chiron in Pisces. But fear of engulfment doesn't seem to be one of your dominant issues.

John: No. It crops up a bit, but it is not a major thing.

Liz: Idealisation can be a Venus-Neptune problem, but fear of engulfment is linked with Moon-Neptune, and sometimes with Moon-Pluto. The other great fear associated with psychopathy is the fear of abandonment, as we have seen. Children who live in terror of abandonment may cope by constantly abandoning others so that they are never at risk. This is connected with the tendency to dissociate. Something within the psychopathic personality says, "I can't cope with this terror any more. I will never need anyone again."

John: There may be something of that in the Venus-Neptune. I remember as a teenager trying to work it out almost schematically. The safe thing to do was to make sure I was the one who was giving. I never, ever received anything, because that way I would never feel dependent. I consciously constructed that system.

What lies beneath

Liz: Fear of rejection is not unique to any particular natal aspect. If the chart contains certain combinations involving the Moon or Venus with Neptune or Pluto on one side and Saturn, Chiron or Uranus on the other, there may be a strong conflict between feelings of dependency and the need for autonomy. This is common enough, and it can create some typical relationship patterns. The moment one starts feeling too attached, one pulls back in order to regain control. Relationship triangles often reflect this dilemma. One's needs are divided between two people, so if one proves to be a disappointment, the other is there to compensate, and one never risks total abandonment.

We all need others and we all fear abandonment. It is the absoluteness of the psychopath's fear that is so destructive, and there is no conscious awareness of it. Most of us, like John, can say, "I have felt this fear. I know what it's like." The psychopath is not aware of feeling fear. Yet the fear is so deep and all-consuming that everything is dominated by it. All behavioural patterns, whether psychopathic or not, serve some inner goal, conscious or unconscious. The psychopath's characteristic promiscuity serves as a protection against abandonment. If one is always hopping from one bed to another, casually exploiting sexual partners but never feeling attached to any of them, one never runs the risk of being vulnerable. Power over others is a highly effective weapon against the threat of abandonment. Why should an individual disconnect from feelings? Because when we need, we are vulnerable, and we might be humiliated or abandoned. Even the low boredom threshold of the psychopath is related to this all-consuming fear. To become too attached to anything, whether it is a person or an object, means one is vulnerable. If we wish to create anything, we must run the risk of criticism and rejection. The psychopath's creativity is expressed through manipulation. All that intelligence and ingenuity are mobilised to serve as protection against the one global, intractable fear.

Audience: What would you expect to find in Hannibal Lecter's chart?

Liz: Hannibal is an imaginary figure, a character in a novel and a film. But if I were looking for signatures of extreme cruelty and violence, I would expect a severely threatened Moon and a very unhappy Mars. I might also look for a powerful angular Venus, or a Venus-ruled sign on the Ascendant.

Audience: Where are the aesthetics in eating people?

Liz: You'd be surprised. It depends on the recipe. But it is not coincidental that Venus is emphasised in the charts we have looked at. These people are born with an overwhelming craving for beauty. The world they meet seems so black and dreadful that their capacity to relate emotionally is severely damaged. We do not know whether the damage is permanent. The psychopathic personality is usually of at least average, and frequently above average, intelligence. Obviously many violent criminals lack intelligence, but they are not usually psychopaths. They are just stupid and violent. If an individual is perceptive to an unusual degree, but the environment they are born into is severely disturbed and their first encounters with life are appalling, this fine intelligence becomes dissociated from the heart. The intelligence no longer serves the whole person. It only serves the pathology.

Something happens to these people which deforms natal aspects that might otherwise be very creative. Perhaps the aspects themselves suggest a propensity to experience suffering and frustration in a particularly intense way. Perhaps fixity and tight orbs contribute to the inability to process difficult childhood experiences. All the charts we have looked at today, with the exception of John's, have outer planets on angles, strongly configured with the Sun or Moon, and we have seen that receptivity to the collective is another important factor. Once these people are twisted out of shape, they can't untwist. And it happens so very early. I don't know whether there is a genetic component in psychopathy. Certainly there are astrological components which reflect certain kinds of sensitivities and certain kinds of defences, which in the majority of people would lead to no more than the garden variety neuroses in which we all partake. And in case you haven't worked it out, there is no such thing as normal. But psychopathy is a long way from the neurotic behaviour of a complaining Moon-Saturn or an irritable Mars-Chiron or an anxious Moon-Uranus or a mistrustful Venus-Pluto. The astrological signatures are the same, and so are the psychological dynamics which astrology portrays. But some appalling and irreversible dislocation happens in the psychopath, and these aspects are transformed into something frightening.

Audience: I wonder about the relationship between apparently normal, conventional people who have these planetary configurations, and psychopaths with the same configurations. I don't mean that the normal ones are really psychopaths, but when people are being overly normal and conventional, the disruptive energy must go somewhere. Maybe that creates a sort of polarity with people who are psychopathic.

Liz: This is what I was saying earlier. In some ways, psychopaths are the mouthpiece for something in all of us which we cannot face or deal with. We cannot separate the psychopath's chart from anyone else's chart, and we cannot separate them from the society in which they live. If you squeeze a balloon on one side, a lump of air pops up on the other side. Any behaviour which excludes the whole human being squeezes the balloon, and the distortions reflect our secret selves *in extremis*.

Audience: Those boys in the James Bulger case: are they psychopaths?

Liz: I don't know.

Audience: How would you know if a client was psychopathic?

Liz: Possibly with hindsight. Possibly never. The psychopath does not enter the room and say, "Hello, I'm a psychopath," and they are, as a rule, very convincing in superficial social contact. There may be nothing in the behaviour that suggests psychopathy. Psychopathic tendencies usually reveal themselves quite early in life, but the astrologer is not ordinarily privy to that knowledge.

Audience: How would you know as an astrologer?

Liz: I wouldn't know as an astrologer. I have been telling you that all day. I would have to rely on my human instincts, and observe whether the hairs on the back of my neck stand up because something doesn't feel right. Sometimes one gets a whiff of something chilly and strange. One can "smell" the lack of real emotional connection, if one is paying attention. But it is very unusual to encounter a full-blown psychopath. We are more likely to encounter elements of it within an apparently civilised personality, including our own.

Audience: I read an interesting article by a journalist who worked on the hunt for the Yorkshire Ripper. It took such a long time to catch him, because the police were looking for a psychopath. He was interviewed twice, and both times they let him go. He kept slipping through the net because he looked like everyone else.

Liz: Yes, that's the punch-line, I suppose. He didn't just *look* like everybody else, he *was* everybody else, with just a little piece missing. We should probably all get down on our knees and thank the gods that whatever seems to afflict these people does not afflict the rest of us – at least, not to the point where we begin to destroy others.

Audience: Why are we reacting with such shock and murderous rage toward Jamie Bulger's killers?

Liz: Perhaps because they remind us of what we ourselves could so easily become. These two killer-children also trigger a deeper collective issue. Any murder is horrific. But what we deem to be shocking changes according to the prevailing *Zeitgeist,* and certain things are more horrific to us at the moment than others.

Audience: Exactly. That's why I don't understand why Jamie Bulger's murder seems so much worse to people than other horrible murders. I know it might sound hard, but why is the murder of a child worse than the murder of a teenager, or a young adult, or a middle-aged person?

Liz: It depends on what we project onto all these different victims. Children who kill children are shocking to us because we project our lost innocence on the young. We want so much to believe that they are blameless. In literature there have always been morally questionable and even "evil" children, and some novels deal with the essential amorality of children: think of Golding's *Lord of the Flies*. But in the last couple of decades, our perspective on children has shifted quite dramatically. As we become more alienated and cynical as a collective, we long for the golden age of innocence which we have lost, and we project it onto children. If a parent kills a child, we say the parent was evil and the child was innocent, or we say society is evil and both the parent and the child are victims. But if a child deliberately kills another child, we don't know how to deal with it. What shocks us depends on where our own issues lie, and this changes all the time because the collective is in a state of constant flux.

We have reached the end of the seminar now. Thank you for your honest input, John, and thank you all very much for participating.

Part Two: Sanity and Madness

This seminar was given on 25 June 2000 at Regents College, London as part of the Summer Term of the seminar programme of the Centre for Psychological Astrology.

All the world's mad but me and thee

Let's start the day with a simple question. How many of you consider yourselves sane? Only one? That's very encouraging. It is important for us to look at sanity and madness from an astrological perspective because practicing astrologers will inevitably, sooner or later, encounter clients who are on the edge of a psychotic episode but who fear falling into the hands of the psychiatric establishment. We will also meet clients who have experienced one or more breakdowns and are seeking a deeper understanding of what they have been through. And we will encounter concerned parents who want a chart done for a schizophrenic child, or a partner who is in the throes of a serious psychotic episode. As astrologers, we encounter the issue of madness constantly in our work. And those of you who are prepared to be honest will acknowledge that we ourselves, in company with all those who work in the helping professions, are not necessarily always able to cling to what we call sanity. As the saying goes, "All the world's mad but me and thee, and sometimes I wonder about thee."

I chose the title of this seminar very carefully, in part because the word "madness" is no longer deemed appropriate when discussing this subject. We are allowed to call historical figures mad if enough centuries have elapsed, but we are not supposed to use this word about people we know. We are supposed to say things like, "He's in a very disturbed state," or, "She's having some difficulty in adaptation." Because of the stress of not being able to call madness by its name, we unleash our bewilderment privately and use less polite expressions, such as, "He's absolutely barking," or, "She's gone bonkers," or, "He's in la-la-land." Or we resort to sardonic euphemisms: "The lift doesn't go to the top floor any more," or, "There's a screw loose somewhere." We use phraseology which is meant to defuse and keep at a distance an experience which is quite terrifying, not only to the person undergoing it, but also to the observer. There is something about mad states which frightens the life out of people who have never been overwhelmed by the condition that is overwhelming the mad person.

So, at various times during the day, I am afraid I may stumble into serious political incorrectness. We can't deal with this subject by speaking in hushed voices and adopting a theatrically caring tone. We need to bring in an essential ingredient which mad people themselves often have in abundance: humour. We may be very mistaken in defining mad states as something separate from the way the rest of us experience life. Most of us cannot cope well with madness in other people, and it is rather naive to assume that we can care for mad people "in the community" without any prior training or knowledge. Our confusion is made worse by the increasing social pressure to use phraseology which drains all meaning from the way we describe our experiences. Last night, someone showed me a cartoon which I found very refreshing. It was a picture of two cows. The first one was saying to the second one, "What do think of all this business of mad cow disease?" The second cow replied, "Well, it has nothing to do with me. I'm a helicopter." An ironic sense of life's absurdity can help us work more creatively with the material under discussion today.

First we will look at how madness has been interpreted over the centuries, beginning with ancient cultures. Then we can look at how our view of madness has changed according to the perspectives of psychiatry and depth psychology. Finally, we need to consider the question of whether states of madness, temporary or permanent, are in any way related to anything we can see in the horoscope. What does madness look like astrologically? Is it inevitable in the people afflicted by it? Does it have any creative potential? Can the timing be predicted? We need to examine not only birth charts, but also the transits and progressions that might be active when someone goes mad.

Psychiatry's split

I want to make it clear from the outset that I am not attempting to denigrate the psychiatric establishment in my approach today. This is not a seminar on clinical diagnosis or treatment, nor is it an attack on the medical view of madness. It is intended as an imaginative exploration of madness through the language of myth and the symbolism of astrology. Although I have some experience of clinical psychiatric work, I am not medically trained, and I would not presume to advise a client to abandon any treatment prescribed by their psychiatrist. But as astrologers, we need perspectives other than that of psychiatry in order to understand more deeply the nature of madness and its possible causes. During the course of the day I will be highlighting some alternative ways of viewing madness, which might or might accord with the established medical view. There has been a serious split within the psychiatric establishment for many decades concerning madness, and we should not imagine that any uniform opinion exists among psychiatrists that will answer any of our deeper questions. I will read you a quote from Thomas Szasz, Professor of Psychiatry at Syracuse University in New York, who denies that there is any such thing as "mental illness".

> Psychiatry is conventionally defined as a medical specialty concerned with the diagnosis and treatment of mental diseases. I submit that this definition, which is still widely accepted, places psychiatry in the company of alchemy and astrology and commits it to the category of pseudoscience.[1]

It is reassuring to know that Szasz classifies psychiatrists with astrologers. In any event, he insists that mental illness is a myth fabricated by psychiatrists for reasons of professional advancement, and endorsed by society because it sanctions easy solutions for problem people. It is unnecessary to add that many of his fellow psychiatrists consider Szasz himself to be mad, although he also has his supporters. At the opposite extreme is the school of psychiatry which perceives

---

[1] See Thomas Szasz, *The Myth of Mental Illness* (1961) and *The Manufacture of Madness* (1970).

mental illness to be not only a real psychopathological entity, but a condition with an entirely organic basis. On this side of the fence there is no room for the perspectives of dynamic depth psychology, let alone astrology, since all states of consciousness, be they "normal" or "abnormal", ultimately have their source in the chemical output of the human brain, and must be treated accordingly with the appropriate medication. Although I have some sympathy with Szasz' perspective, we need to be pragmatic about the individual clients who come to us for insight. Even if we do not believe there is such a thing as mental illness *per se*, in practice we must deal in a realistic and constructive way with those astrological clients whose psychological disturbances are destroying their lives.

Certain of the more florid states that psychiatry deals with, such as schizophrenia and manic depression – which has recently changed its name to bipolar disorder – are generally understood to be states of madness. Other states, which might or might not be madness, may not be interpreted as such: for example, someone who has a powerful religious experience and then feels impelled to offer the Truth to others, whether invited to do so or not. Is this madness? If so, what is its nature? And if not, what is it? Is fanaticism "sane"? At various times in history, such a state of absolute conviction has been considered a visitation from God; the person has been specially blessed, or is a saint. Even today, in some societies, it is possible to have an intense religious experience, go out into the streets preaching – or even blowing up recalcitrant unbelievers – and still be considered normal.

What if someone from another culture, such as India, has had a transcendent experience and spends the rest of their life in profound meditation, abjuring all material goods and refusing to relate to the outer world? Is this person mad or enlightened? Is it possible to be both? Are they secretly the same? Religion and madness, as we shall see, have always had a peculiarly intimate relationship. And what about political fanaticism? Was Lenin mad or sane? And what about Hitler and other psychopaths? We ourselves are often called mad because we "believe in" astrology. Even if people don't say this directly, they often imply that there is something definitely disturbed about an individual involved in a subject not sanctioned by the prevailing world-view. Szasz' comment is particularly relevant here. On the other hand, mad states are unmistakable when they are severe, as any of you who have experienced or observed such states will know. There is no point in pretending that this individual is fine, because they obviously are not. But what makes them different from the rest of us?

Audience: I think the outer planets have a lot to do with it.

Liz: You are suggesting that astrological factors are relevant. That is what I would like to explore today. There are certain configurations in the chart which might suggest a difficulty in processing certain kinds of experiences, and when this vulnerability is combined with the right environmental factors, psychological states may result which are out of touch with what we are pleased to call reality. But even that careful statement is fraught with difficulties. Although we will see some very interesting patterns in the horoscopes we examine today, we will still not be able to conclude from the chart that any individual is or will become mad. But before we start exploring the astrological picture, I would like to look briefly at how madness was perceived centuries ago. Although this isn't intended to be a definitive history, there are insights into madness which the Greeks possessed that can help us to a deeper understanding of the astrological as well as psychological factors involved.

Madness through the centuries

The punishments of the gods

The Greek approach to madness developed over the centuries from the archaic period to the classical, moving from an intuitive religious perspective to a more scientific one. But Greek science still embraced a world-view in which, as Thales once said, all things are full of gods. Greek drama combines both dimensions, and both are relevant to our astrological understanding. In early Greek epics such as the *Iliad*, human beings are portrayed as mere puppets in the grip of terrible forces beyond their control, and madness is only one of many possible visitations from these powers which avenge and destroy. Individual conflicts and deliberations of conscience are ineffectual in the face of such divine potency. This attitude began to shift by the 5th century BCE, and in the plays of Aeschylus, Sophocles and Euripides we see madness arising not only from the ineluctable decrees of the gods, but also from human *hubris* and human conflict. Figures such as Oedipus and Orestes are certainly the innocent victims of divine vengeance, but these characters also reflect, agonise and make choices which can either save or destroy them. They torment themselves and thus help to invoke their own madness. This combination of the rampaging of an irate deity and a conscious human response to that deity is highly relevant to our understanding of how particular astrological configurations may be related to states of madness and their potential transformation. I will deal with this in greater detail later.

The archaic Greek view, inherited from Sumerian and Babylonian antecedents, perceived madness as a condition of possession by a god or spirit. The mad person is an individual whose rational consciousness had been supplanted by an energy which, although not necessarily benefic, is nevertheless divine. This state of divine possession included not only destructive compulsions but also altered states such as the prophetic trance of the seer. Conditions which we might now understand as at least partially physical, such as epilepsy, were also thought to be divinely inflicted. In the archaic Greek world, any person at any time could be vulnerable to invasion by a deity. But by the classical age, the criteria for a deity taking possession of a human became more selective. Usually the individual, or his or her family, offend the deity in some way. This is a very sophisticated definition of madness: certain primal powers, which we might now call archetypal, are angered by human attitudes and actions. The individual has dishonoured or failed to acknowledge some fundamental divine principle in life, and the divinity retaliates by inflicting madness on the offender. If the individual is not personally culpable, their mother or father, grandfather or great-grandmother invariably is. Thus madness, in the Greek world-view, can be the result of psychological inheritance.

Although we have embraced many definitions of madness since ancient Greece, we would do well to remember this one as we proceed through the day. Although it may not give us the whole story, it is an approach which can be integrated into our astrological understanding of the planets as archetypal principles. When thwarted or "offended", they may extract a very high price. In tribal societies, supernatural possession is still seen as the cause of madness, although this may include possession by an evil spirit or the angry ghost of an ancestor. Here the Greek idea of madness involving an irate deity is expanded to include an offended ancestor whose spirit afflicts the living. We might keep this in mind, too, as families seem to have presiding "spirits" or creative daimons which demand fulfillment and which, if thwarted, may turn destructive. Whether these supernatural forces are perceived as divinities or spirits, propitiation and exorcism are the two mythic means by which states of madness might be redeemed.

Greek humours

The Greek philosophers who emerged from the 6th century BCE onward viewed the cosmos more rationally, as an orderly and unified system rather than a playground for unpredictable daimonic powers. This reflects the gradual increase of emphasis on individual consciousness. Although the irrational was recognised, honoured and feared, nevertheless the power of individual reflection, resulting in self-knowledge and a "right" relationship with the divine realm, was understood to be the key to human psychological health. From the 4th century BCE, Hippocrates and his followers "naturalised" madness and brought it down from the realm of the gods to the realm of the body – although the body, too, was understood to be made of divine stuff and under the governance of astrological influences. Hippocratic medicine explained health and illness in terms of the four humours, present in blood, yellow bile, phlegm and black bile. These fluids influence the rhythms of development and change within both body and psyche. The humours are reflected on the macrocosmic level by the four elements: blood is equated with air (the sanguine temperament), yellow bile with fire (the choleric temperament), phlegm with water (the phlegmatic temperament), and black bile with earth (the melancholic temperament). These ancient links between physiology, psychology and astrology are of great importance to us in understanding the ways in which planetary pictures reflect all levels of the human being.

The plunge from health into illness, physical, psychological or both, was understood to occur when one of the four vital fluids either accumulates at dangerously high levels, or sinks to dangerously low ones. Greek physicians believed that mania results from excesses of either blood or yellow bile, while depression arises from a surplus of black bile. If we translate this in terms of the natal chart, an over-emphasis or under-emphasis in any particular element may be one of the factors we need to consider in terms of the possible astrological significators of madness. We will see how relevant this might be when we begin to look at some charts. The Greeks believed these imbalances, although inherent, could be helped through a wide range of treatments covering both physical and psychological ground: diet, exercise, music, medical or surgical intervention, herbal remedies, and what we might now call the therapeutic catharsis. Mania and melancholia were of particular concern to Greek physicians, and even modern psychiatry admits its debt to them. Aretaeus of Cappadocia, a contemporary of Galen who lived in the 2nd century CE, is credited with identifying what is now known as manic depression or bipolar disorder.

Medieval Christian madness

Medieval medicine followed the medical traditions begun by Hippocrates, Galen and Aretaeus. Diagnoses were quite sophisticated: for example, Bartholomaeus Anglicus taught in the 13th century that melancholia included such conditions as anxiety, hypochondria and depression. But such knowledge was limited to the well-educated, and they had to tread carefully because of the omnipresent threat of being accused of religious heresy. Possession by the devil was a more popular perspective on madness, particularly among the uneducated and during periods of social upheaval such as the Inquisition, the outbreak of the Black Plague, and the witch-hunts of the early 17th century. Possession by a god now became possession by a demon and, as in primitive tribal societies, exorcism was the chief means by which the evil power could be expelled from the mad person. The old pagan gods were translated into forces of evil by the Church, but madness was still perceived as supernatural intervention. The Renaissance brought a resurgence of interest in the classical world-view and further developments in the classical medical tradition, but the religious wars of the 16th century and the Thirty Years War in the 17th century ensured that views on madness remained split between physicians on the one hand, following the classical tradition based on the humours, and the remainder of the populace following the teachings of the Church and living in terror of demonic possession.

The discovery of the unconscious

Once we begin to move into the modern era, we find concerted attempts on the part of medicine to dispel the idea that madness is connected with anything supernatural or divine. Mesmer, who lived at the end of the 18th century and was a bridge between the ancient world and the Enlightenment, is usually considered the "father" of modern dynamic psychology. From his time on, madness was no longer perceived as an invasion from another realm. Instead, it was understood to be the result of a malfunction in the individual's physiological or psychological adaptation, either because of organic causes such as syphilis or because of some traumatic experience which has distorted the development of the personality. The idea that madness is linked with a transgression of some kind is a concept belonging to both the ancient and medieval worlds, and this moral element vanishes after the Enlightenment. Early research by the great explorers of the psyche, such as Janet, Charcot, Breuer, Freud and Jung, focused on two main expressions of madness: hysteria and *dementia praecox* or "premature dementia", which we now know as schizophrenia. The term *praecox* was used because the symptoms of schizophrenia so often appear in young people. These conditions were of particular concern because they appeared to have no organic basis yet seemed incurable.

Out of all this early research emerged the concept of the unconscious and the idea of the invasion of the ego by an unconscious complex. The ancient gods were still alive and well, but they were redefined as forces within the psyche. Although Freud was careful to avoid attributing any numinous element to these forces, Jung was not averse to making the connection between the ancient deities and modern   psychological terminology. In states of madness, the unconscious was understood to rise up and take possession of the personality. Why should this happen to some people and not others? The cause was initially sought in early traumatic experiences, usually interpreted as sexual in one form or another, which created splits or dissociated "pockets" in the unconscious which eventually gathered an enormous energy charge. The energy would eventually build up to the point where the ego could not contain it any longer, and a state of madness, temporary or permanent, would ensue.

This model is still relevant in modern depth psychology. Organic psychiatry, on the other hand, has gone its own way and has opted for an organic explanation of mad states. Either there is a genetic component which indicates a predisposition for madness, or there is some kind of chemical imbalance which affects the brain and the perceptual functions so that a state of madness ensues. This imbalance may be partly linked to genetic factors, but it may also be induced by particular pressures from the environment, and even by diet or hormonal shifts connected with major life changes such as puberty or menopause. Either way, organic psychiatry, which is a branch of medicine, continues to assume an organic basis. Madness lies in the physical brain, not in some mysterious entity called the psyche, which, after all, is deemed to be only a by-product of the brain anyway. This is the prevailing view of madness at the present time, and treatment, like the assumed cause, is organic and based on altering brain chemistry through the intervention of medication.

Modern definitions of madness

According to the prevailing perception, a mad person is someone who has lost touch with what we define as reality. Now, that is a very dangerous definition, and we can all shoot holes in it, but it works for the medical establishment. If a mad person is rushing about murdering people, they are seen as a threat to society, and they must be locked up. This threat can sometimes be very real, because some mad states do involve violence and the destruction of innocent bystanders. If a person attempts suicide, they are also seen to be mad, at least temporarily, which is another very dangerous assumption. Other mad states harm no one, but they unsettle passers-by. Climbing Nelson's Column naked and claiming loudly that one is the messiah doesn't actually hurt anyone, but it is deemed to be mad, unless it is a political statement, in which case it is deemed to be sane but illegal.

Once the individual breaches the barriers of what we define as normality, they are taken in for diagnosis and treatment. The outcome depends heavily on where they land – which hospital, and what kind of training the psychiatric staff have had. Some mad people wind up somewhere other than a psychiatric hospital: many, understandably terrified of the lottery of psychiatric wards, find their way into a spiritual commune or ashram. No clinical diagnosis is made in such places of asylum. But once a person can longer cope, either they need to be removed for the protection of others, or they need to be removed – or remove themselves – for their own protection. We have social, legal and medical mechanisms by which mad people are removed from this threat to both themselves and others. They are given treatment and, in theory, released when they are able to cope better. This is a pragmatic rather than a philosophical issue. Although we all know how very imperfect our social, legal and medical mechanisms are, that is not what we are concerned with today. We are exploring what madness means on a more profound level.

Essentially we have two definitions of madness, one organic and the other dynamic. Astrology does not have much to say about the former, but it has a great deal to say about the latter. That does not mean there is no truth or value in the organic approach. Body and psyche are an inseparable unity, and we cannot pretend that psychological distress does not have any physical concomitants or repercussions. It is fashionable in esoteric circles, particularly those concerned with "New Age" psychology, to condemn the psychiatric definition of madness altogether. This is very foolish. There are times when medication, the main instrument of psychiatric treatment, is necessary and helpful, because it may prevent the individual destroying themselves and others, and can make possible a period of relative tranquillity during which therapeutic work might become possible. Although we will be exploring the inner meaning of mad states today, it is important that we recognise that medication is not an evil, unless it is used indiscriminately and without deeper understanding. Many astrological practitioners do not have to deal with mad states, except in the occasional client, and they are extremely negative about the psychiatric approach. This is very naive.

Once upon a time, there was an old-fashioned word called "asylum". This word comes from a Greek root which means "inviolable". It goes back to the ancient idea that one could claim sanctuary in a sacred building such as a temple or shrine. They then became inviolable because they were under the protection of the deity. The idea of inviolable asylum continued into medieval times, when the temples were replaced by churches. If someone was being pursued by the mob, they could enter one of these sacred places and place their hand on the altar, and no one could touch them until a just process of law was implemented. Asylum was a place where one could seek protection from a rabid mob. Later, asylum became a term associated with lunatics. Lunatic asylums were places in which we incarcerated people, not to give them a place of protection, but to protect ourselves from them. Instead of keeping others out, the asylum kept the mad person in. But the original idea of asylum is deeply relevant for anyone in a mad state. It is essential to have a place where one does not feel pursued and hunted. It may then be possible to deal with whatever one is dealing with, in the knowledge that one is safe.

Audience: I thought for a minute that you said "saloon" instead of "asylum".

Liz: That's the room in the pub where they keep the television.

Audience: They are both Neptunian.

Designer labels

Liz: Yes, I suppose they are. Spiritual communities, which are also Neptunian, have always been places of asylum. Such communities may have many problems, but people who are in a mad state can enter this kind of environment and feel safe because their behaviour is contained without judgement or enforced treatment. We no longer have this concept of asylum. Our psychiatric hospitals are filled with people we have incarcerated not for their sake, but for ours. Now we are throwing them out. We have adopted the "care in the community" approach, which is a wonderful idea if there is a real community which can offer genuine care. In a city like London, there is not much sense of community. Where do these people go when they have had their asylum taken away? There is little understanding of this situation, and the voice of depth psychology is a very small voice which isn't audible at a distance. One of the results of our collective inability to deal with the mad members of the community is that more and more people who are hovering around the edges of madness are coming to astrologers, because they feel they can gain some insight without being given a clinical label. Clinical labels are devised primarily for the benefit of the doctor, and they describe a set of symptoms rather than giving us any understanding of the deeper patterns involved.

In America, manic depression is no longer called manic depression. As I mentioned earlier, it's now called bipolar disorder. The word "manic" now seems to have become politically incorrect because it implies "maniac". "Manic" is, in fact, derived from a Greek root, *mania*, which is a particular state of madness imposed by Dionysus. There is another, nastier element in this business of labels, and that is the role of the pharmaceutical business. It is, of course, a lucrative business involving giant multinational companies, and new medication is being developed all the time to deal with various states of madness. If a new medicine appears on the market which seems promising in alleviating the symptoms of schizophrenia, then it is relevant to diagnose as many people as possible with schizophrenia because then the drug can be prescribed and tested. This may sound dreadfully cynical, but it is part of the way in which we deal with madness at the moment.

Medication goes through phases of fashion, and clinical diagnoses also go through such phases. Labels are a big problem because, once someone has a psychiatric label, they cannot get rid of it. As a collective, we have many ignorant assumptions about the nature of conditions such as schizophrenia and manic depression. Yet we have little insight into the real nature and cause of these states. We are taught that they are incurable, but this is not always the case. If someone carries such a label, they have a stigma which they can never remove. The whole diagnostic system is fraught with difficulties. Diagnosing madness by grouping symptoms can, in theory, facilitate the appropriate kind of treatment. But mad people in psychiatric wards often mimic each other's symptoms. Moreover, the particular orientation and training of the consulting psychiatrist will affect the behaviour of the patients in his or her care. Mad people can exhibit extraordinary sensitivity, and they are often open to the unconscious psyche of the person who is treating them. This should not be astonishing if we think of madness as the flooding of the ego by the unconscious. If a particular doctor sees every mad state as a form of schizophrenia, that doctor's patients will very obligingly present the symptoms of schizophrenia. They will try to please because they know their lives are in the hands of the doctor, and they will obligingly provide what is expected of them. This really complicates the issue, because symptoms may be as variable as a scientific experiment is variable according to the attitude of the observer. If symptoms are not really very useful in terms of categorising states of madness, how are we to differentiate between these states in a way which furthers our understanding while according respect and dignity to what the individual is experiencing?

The madness of Dionysus

Now I want to talk about the Greek deities in more detail, because this can help illuminate certain patterns of madness from an archetypal as well as a planetary perspective. Rather than going through a list of psychiatric diagnoses defined by groups of symptoms, I will look at archetypal pictures instead, because these can lead us to the core rather than to the outer manifestation of mad states. Whether and how such insight might be relevant to treatment is a question I will leave open. In Greek myth, not all deities afflict human beings with madness.

The ones who do may further our understanding of the nature of madness. We will begin with Dionysus, the god most commonly associated with madness. The Greek word *mania* is related to *mainas* or maenad, one of the ecstatic female followers of Dionysus. To the Greek mind, the state of mania is a state of possession by Dionysus. Dionysian mania can be ritually contained, in which case it is a desirable state which can transform the personality. Or it can be uncontained, in which case it is ultimately destructive. In Dionysian mania, we are taken out of ourselves and become one with the transcendent spirit of nature, the life force itself. Dionysus is the god of divine inebriation.

Hallucinations are frequently associated with Dionysian madness. The experience of being fused with the god means one is godlike oneself. One can be and do anything; one is superhuman. Sexual ecstasy, music and dance are also associated with Dionysus. The Dionysian experience of madness involves possession of the body as well as the psyche, and there is a compulsive need to express the ecstasy through physical movement. In the Greek world, when Dionysian ecstasy was contained within a ritualised setting, the initiate was washed clean and could return to the everyday world feeling reborn. When the god becomes angry, as he often does in myth when he is not given his due, he still imposes ecstasy, but it is not contained within the ritual framework. The victims of Dionysus' anger wander about hallucinating and mistaking their fantasies for concrete reality, and ultimately they destroy others and, eventually, themselves. Do all of you know Euripides' play, *The Bacchai*? I recommend that you read the play, or see a production of it when it comes around. Dionysian madness may be in evidence in the psychiatric world as hysteria, but manic depression could also be related to the archetypal patterns symbolised by this god.

Audience: Does it have anything to do with repressing the world of the emotions and instincts?

Liz: Yes, it has everything to do with these things, although that is not all. Euripides' play is a remarkable portrayal of the psychological process through which a certain kind of madness is generated. The protagonist, Pentheus, king of Thebes, is like the rational ego. He is disciplined, orderly, fundamentally decent, but arrogant in his assumption that his world-view is the only right one. He suppresses the women in his kingdom and does not respect their emotional needs. Just as Pentheus is himself a symbol, so too are the women of Thebes. The king, the women and the god may be understood as dimensions of the psyche, and we may equate the king with ego-consciousness, the women with the instinctual realm, and the god with the divine life-force which animates both.

The denial of the irrational

Audience: So Pentheus is inhibited by social codes.

Liz: Not really. We are dealing with a battle between a king and a god, and Pentheus is no puppet of the collective. He creates the social codes, rather than being inhibited by them. It is his fundamental perceptions which lead him into conflict with the deity. What is being denied here, that causes the god to became so enraged and take his revenge so cruelly?

Audience: Chaos.

Liz: That's a little nearer.

Audience: Emotions. Instincts.

Liz: Yes, but as I said, it's more than that. Here is Euripides' statement, which says it all:

> If any man derides the unseen world, let him ponder the death of Pentheus, and believe in gods.

Now, the "unseen world" to which Euripides refers is not concerned with organised religious rituals, where one goes to Church on Sunday and listens to a boring sermon from the local vicar, has a good gossip with the neighbours, and feels righteous for the rest of the week. It is not about so-called spirituality either, where one meditates and talks about the spiritual path and feels righteous for the rest of the week. It is not about righteousness at all. Nor is it restricted to the emotions and the instincts. The unseen world is the world of the imagination, the realm of the irrational, and it is full of chaos and frightening oceanic currents and boundless depths. Dionysus both symbolises and requires the kind of perception which recognises the numinous in everything: *really* recognises it, not just pays lip service to it. Moreover, the numinous is not necessarily "good" or "light". Dionysus is also an underworld god, a god of sexual and drunken ecstasy, and his followers, when they are in his ecstatic trance, tear wild animals and even humans to pieces and smear themselves with the bloody remains. This is not a god to joke about with.

In the Dionysian state of ecstasy, one throws away one's persona, one's position in society, one's dignity and correctness. Certain societies understand this, which is why they have annual carnivals. They may no longer have a Dionysia or a Saturnalia, but they have a modern equivalent. At carnival time in Rio, in Venice, in Zürich and Basel, people go out on the streets and get drunk or stoned. They dress up in extraordinary costumes, and they behave in a way that they would never dream of doing on any other occasion. They wear masks so that they are no longer identified with their ego-image. They indulge in sensual and emotional experiences of a totally abandoned kind, and the release allows them to feel renewed. Music and dance have always been a fundamental part of this kind of release, from the "love-ins" of the 1960s to the modern "rave". Now, what might this look like if we think in astrological terms?

The divine inebriate

Audience: Neptune in Scorpio.

Liz: Certainly Neptune is one factor – not the only factor, perhaps, but an important one. And it is not a coincidence that the great love-ins of the 1960s occurred when Neptune was transiting through Scorpio. The god himself is, in large part, a Neptunian deity. But there is also a

Jupiterian component, reflected by the fact that his father is Zeus, and Roman frescoes portray him presiding over the "celestial banquet" of the souls of the dead who have risen to the Olympian heavens. And Dionysus is also *chthonios*, born to Persephone in the underworld and sometimes called Zagreus. Aeschylos, in one of his *Sisyphos* plays, makes Dionysus-Zagreus the son of Hades. Euripides calls him "night-wandering Zagreus, celebrating the feasts of raw flesh". His state of inebriation is not only Neptunian. It is a combination of several different qualities including those of Pluto, all of them related to excess, intensity and loss of boundaries.

Audience: What about Uranus? That seems to me to have elements of madness in it.

Liz: Uranus can reflect a certain kind of mad state, as we shall see, but it is not Dionysian madness. The condition of Uranian possession is not emotional or sensual. It may be visionary, but it is not a body experience. Dionysian states are deeply rooted in the body. At the same time, a strongly Uranian personality, with its emphasis on the world of the mind, may be particularly subject to the eruption of an angry Dionysus in the form of a dislocated Neptune, if this planet is also strong in the chart but suppressed or denied.

Audience: Problems with Saturn must also be involved.

Liz: Yes, they are usually involved as well. It is never just one factor. The relationship between Dionysus, Pentheus and the maenads, when viewed astrologically, involves several planetary factors.

Audience: How do you spell the king's name?

Liz: P-E-N-T-H-E-U-S. Interestingly, it's the Greek word for "grief". We can look at the relationship between Dionysus and Pentheus on an individual psychological level and say, "Here is a person who either deliberately or because of family pressures has blocked or denied a very powerful life-force, which eventually erupts and destroys him." But we can also look at this dynamic on a social level, which is what Euripides did. Pentheus is not only the individual ego; he is also an image of society. He is a king, so he symbolises the presiding values in a given society. He is the law-maker, like Freud's superego. We may also understand him as reflecting the Saturn principle in collective life. He represents the structures which define human behaviour in a particular social context.

Who are the women whom he suppresses and whom Dionysus releases? Yes, they are the emotional and instinctual side of the individual, but they are also forces within any group or social structure. These forces are denied and stifled by the ruling social attitudes. When we look at it from this perspective, we move straight into R. D. Laing's territory. Ronnie Laing seems to have suffered from Dionysian difficulties himself during the course of his life, and he understood something very important about this kind of madness. It is not only the particular problem of an individual who has suffered from a dislocation between the rational ego and the instinctual energies of the unconscious. The family and, ultimately, the whole society in which the individual is embedded, are also disconnected, and particular individuals are like safety valves for the pressure that builds up. They are the scapegoats and vessels for what is, in effect, a collective madness.

Although *The Bacchai* gives us extremely important insights into individual psychology, Euripides was also making a profound social comment which is very relevant to our own contemporary Western culture. We do not have ritualised Dionysian revels. We have football matches, rock concerts and raves, but we do not understand the religious content in such experiences, and so they lose both their dignity and their deeper cathartic value. Rather than individuals taking responsibility for the correct ritualising of their own Dionysian experience, we simply ensure that there are enough police around to make sure things don't get out of control. Of course they get out of control quite often. Dionysus always outwits the police, as Pentheus discovered. Ritualising Dionysus does not lessen the intensity with which the individual or the collective experiences the god's ecstasy. But it does sanctify or make sacred an inner experience which, devoid of such recognition, becomes debased and often destructive.

Madness and the artist

Audience: Why are so many artists mad?

Liz: This is a question which has been the subject of debate for many centuries. It does seem that art and madness go together, and this is the realm over which Dionysus presides. The artist needs to live close to the archetypal realm, because that is the source of creative inspiration. Without this contact, the artist cannot mediate the images of the collective unconscious, and inspiration dries up. But as they say, one must have a long spoon to sup with the devil. The receptivity which allows the artist to retain a connection with the archetypal realm may also reflect an ego that is too porous, and the personality is at risk of being fragmented or overwhelmed by the collective energies and images which are being mediated.

We expect and forgive madness in artists because we know there is a connection between the two. We don't excuse madness in people who are mad but don't produce art. This is a rather ignorant attitude, but nevertheless it is a common one. We are perfectly all right about Van Gogh cutting off his ear, because he was a great artist. That somehow seems to justify the mad behaviour. But does an artist have to be mad in order to be gifted? Does madness unlock genius, or the other way around? Is it a matter of talent or a matter of receptivity to the collective psyche, or is it a combination of the two? If you are interested in this issue, you should have a look at a book by Erich Neumann called *Art and the Creative Unconscious*, in which he explores the psychology and psychopathology of Leonardo da Vinci.[2] The ego of the artist needs to be receptive, if not actually weak. Receptivity is not mutually exclusive with an ego strong enough to allow the individual to live a rewarding and relatively balanced life. But it may be mutually exclusive with so-called "normality". Psychologists have never been able to agree whether one is born with such receptivity, or whether it is the result of a particular kind of childhood "damage" which blocks ordinary channels

---

[2] Erich Neumann, *Art and the Creative Unconscious*, Princeton University Press, 1959. Also see Liz Greene, Chapter 10, "Neptune and the Artist", in *The Astrological Neptune and the Quest for Redemption*, Samuel Weiser Inc., 1996.

of fulfilment but opens other, deeper channels in their place. As astrologers, we do know that astrological placements such as a powerful Neptune or Uranus reflect both inner states and outer experiences, and thus inherent character, the perception of outer experience and the experiences themselves are part of the same archetypal pattern. It could be argued that really stable, "normal" people do not create. If one is not receptive to something beyond the personal, one may be a fine craftsman, but one will not be an artist.

The madness of Aphrodite

Now let's move on to Aphrodite, who is notorious in myth for inflicting states of madness. It should be fairly obvious what kind of madness this is. Aphrodite takes revenge on those who deny or misuse their passions, and afflicts her victims with erotic madness. She does this to Pasiphaë, the wife of King Minos, filling her with obsessive lust for a bull. Aphrodite also afflicts Hades with an overwhelming passion for Persephone, which results in his abducting and raping her. This is the goddess' vengeance on Demeter, Persephone's mother, for her intransigent resistance to sexual pleasure. Aphrodite's madness is connected with erotic obsession, often for an unsuitable or unresponsive object. This most beautiful but most easily angered of deities may be glimpsed in many other distorted states, such as compulsive paedophilia and the strange homocrotic obsession with religious overtones known to the psychiatric world as Clerambault's syndrome. Literature throughout the ages has always been full of portrayals of the madness of Aphrodite.

The astrology of erotomania

Ordinarily, we don't think of erotic obsession as madness. We think of it as falling in love, even if the love is clearly not reciprocated. We don't consider the state of being in love as a state of madness because, in the majority of cases, we can still more or less cope with life.

We can get dressed, go to work and communicate with our friends. The Austrian novelist Robert Musil informs us:

> There is still a great deal unknown about this phenomenon capable of transporting an ordinarily "civilised" man and woman into a state which under other circumstances we would associate only with a frothing lunatic.

But we still believe ourselves to be sane, even though, in a specific sphere of our life, the ego has lost its capacity to mediate between the unconscious and the outer world. In such a state, the beloved object is not a real person. He or she is perceived as semi-divine.

The word "madness" tends to crop up when there is an obsessive passion which becomes destructive: for example, the stalker who becomes obsessed with a particular film star or musician, follows them everywhere and harasses them unceasingly. Then we can recognise that the person's level of sanity may be questionable. The French legal system displays some sophistication in describing crimes committed in this state as "crimes of passion". They are treated somewhat differently from a premeditated murder, because it is understood that this is a state of madness. A man comes home and finds his wife in bed with his best friend and murders them both in a fit of jealousy. He has destroyed two human lives, but he is not a criminal. His crime was not premeditated. It was an expression of his passion, and thus he was temporarily afflicted with "diminished responsibility". In other words, the ego was out to lunch. In this legal differentiation, there is some understanding shown of the way in which Aphrodite can inflict human beings with states which are truly disconnected from reality. Now, what might we look for astrologically?

Audience: Venus-Neptune?

Audience: I would have thought obsession is connected with Pluto.

Liz: Yes, I am inclined to look for Pluto-Venus contacts, in addition to patterns which reflect certain kinds of childhood experiences. But I am not excluding Neptune, especially when religious or spiritual overtones are mixed up with erotic obsession, as is often the case with the "soul-mate" type of obsession. Usually we will find a combination of factors which look just like the factors in the charts of people who are not in the least bit mad in their attitudes or expressions of love.

Audience: What about Venus-Saturn?

Liz: Venus-Saturn contacts can reflect great insecurity and a low sense of self-esteem. That is not, in itself, conducive to erotic obsession. But Venus-Saturn can play a part when the individual is compulsively driven to set up situations in which they are repeatedly rejected. Some obsessions have this basis, especially when there is an Oedipal conflict in childhood involving a parent who was never available. Venus-Saturn crops up regularly when there is an obsession with an unobtainable object. It is not an aspect of passion, but it can be an important factor in what Freud called "repetition compulsion". In cases of erotomania, other aspects are usually present as well, often involving Neptune or Pluto. The Moon in hard aspect with Neptune or Pluto may be relevant to erotomania, and sometimes the Moon is triggered by transits from one or both of these outer planets when an obsession begins. This is because this form of madness is connected with the body and the instincts, both part of the lunar realm. The Moon may play an important part in the madness of Aphrodite. But I would remind you all again that such aspects, in themselves, do not indicate madness. It is the chemical mix between inherent temperament and environment that seems to provide the key.

Audience: I have Venus in Pisces, at the receiving end of a yod with Neptune and Pluto. I am a good example of what you are talking about. For many years I was completely obsessed with a particular rock band. I used to follow them around to every gig they did. When I look back on it, I can see that it was really a mad state.

Liz: Thank you for talking about it. Normally it is not a state which people care to discuss in a group setting. It is extremely painful for the person experiencing it, because it is an obsession. And yes, it is a mad state, even though the rest of the personality may be quite well adapted and functioning in the world. You seem to have a strong enough ego to look at your behaviour and recognise the madness in it. Erotomania, in clinical terms, often involves the absolute conviction that the love object reciprocates the passion, even when the beloved is utterly out of reach or repeatedly says, "I want nothing to do with you. Sod off!" The obsession has interfered with the ego's adaptation to reality to such an extent that the person rationalises all obstructions to fulfilment as lies or temporary difficulties which will eventually be overcome.

Aphrodite's madness as a delusional system

Many years ago, a woman came to see me for a chart reading. She was not recognisably mad. She could communicate perfectly well, she looked presentable, and she was able to maintain a good job. Only my intuition told me something was very seriously wrong, but at first I could not work out what it was. Eventually she revealed the real reason she had made the appointment. This reading took place many years ago, before the marriage of Prince Charles to Lady Diana Spencer. My client told me that she knew it was her destiny to marry Prince Charles. But there was a difficulty: the Queen was trying to have her killed. She knew that the Prince reciprocated her love. Although they had never met, he knew who she was, and recognised she was his soul-mate. It was only a question of time before the two would meet, but my client had to find a way to avoid the Queen's spies.

Yes, you are allowed to laugh, but laughter is one of our defences against the horror of this kind of state. Let's consider first what psychiatry has to say about it. The central theme of the delusion of erotomania concerns idealised romantic love and spiritual union, rather than a genuine sexual attraction. The object of affection is usually of a higher status and is often a complete stranger, usually known through the media. Efforts to contact the love object are common, and the result may be stalking, but the person may keep the delusion a secret, as did my client. From the evidence of forensic samples, men rather than women afflicted by this kind of madness most often fall foul of the law, usually during misguided pursuits to "rescue" their beloved from some imagined danger. Women tend to keep quiet about their obsession, although women too may try to contact the love object through persistent letters and telephone calls. What differentiates this state from simple romantic fascination is that it is an immovable obsession. Rejection does not deter it, nor does the complete impossibility of circumstances. Erotomania is very frightening to the recipient because of its absoluteness. In extreme cases, it can lead to violence, as demonstrated in films such as *Play Misty for Me* and *Fatal Attraction*.

Audience: Wouldn't this be the behaviour of a psychopath? They often stalk women.

Liz: Psychopaths do not believe themselves in love with their victims. They feel nothing at all for the people they destroy. Erotomania is full of feeling, but it is feeling divorced from reality. When I asked my client about her family background, she was quite articulate. Her parents were obsessively religious, and she was raised in one of the more unpleasant fundamentalist Protestant sects: no music in the house, no singing, no dancing, no laughing in an unseemly way. And, of course, no discussions about sex, or even about normal bodily functions such as menstruation. All things of the body were deemed a sin. My client had been brought up in an environment so utterly destructive to pleasure, joy and self-confidence that I think any of us would have developed some form of madness if subjected to it. If she laughed, she was beaten. If she exhibited any sort of interest in boys, she was beaten. Did any of you see the film, *Carrie*? If so, you get the picture. Unfortunately my client was not able to become telekinetic; she could only go mad. Her madness is not easily classifiable, since it involved not only erotic obsession but also what is known as a "delusional system". This is defined as a form of paranoid schizophrenia. Diagnoses such as this do not, however, help us to understand her mental state at a deeper level.

Now, bear in mind what I keep repeating about the chemical mix between inherent character and environment. The first thing I noticed about the chart was a complete absence of the element of earth. I also found a Sun-Saturn-Pluto conjunction in Leo in the 5th house, square a Moon-Jupiter-Chiron conjunction in Scorpio in the 8th. These configurations are not a signature of madness. But they are certainly a signature of someone who has a lot of Aphrodite in them: powerful passions and great intensity of feeling, emphasised by Venus in Cancer in the 4th house trine the Moon-Jupiter conjunction in the 8th. It is likely that she was deeply attached to her father as a child, and this Oedipal fantasy was projected onto the figure of Prince Charles. No prizes for guessing who the malevolent Queen stands in for. When someone with such a fixed, intense and passionate nature grows up in the kind of environment my client was subjected to, it is a recipe for total psychological disaster. The surprising thing was not that she was mad, but that she was actually up and walking, held a job, and could communicate in a sane and articulate way. I learned a great deal about Aphrodite's madness from this client.

Audience: How did you react to what she told you?

Liz: With great sadness and pity. She told me about her background before she told me about her secret, and it was apparent that this was a case of the sins of the parents being visited on the child. It would have been pointless to say, "What nonsense!", because she would simply have left. Nor would it have been helpful to tell her she was mad. As an astrologer, my responsibility was to try to help in whatever way I could. On the other hand, it would have been destructive to collude and say, "How wonderful. Send me a wedding invitation." I tried to walk a tightrope between the extremes of denying and colluding with her obsession, and stayed on the safer ground of communicating with the sane parts of her. What was her job like? What were her interests? Were there ways in which she could begin to develop some sort of ego strength around this pocket of madness? The obsession was, in fact, a necessary defence system, and attempting to dismantle it before she had developed the healthier parts of the personality would have probably pitched her into full psychosis or a suicide attempt. If she had not had this great hope, she would have destroyed herself. Her obsession gave her the will to live. I believe her real reason for coming was that she knew, on some level, that she was in a desperate state, and she wanted some kind of help. But she had no concept of what "help" might mean.

The family scapegoat

Audience: What you seem to be describing is a madness which compensates for something horribly damaged in her.

Liz: Yes, the "delusional system" is a compensation for deep feelings of sin and shame. It is also a defence against violent, murderous rage toward the mother. This murderous rage comes from something within her which has been horribly abused. Here we can see what the Greeks understood as an angry deity who visits punishment on the next generation. My client was psychologically violated in a particularly savage way, by parents who were clearly mad but perceived themselves as righteous, religious people. It is a bit like the line from that old American quiz show called *To Tell the Truth*: "Will the real mad person please stand up?" If we were not trying so hard to be politically correct in order to avoid offending people's religious sentiments, we would admit that parents who espouse a religious sect which inflicts such psychological damage on their own children are obviously mad, and may even be psychopathic.

     States like this arise because the ego is badly damaged and the relationship between the ego and the unconscious has been severely disturbed. The chart alone, without a knowledge of the family history, cannot tell us this. Many people were born under that configuration of Sun-Saturn-Pluto square Moon-Jupiter-Chiron in Scorpio, but they are not all waiting in white dresses outside Buckingham Palace. The chart can tell us that this individual will not cope well with the specific nature of the environment she experienced. The lack of earth is important here, because a weakness in this element can reflect an uneasy relationship with one's physical body, and my client was brought up to believe that her body was dirty and full of sin. Configurations such as Sun conjunct Saturn-Pluto, and Moon conjunct Chiron and square Saturn-Pluto, suggest that she was peculiarly sensitive to the unconscious undercurrents in her early environment, and also that she was the recipient of a particularly dark and difficult family inheritance. If she had been raised in another environment, the lack of earth might not have been such an issue. If she had grown up in an Italian family where everybody screamed and shouted and threw things and hugged each other and openly admired beautiful bodies, she might not be mad. She would be very intense and undoubtedly difficult to live with if one were a Gemini or an Aquarian, but what else is new? And "environment" doesn't only mean family. It also means one's culture. A bad mismatch between inherent temperament and culture has occurred in my client as well. Certain cultures honour Aphrodite, but others do not.

Audience: Do you know what happened to her when Prince Charles married?

Liz: Yes. I hadn't heard from her for several years, and then suddenly she appeared again, about a year after the royal wedding, wanting an updated reading. The marriage had not pitched her into psychosis as I had feared. She told me she had been mistaken: she was not supposed to marry Prince Charles after all. She was still an extremely disturbed person, but there seemed to be a glimmering of awareness and a willingness to concede that perhaps her delusional system had, after all, been a delusion. She admitted that she did not know what her real destiny was. Something had begun to change. She had not had treatment of any kind. Time itself had proved to be a healer, and the incredible strength of that Sun-Saturn-Pluto conjunction no doubt helped. She still had her job, and was beginning to consider that maybe there might be an ordinary human male out there somewhere whom she was destined to meet. I have not heard from her since. She may well be practising as an analyst now.

Personal and archetypal roots of madness

Audience: You were talking in the beginning about when the gods aren't respected. I think they are not always respected in some psychological schools. I am on a training course in psychoanalysis at the moment, and I can feel some very profound images coming through. But I can't talk about them in the framework of the school's theories and methods. What kind of revenge do the gods take on psychoanalysts who don't honour them?

Liz: The same kind that they take on everyone else, I suppose. Any healer – medical, psychological or spiritual – who does not recognise the archetypal levels of the psyche may have difficulty in comprehending the deeper roots of madness. That doesn't mean that every psychoanalyst is demoting the gods just because they don't talk about them. It depends on the attitude of the analyst, rather than the language. Freud made his psychoanalytic terminology deliberately neutral and quasi-scientific because it was developed at a time when his work was held in great suspicion. This language may suffice if respect for the archetypal realm is implicit in the dialogue between the analyst and the client. Freud presented himself as a rationalist and a materialist for most of his life, but if we read between the lines, he describes the *id* in an essentially religious way. Although his language is not religious, the awe and respect he had for the unconscious psyche is, in effect, the kind of honouring that the gods require. I have known so-called archetypal psychologists who talk a lot about the gods, but who do not feel their presence within as a living reality. It doesn't really matter what you call them. They know when they are being insulted.

    The quality of the person who is working with a mad individual is more important than the language or the theoretical framework. And we should not underestimate the importance of the personal unconscious, either, which is where the psychoanalytic approach excels. If I describe the condition of my client as the madness of Aphrodite, I am acknowledging the importance of an archetypal life-force which was violated in her family for many generations. That is perhaps more useful, in terms of deeper understanding, than calling her a paranoid schizophrenic. But the Oedipal dynamic at work between my client and her parents is the personal channel through which the anger of the goddess takes on flesh. In speaking about her "destiny" with Prince Charles, my client was really talking about a father whom she adored with erotic as well as idealised feelings. That is perfectly normal for a child with a 4th house Venus trine an 8th house Moon-Jupiter conjunction in Scorpio. But her parents were not capable of responding to her with anything other than their own sexual conflicts disguised as religious fervour, so her forbidden feelings developed into a fantasy scenario in which the wicked Queen was trying to destroy the destined marriage of soul-mates. Integrating these internal conflicts would require recognising her erotic fantasies about her father, her rage and hatred toward her mother, and her fear of her mother's jealousy. Psychoanalytic language may not call this Aphrodite. But a more prosaic language may be needed in order to explore how the ego has been so damaged that the gods can only enter a person's life by destroying it. Planetary signatures tell us about the archetypal background, but they must be understood in the context of the early environment and the society in which the person is living.

The madness of Hera

In myth, Hera drives Dionysus mad because he is the illegitimate son of Zeus, and she wishes to take revenge for her husband's infidelity by destroying its fruit. She also transforms a number of her rivals into animals. For example, she turns Io into a cow and then afflicts her with swarms of gadflies. There are many such transformations in Greek myth: the sorceress Circe changes Odysseus' men into swine, and Athene transforms the beautiful Medusa into a frightful gorgon. The transformation of a human into a tormented animal or monster is a powerful image of madness, and Hera specialises in this kind of punishment. Her motivation is always jealousy. With the exception of Dionysus and Herakles, both of whom are the products of her husband's infidelities, it is usually her rivals who are the recipients of her anger. The madness Hera inflicts is always related to rage at Zeus' wandering proclivities. These mythic images are telling us something important about a certain form of madness.

Social structure as an archetypal pattern

Hera is the archetypal symbol of the family. She represents the structure and integrity of the family unit as the basis of human society, and therefore marriage and family traditions are sacred to her. Hera's revenge is unleashed when the integrity of the social structure is threatened by behaviour which might destroy the family unit and the social cohesion dependent on it. Social taboos are part of Hera's domain. Parent-child incest and illegitimacy are perceived by her as forms of incipient social chaos. But Hera's relationship with social structures does not mean she is less of a deity than the other gods. She is not a concept artificially imposed through human decision-making. The need to create family structures and hierarchies is inherent in both the human psyche and in nature. We create societies and the laws by which they function, not because we have sat down rationally and worked it out on paper, but because we have an inherent social instinct. So do animals, as demonstrated by a pride of lions, a flock of geese or a pack of wolves. These social instincts are deeply conservative, and serve the preservation of the species rather than a Uranian ideal of progress. When social structures are artificially created according to ideological principles, as was the case with the Soviet Union, things tend to work out badly, and in the end the society collapses. It seems that the healthiest and most productive societies can balance Hera's innate social instincts with enlightened ideas. Hera's domain is inherent and archetypal, and we violate it at our peril.

Audience: What she represents violates individual freedom.

Liz: All relationships, both intimate and social, violate individual freedom, because we are required to compromise and control our self-gratifying impulses if we wish to live in reasonable harmony with other people. When chthonic deities such as Dionysus are suppressed by overly rigid, consciously imposed social rules, it may be appropriate to use the term "violates", because these are instinctual forces, necessary to life, which rise up in anger when they are denied expression. But Hera is also an instinctual force necessary to life. Myths tell us that the gods are always quarreling and finding new ways of resolving their conflicts. Battles result in adjustments and adaptations, which in turn lead to new battles and new adjustments and adaptations. The need for freedom is an instinctual need, and Zeus' constant philandering – which is a reflection of the individual creative urge – reflects this. That is why Zeus and Hera are bound together in an eternal marriage. One without the other would prove destructive to the evolution of life as a whole.

Your statement, taken to its logical end, means that a father should be free to rape his daughter if he so wishes, and any curtailment of this impulse would be a violation of his individual freedom. And a mother should be free to bludgeon her infant to death if she so wishes, because if she is required to endure endless sleepless nights and dirty nappies, that is a violation of *her* individual freedom. I am sure that is not what you meant, but if you are going to blow the trumpet for "individual freedom", you cannot pick and choose which freedoms are acceptable and which are not, unless you are prepared to acknowledge Hera's requirements as well as those of the individual's own will. Hera herself is "violated" by the chaos which ensues when individuals cannot contain their instincts. This is a profound issue, and it is very easy to polarise. But polarisation is not helpful. The Greeks envisaged many deities who interacted in complex and constantly shifting ways, because they understood very well the danger of taking sides.

It is very easy to idealise the chthonic deities and say, "Madness is the result of beautiful life-giving forces being squashed by a heavy Saturnian foot." But Saturn too is a beautiful live-giving force in the right proportions and in the right place, and astrologically this planet reflects the integrity and necessity of structures and boundaries. If the individual's self-indulgence – which is a form of hubris – oversteps those boundaries at the expense of family and society, then something rises up in revenge, which the Greeks envisaged as Hera. It may be wise to look carefully at our own prejudices here. In the astrological world, we tend to identify with the unconventional elements in society, and it is easier to align ourselves with Dionysus than with Hera. But Hera also merits respect, and she too can generate madness if she is demeaned or repudiated.

The form of Hera's madness

Now we need to look more closely at the nature of Hera's madness. What is the myth of Io telling us?

Audience: She is no longer Zeus' special love. She is just a cow.

Liz: Yes, she is just one of the herd, a cow among many cows, and subject to the same gadfly stings as her fellows. Although she has been favoured by Zeus, she cannot expect his protection afterward. Hera is saying to her, "You may think you're really special because you had it off with him, but you're just a mortal. And don't forget it." It is a revenge against the individual who considers himself or herself exempt from the laws which sustain any social group. What might this look like in terms of a psychological state?

Audience: It's the depression of the artist after the creative work is finished.

Liz: Yes, precisely. It is also the self-destructive fears which afflict the *puer aeternus* of either sex. These fears often take the form of an obsession with becoming ill, poor, a failure or a social outcast. Sometimes this kind of obsession can manifest as a terror that one will die young of some horrible disease. Many people suffer such fears from time to time, but sometimes they can be overwhelming, and a breakdown can ensue. Hera vents her rage on her rivals, rather than attacking Zeus himself. This suggests that she takes her revenge through the instinctual realm. Astrologically, what would we look for?

Audience: The Moon.

Liz: Yes, the Moon is related to Hera's realm, perhaps more than to the domain of Artemis, who is usually considered a lunar deity. But Saturn is also very important, particularly when the Moon and Saturn are connected in the chart. And we need to keep in mind the signs that are ruled by these planets. We may see a dichotomy like Moon conjunct Saturn in Capricorn or Aquarius in a fiery or Neptune-dominated chart, or Moon-Saturn opposition Jupiter, Uranus or Neptune. Such conflicts don't necessarily mean Hera will be angered. It all depends on how conscious one is of any conflict in the horoscope, and how able the ego is to contain and work with the conflict.

The terror of the hunted

Earlier, we looked at Pentheus, the protagonist in Euripides' play. He is a very Saturnian figure, and he makes the bad mistake of repudiating the divinity of Dionysus. But he is not portrayed as an evil man, only a misguided one. Behind Pentheus stands Hera, the natural enemy of Dionysus, for society needs leadership, structure and laws. Pentheus does not understand that a balance is required between the two. His ensuing madness is inflicted by Dionysus. Had he taken the side of Dionysus, we could easily imagine him afflicted by the inner torment of the outlaw, compelled to rebel yet living with the constant terror of being caught and judged – which is, in fact, the character of the god's own madness, inflicted on him by Hera. Hera's victims are terrified of life because they feel something is hunting them. This goddess actively pursues her foes, and the sense of being hunted by something is characteristic of her madness. States of extreme anxiety are linked with this mythic figure, and anxiety is one of the major components in depressive breakdowns.

Audience: I was wondering about the issue of an unwanted pregnancy in certain societies, where someone's reputation is destroyed because of other people's moral judgements. It was the case in Britain not so long ago, especially in rural communities, and even now there are parts of the world where women are executed for adultery.

Liz: I am not sure whether it is appropriate to suggest that an unwanted pregnancy is a state of madness. But I take your point.

Audience: It is a confrontation with society.

Liz: Yes. But in such a case, Hera's madness is externalised and takes the form of being hunted by a judgemental collective "out there". The most extreme form of this is the witch-hunt. When Hera goes beserk on a social level, her madness is reflected both in the terror of the scapegoat and in the madness of the pursuing mob, who have moral righteousness on their side. Both hunted and hunter are afflicted with madness. The young girl who gets pregnant in a narrow-minded rural society may go mad and kill herself or her unwanted child. This is one of the themes in Goethe's *Faust*, and even in the 20th century it is not an uncommon event in Western countries. But this conflict is more likely to be internalised now, and we may see it in certain forms of mental breakdown.

Audience: There is a story that Zeus and Hera had an argument about who takes the most pleasure from sex, a man or a woman. Zeus insisted that it was the woman, but Hera insisted it was the man. They consulted the prophet Teiresias, and he said, "If pleasure could be divided into ten parts, a woman would have nine parts and a man would have only one." Hera got very angry because it wasn't her experience, so she struck Teiresias blind.

Liz: "Wasn't her experience"?

Audience: She seems to me to be a pretty frigid goddess.

Liz: You are giving us an excellent example of polarisation. The story is relevant, but Hera's anger, according to Apollodorus and Ovid, is because Teiresias has taken Zeus' side and won him the argument. Hera is not a sexually frigid deity. She just wants the marriage lines respected. She is not averse to sexual pleasure, but she wants it contained within an appropriate social framework so that she isn't humiliated. And more importantly, containment ensures that there aren't hundreds of unwanted babies lying about with no one to look after them. In the world of Greek myth there are no contraceptives, and no one offers free council flats to unwed mothers.

Audience: Saturn in Taurus can create extreme anxiety if the conventions are broken. I think Hera is a Taurean woman, very afraid of losing her security.

Liz: I would agree that there is a Taurean element in Hera, which is emphasised by placements such as Saturn in Taurus or Venus-Saturn contacts. But I get the feeling that you still don't quite grasp what Hera is. You see her as entirely negative.

Audience: She is.

Audience: No, she isn't. She has a sense of justice.

Hera's justice

Liz: Yes, she has a very powerful sense of justice, but it is very personal and feeling-based, not abstract like Athene's justice. When an individual breaks the social code and begins to step over the limits, Hera retaliates. In this sense she is Saturnian: she is opposed to excessive individualism.

Audience: You are blaming the mortal women. What if they had no interest in Zeus in the first place?

Liz: I am not "blaming" anyone. I am trying to get to the core of a myth and its relevance to states of madness. This is clearly a very emotive issue. Hera's attack on Zeus' women is, from her perspective, justifiable because these women aspire to be her equals. But they are mortals, not gods. And they are not uninterested in Zeus. They are seduced, not raped. When Zeus comes along and says, "What are you doing later?" they could go to the nearest shrine of Hera and say, "Help! I am putting myself under your protection." But they don't. There is a taboo involved here, and it is an Oedipal taboo, because Zeus is called "Father of All". It isn't simply an issue of sexual promiscuity. It is about the individual who sees himself or herself as godlike, and exempt from the laws that bind ordinary mortals in their social and personal relationships. When these laws are violated, Hera takes revenge. One manifestation of her revenge is a kind of madness which counteracts inflation by creating enormous insecurity. Feelings of inferiority and dread rise up and spoil the self-aggrandising tendencies that are running amok. Families as well as individuals can see themselves as exempt from ordinary social laws, and so can nations. Hera's revenge can be visited on collectives, too.

Audience: In America right now, there is a big backlash against the kind of individual freedoms which were so important after the 1960s.

Some states are reviving their anti-homosexuality laws, and the whole climate has become very traditional and family-orientated.

Liz: This could be interpreted as Hera's backlash. Whether such a backlash is right or wrong is not the point. It is probably inevitable, because the pendulum has swung too far in one direction and now it must swing back in the other. A nation, like an individual, can suffer from an unformed or damaged ego-structure which proves unable to hold the balance between two colliding archetypal powers. The origins of madness in society, in families and, ultimately, in the individual, cannot be reduced to the simple idea that the ego is blocking something in the unconscious. Two equally valid, equally powerful archetypal drives within the psyche are at war, and the ego must find a way to mediate between them. When this is not possible, psychosis may ensue.

Although a rigid ego is often a major component in madness, focusing solely on this misses the archetypal nature of the conflict. Even my client is not merely a victim of terrible parenting which damaged her ego-development. She carries her own archetypal conflict within her. The Saturn-Pluto conjunction sitting on the Sun and squaring the Moon is her Saturn-Pluto, not her parents', and in the midst of all that Plutonian passion there is also something Hera-like in her that wants clear structures and rules. Planetary conflicts like this describe a battle between archetypal powers, and neither side is wrong or pathological. But human consciousness gets caught in the middle. It is the function of the ego to mediate and, ultimately, transform these forces through giving them creative form. We may not be able to do this because we do not have a solid enough sense of self to hold the middle ground. But we can exacerbate the conflict by siding with one archetypal power against the other, even when we are conscious that both are within us.

Hera and feminism

Audience: A lot of Hera's concerns are the concerns of my mother's generation. Like lots of women of that generation, she was stifled and eventually destroyed by trying to stay in an unhappy marriage. She was always treated as inferior, and she believed it. I find it very difficult to honour what Hera represents because I don't want to live that kind of life. I am curious about the issues of feminism here.

Liz: It sounds as though your mother identified with Hera at the expense of other, more important aspects of her personality. That is not what I mean by "honouring". Your mother was held in bondage to collective opinion, rather than living her own individuality. Some women are more Hera-like, and conventional married life accords with their own individual values. Others feel suffocated and must break free. I cannot give you a universal, fits-all-sizes formula to deal with the archetypal patterns that Hera symbolises. It depends on the individual and the individual chart. Hera doesn't represent one particular thing for all women, because every woman must express the archetype in an individual way. And Hera is not equally important in every woman's chart. As far as inferiority is concerned, Hera is the queen of the gods, and this position of cosmic rulership hardly implies that women are "inferior". She is Zeus' equal and in many respects his superior. Her emphasis on the sanctity of social codes reflects a perspective in which individuals must acknowledge their responsibilities to the people with whom they live. But such acknowledgement may be expressed differently by different women, and marriage is only one form of it.

When enraged, Hera can be vindictive, as are all angry deities. But her viewpoint reflects as valid an element in human psychology as any other deity. This perspective has nothing to do with feminism or patriarchy. It is an acknowledgment of the sanctity of individual boundaries on the social and family level of life. It is worth noting that the Roman astrologer Manilius, who assigned a series of zodiacal rulerships to gods rather than planets, gives Aquarius to Hera, whom the Romans called Juno.[3] Interestingly, he also assigned Pisces to Neptune, eighteen hundred years before anyone knew the planet existed. Although his rulerships are not viable in practical astrological interpretation, the symbolic connotations are highly relevant, as these zodiacal deities contain something of the essence of the signs they rule. Aquarius, as we know, is concerned with the functioning of the group on a social level. It represents those social systems which are imposed

---

[3] See Manilius, *Astronomica*, 2.450.

on group behaviour and which allow solar, 5ᵗʰ house individuals to relate to each other in the context of a collective. Our old planetary ruler for Aquarius is, of course, Saturn, and as we have seen, Hera has many Saturnian qualities.

Audience: She seems to have to do with possessiveness.

Liz: Not in the usual sense. It is very interesting to see your reactions to this unpopular deity, because they are so highly coloured by the presiding ideology of the late 20ᵗʰ century. Hera's perspective runs very deep in all human beings. Debating whether this perspective is "right" or "wrong" is a pointless exercise. It is an archetypal perspective, and all archetypal perspectives are "right" provided they remain in balance with other perspectives. As I said, that is what the Greek image of the Olympian pantheon is about. The gods squabble and fight, but ultimately they are a family who find constantly shifting creative resolutions to their conflicts. Arguments about patriarchy and the inferiority of women are relevant to certain of the male deities, one of whom – Uranus – has a particular dislike of anything incarnate in flesh. But this has little to do with Hera. If our heads are filled with nothing but political polemics, we will find only negative qualities in Hera. Then we say she is oppressive. But the term "oppression" is often trumpeted simply because we are not getting what we want.

Audience: I still think she is unfair and sexist.

Liz: All the gods are unfair and sexist in one way or another, and we could say the same of the planets in astrology. They represent natural forces, each of which seeks to fulfil itself according to its own nature, and sooner or later they will come into conflict. Each of the energies symbolised by the gods is directed toward the full expression of its own being, and they are all lopsided. Whichever deity or planet we identify with, the others will seem wrong or repressive when our desires conflict with theirs. This discussion has been very revealing, because it highlights where we ourselves tend to polarise. The person who goes mad has polarised to an extreme degree, and whatever deity is favoured, the rejected one will always retaliate by forcibly demanding entry into the ego's world. Of course it is sexist, if you want to see it that way. We could also say that Saturn is paranoid, the Moon has an eating disorder, Mercury is a pathological liar, Venus is promiscuous, Jupiter is manic depressive, Neptune is a druggie and Uranus is a psychopath. They have all got problems, just as we do.

Audience: So you are saying that madness and sanity depend on the interaction between these principles and the ego, and moral judgement is not relevant.

Liz: Yes, I am saying something like that. States of madness, whether they slide into the destructive realm of criminal insanity or whether they are essentially benign, reflect the eruption of archetypal forces, which the Greeks envisaged as gods. None of these gods is intrinsically evil or pathological, but they have natural antipathies and are always struggling for supremacy. The conscious ego stands in the midst of these powerful forces and acts as both a lightning conductor and an alchemical alembic. If the ego collapses in the face of these collective forces, the ensuing state is what we call madness.

The madness of Artemis

We do have a lot more to get through before we break for lunch, so let's look at two more female deities associated in myth with madness: Artemis and the Erinyes. Artemis, like Hera, sometimes transforms her victims into animals when she is outraged. She is usually known as a lunar deity, but as Hekate, a chthonic underworld goddess, she is more Plutonian than lunar. Although Artemis is a goddess of childbirth, she is certainly not related to the cuddly, bread-baking image of the Moon which is so ubiquitous in traditional astrological texts. The dimension of the Moon concerned with family bonds is Hera's domain, while Artemis-Hekate is the wild, dark side of the Moon, the "mistress of beasts". Her realm is the heart of the primordial forest, where human beings are not meant to walk. Artemis as Hekate is often shown with a triple face, representing the three phases of the lunar cycle: the crescent, the full Moon and the dark Moon. Artemis-Hekate presides over sorcery, magic, the secrets of the underworld and the realms of the dead. These domains are forbidden to humans. Artemis is sometimes represented as a virgin goddess, which means she is inviolate. What are we looking at psychologically?

Audience: It sounds as though she is connected with Lilith, the Dark Moon.

Liz: Yes, she bears a family resemblance to Lilith, although I generally don't work with Lilith in natal charts. As with other hypothetical planets, I have problems interpreting something which is not actually there, since this raises questions about the source and validity of the purported placement of the "planet" in the zodiac. I associate Artemis-Hekate with Plutonian qualities, or with a combination of Pluto and the Moon. Artemis is not an intrinsically evil or destructive deity. She is a beneficent protector of children and animals. But like the other deities we are exploring in the context of madness, she can be vengeful if crossed. Her greatest enemy in myth is arrogant males...

Audience: Ha!

Liz: ...Who, through pride and greed, demean her or violate her sacred precincts. There are many myths about the rage of Artemis. One of her victims is King Agamemnon. Before he sails for Troy to fight the Trojans, he shoots a deer, and then offends Artemis by boasting that not even the goddess is his equal in the hunt. In revenge, she turns the wind so that the Greek fleet cannot set sail. When the oracle is questioned, Agamemnon is advised to sacrifice his daughter Iphigeneia in order to earn the forgiveness of the goddess. He carries out the sacrifice, and the wind does indeed turn in his favour, but the slaughter of his child unleashes further tragedies. His wife takes revenge on him by murdering him in his bath, and their son, Orestes, takes revenge on his mother by murdering *her*. Then Orestes himself goes mad. Although the goddess appears to be placated by the sacrifice of Iphigeneia, she has no intention of relenting.

Revenge against hubris

Audience: What else could Agamemnon have done?

Liz: Sacrifice his greed and forego the chance to invade Troy, a city which Artemis favoured. That was the real message, but he was too arrogant to read it correctly, and preferred to kill his own daughter instead. Artemis also targets Orion, the famous hunter. He, like Agamemnon, makes the mistake of boasting in one of her sacred groves: he claims he is a match for any animal on earth. The goddess then sends a giant scorpion to destroy him. A certain kind of boasting seems to trigger her rage, and the boasting usually involves a claim of superiority over the natural world. Artemis seems to remind us of the limits of human knowledge and power. She tells us, "You can acquire impressive technology and a certain degree of control over nature. But there are mysteries you must respect because they are beyond the range of human knowledge. The natural world is sacred, and not to be treated as fodder for human greed."

Artemis rises up against humans who do not respect her domain. It may be that her rage is visible in those occurrences where nature retaliates against us because we have violated it. I started off the seminar with a joke about BSE, but this kind of epidemic, rooted in human stupidity and carelessness, could be imaginatively interpreted as an example of Artemis on the rampage. She targets both collectives and individual humans who offend her. She turns Aktaion into a stag, and then sets his own dogs on him. This particular myth tells us a lot about the deeper nature of this mysterious deity's madness. According to Euripides, Aktaion, like Agamemnon, claims to be a better hunter than Artemis herself. When he blunders into her sacred grove and discovers her bathing, he stands ogling her rather than turning his face away, thus adding insult to injury. His dogs are "mere" animals, who are subservient to his will. Suddenly he is transformed into an animal himself, and his own animals tear him to pieces. Artemis revenges herself through the very nature we believe we can control. The natural opponents of Artemis in the modern world are those who attempt to manipulate the natural order. I am sure we can all think of lots of examples. A certain kind of madness afflicts these individuals, and they often bring about their own downfall. What does her madness look like in human form?

Audience: It seems to have to do with self-destruction.

The sting of the scorpion

Liz: Yes. What is interesting about Artemis is how very subtle she can be. Both Agamemnon and Aktaion are destroyed by an aspect of themselves. Because Agamemnon sacrifices his daughter out of greed, he unleashes the vengeance of his wife, and thus architects his own death. Artemis doesn't kill him herself. She sets him up, and uses his own personality as the means of his downfall. She knows that he is so arrogant that he will choose military glory over his daughter's life. She doesn't kill Aktaion directly, either. She reveals the animal side of his own nature, and then steps back and says to the dogs, "Go for it, Fido!" Even her destruction of Orion may be viewed in this light. He boasts that he is a match for any animal on earth, so she unleashes a creature from the underworld which he cannot hope to defeat. It is an interesting choice, if we think astrologically. Orion, before he takes on Artemis, has a rather unpleasant history of rape, and his sexuality is closely connected with his arrogance. Of all the possible creatures the goddess might have chosen to work her will, she selects one which symbolises both sexuality and death. In a way, the scorpion is an aspect of Orion himself. The madness of Artemis is truly Plutonian: the exacerbation of an already self-destructive quality, to the point where it becomes lethal.

A good example in modern times is Hitler's misguided invasion of Russia in the summer of 1941. Evidently his astrologers neglected to mention that, like the giant scorpion which destroyed Orion, transiting Pluto had crept up to Hitler's MC. Or perhaps they did tell him, and he had them shot. If he had not attempted this invasion, we would no doubt all be speaking German. The war was going badly for the Allies at the time, and if Hitler had not withdrawn from his attempted invasion of Britain, the outcome would have been rather different. But some madness suddenly took hold of him. There is a long history of people trying to conquer Russia, and they have always failed. Napoleon also tried and made a mess of it. The Russian winter is the most powerful opponent in the world, yet both these conquerors apparently forgot this obvious fact. When Artemis attacks, something that was previously held in check begins to inflate, and the person believes they are capable of conquering anything, including nature itself. At that moment they put their foot on the banana skin, and over they go. It is through the madness of one's own hubris that Artemis destroys.

The madness of Uranus

We have had a look at Neptune in the context of Dionysian madness, and Pluto in the context of Artemis'. Now we need to look at Uranus in relation to mad states. All three outer planets reflect collective needs, aspirations and ideas. They symbolise energies in the group psyche which are enormous and undifferentiated. When an individual is strongly aligned with the outer planets, ego-consciousness is critical, because the ego must be strong enough to contain and mediate the collective forces. If the ego cannot deal with these energies, the personality may be overwhelmed, and the individual is "possessed" by collective emotions and ideas which are very archaic. The individual is then no longer an individual, but becomes a mouthpiece for the collective. The artist is also a mouthpiece for the collective, and so are many political leaders; and as we all know, quite a few artists and political leaders are mad. But many people who are neither artists nor politicians become unwilling mouthpieces for collective energies because the ego is unable to mediate. Uranus symbolises our collective ideas of progress, and when it takes possession of the individual ego, it reflects a particular kind of madness which involves a global vision of perfect order. Uranus at its best, mediated through a conscious ego with individual values, can contribute brilliance and creative inspiration in spheres such as science, psychology, sociology and astrology: all fields where a system of ideas reflects progress toward a perfect cosmic order and design. If it subsumes the ego, Uranus may still be brilliant, but it can also be exceedingly destructive because it is so disconnected from living human reality.

I have often mentioned the rising Uranus in Hitler's chart, which tells us a lot about both his brilliance and his malevolent fanaticism. Have any of you seen a Nazi propaganda film called *The Triumph of the Will*? When Hitler gets onto the podium, we initially see a human, albeit a twisted one. But as he begins to speak, something else comes into play. His gestures become jerky, like those of an automaton. His face changes, and his eyes glaze over. Something is coming through him which is no longer human, and certainly not individual. It is a collective idea, which has taken possession not only of him but also of his audience. Here is Uranus, manifesting with all its archetypal power through an individual human psyche, and it carries with it the vision of a perfect society where all inferior, corrupt elements have been purged.

Sometimes the Uranian vision can be glimpsed in schizophrenia. The fantasies of many schizophrenics are concerned with beings from a higher order, usually extraterrestrial, who give instructions on how to eradicate all the sinful and vile elements in human society. Sometimes these fantasies are bizarre but harmless. But sometimes they can lead to violence, because they may take the form of "voices" which demand that certain types of humans be killed in order to purify the planet. On a more creative level, the Uranian world also animates the work of our best science fiction writers, and here Uranian madness finds its most creative expression through the mediation of the artist. Frankenstein's monster is a Uranian vision, and, not surprisingly, Mary Shelley, the author of *Frankenstein*, had the Sun conjunct Uranus.

Uranus and the psychopath

Uranian madness reflects a cosmic vision of perfection. It is devoid of feeling and human contact: in other words, it is utterly dissociated. It is possible that the state which we call psychopathy, which in the old days used to be called moral inferiority, is related to such states of complete dissociation, and Uranus, along with Chiron and Saturn, seems to occur with unusual frequency in connection with the Moon in the charts of psychopaths.[4] Psychopathy is now considered a

---

[4] See Part One of this book.

personality disorder, and it is not usually referred to as madness. This is probably because the psychopath, far from being unable to cope with reality, can usually cope terrifyingly well. But there is no emotional connection with other living beings, and consequently no remorse when acts of destructiveness are committed. There are varying degrees of psychopathy, and not all psychopaths are cold-blooded killers. But there seems to be no treatment for psychopathy. In order for therapy of any kind to be effective, there must be a working relationship between the patient and the therapist, as well as a genuine wish to be helped. The psychopath neither wishes to be helped nor seems capable of forming any kind of relationship with anyone at all. Conning the therapist is part of the fun.

Psychopathy is indeed a mad state, perhaps one of the maddest, but it is often unrecognisable as such because the psychopathic individual is often very charming and believable. They do not appear mad in the context of our prevailing definition of the term. There is an ongoing debate about whether psychopathy is genetic or linked to environmental pressures. As astrologers, we can only recognise that there is often a Uranian element in psychopathy, which means that at least part of the equation is inherent. Uranian psychopathy is particularly evident in the practice of genocide. When any leader justifies the end by the means – the you-have-to-break-eggs-to-make-an-omelette routine – the ego has been shunted out of its seat, and Uranus has taken control.

When the collective goes mad

When we consider the ways in which we are poisoning our planet, even though we are fully aware of the future consequences, we can see this Uranian element run amok. It is a kind of madness, because it is disconnected from the reality of life. In genetic experimentation we can also see glimpses of Uranian madness, as we can in political ideologies which trample on individual feelings and rights in the name of social engineering and an ideal of a perfect society. Where do we draw the line between valid scientific experimentation and the kind of inflation expressed by such dissociated vision? If an idea takes over so completely, the human component is demeaned and eventually destroyed. What makes Uranus rise up as an angry deity?

Audience: Too much Saturn.

Liz: Yes, that is one of the chief triggers. Much of the madness I have just been describing comes from too much Saturn, rather than from Uranus expressed in a conscious and creative way. It arises from the greed in human nature, because genetic engineering is big business. The real root of Uranian madness is not idealism. It is our short-sighted materialism and desire to control life. Uranus can also be kicked into a fury by too much identification with the emotions and the instincts. If the primal instincts have taken over, and a collective descends into darkness and despair, the mad Uranian dictator will rise up in response to the collective need for a perfect world. A good example of this is Germany in the 1920s and early 1930s, and Hitler, a psychopath with Uranus closely conjunct his Ascendant, rose to power as the answer to collective Uranian needs. If a family descends over many generations into poisonous power-battles and emotional chaos, the mad Uranian child will rise up in response to a profound need for distancing and detachment. A family which is too enmeshed is a breeding ground for Uranian madness. In this kind of emotional swamp, the god will rise up and shatter the family unit through the Uranian propensities of one of its members. Such a Uranian vessel is often diagnosed as schizophrenic.

Bondage to fundamentalist religious structures can also arouse an angry Uranus, as can bondage to a social hierarchy based on ancestral privilege. In Russia in 1918, a characteristically Uranian form of madness erupted: the Bolshevik Revolution. The same might be said of the French Revolution, which was hardly a sane and measured expression of social change. Sanity was restored only after the streets ran with blood and the thrill of the guillotine became just another day's routine. These are collective forms of madness or, put another way, a collective gone mad, and Uranus excels at this kind of eruption wherever the life-force is held in bondage to Saturnian structures or primordial Plutonian survival needs.

Michael Jackson: obsession with perfection

Audience: The way Michael Jackson has violated his own body for an ideal look is a Uranian thing.

Liz: Yes, although he is certainly not mad in the sense of not being able to function in the world: he can express his creative talent in a disciplined and innovative way. The correct term might be "obsession with perfection". I have his chart with me, so we can have a quick look.

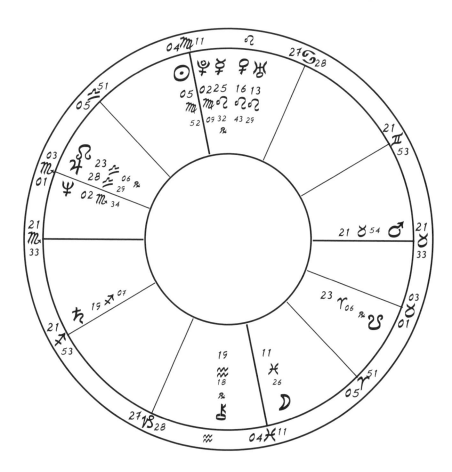

Michael Jackson
29 August 1958, 12.44 pm, Gary, Indiana, USA

Audience: Is the obsession with perfection connected with his Sun-Pluto in Virgo?

Liz: The obsession part is Plutonian. The perfection part is Uranian, and I am also inclined to link it with the Venus-Uranus conjunction in Leo, opposite Chiron. Uranus, as we all know, is the great mythic perfectionist, who condemns his earthy children to Tartarus because they are ugly in his eyes. Uranian madness is often connected with a vision of perfection which makes it impossible to accept life as it is. And Venus opposite Chiron in Aquarius suggests a deep wound to Michael Jackson's sense of self-worth, linked with being somehow socially outcast or "different". Venus-Chiron, like Venus-Saturn, often carries a feeling of physical inferiority or unattractiveness. The Sun-Pluto conjunction and the Moon-Pluto opposition, underlined by the Scorpio Ascendant, certainly reflect an obsessional nature, and the placement of this configuration along the MC/IC axis suggests that it is an inherited obsession. It comes down through the parents, and is connected with image or status in the eyes of the world.

Michael Jackson has done his utmost to transform himself from an attractive and energetic black man to a strange, androgynous white creature, and the racial issues behind his constant attempts to alter his physiognomy are obvious. These racial issues must have been powerful in his parents' lives, demonstrated by his father's tyrannical determination to make his children celebrities rather than allowing them to be ordinary children. As a Virgo with the Moon in Pisces, Michael would have been a highly sensitive child, very vulnerable to criticism and very much in need of being liked and accepted. Although by his teens he had already achieved considerable acclaim as a talented performer, the wound does not seem to have healed. What he has done to his face is deeply self-destructive.

Audience: I have got the Moon with Uranus and Pluto in Virgo in the 3rd house, and I think sanity has something to do with the issue of boundaries. I don't think I'm mad. When a person doesn't breach the boundaries, aspects like this are easier to work with.

Liz: With that conjunction in Virgo, clear boundaries are a means of grounding outer planet energies which might otherwise be utterly terrifying. The Moon tells us about what we need in order to feel safe and grounded, and your definition of sanity, and the path through which you feel you can maintain it, reflect your Virgo Moon. Everyone here today will have one or another of the configurations we are looking at. No one in this room is exempt. Now, that may mean we are all mad. Alternatively, we have each found a way to mediate such configurations, according to our individual nature and needs. An individual with an identical configuration, who has not been able to find a means of containing and mediating these powerful unconscious energies, may slip into madness, temporarily or chronically. That is the only real difference between the sane person and the mad one. The sane person is able to swim in those currents, but the mad person goes under. Probably every person in this room, at some time and however briefly, has been in a state which could appropriately be defined as mad. It may last five minutes, or half an hour, or a week. It is a disconnection from ego-reality because the ego has been overwhelmed by the unconscious. But we are somehow able to preserve the ego's integrity long enough to come back again without having been noticed. Then we have the luxury of saying, "I am sane."

The madness of the Erinyes

Let's look now at the Erinyes, otherwise known as the Furies. The Greeks referred to them with the euphemism "Eumenides", which means "the Kindly Ones". I don't need to spend a lot of time on them, because most of you have a sense of what they are. They are related in some ways to Artemis-Hekate, because they are underworld deities. They are goddesses of natural justice and the protectors of mother-right, and they rise up when a mother's honour has been violated. In myth they are best known for their pursuit of Orestes: they hunt their victim like a pack of hounds, and punish him by inflicting madness. The Erinyes drive Orestes mad because he has murdered his mother, and they drive Oedipus mad because he has had sex with his mother. Any violation of the sanctity of the Great Mother invokes the wrath of these creatures, and their madness takes the form of horrible nightmares. They are an image of acute paranoia. It should not be difficult to work out what kind of planetary components are involved. Pluto is obviously the prime suspect, especially when it is linked with the Sun, the Moon or both.

Fear of the dark

The Erinyes, like Artemis-Hekate, don't like the Uranian realm much, but they are equally antagonistic to the Sun-god. The Great Mother is an image of the collective cyclical life of nature, and at this level we are not differentiated as individuals. We are merely one of many species, doomed to be born, reproduce and die. Our aspirations toward individual fulfilment are allowable as long as we accept our *moira*, our fate as mortal creatures. A powerful Pluto, angular or linked with the luminaries in an airy or strongly Uranian chart, can sometimes be connected with their very special form of madness. Whenever we feel that people are out to get us and the world is full of dark, invading forces, we are confronting the Erinyes. We may also meet them in our fears about our bodies, and our expectations that if anything good happens to us, it will be wrenched away. If we experience such feelings, it is a good idea to try to explore where we might have offended the realm of the instincts, where we are still frightened of mother's punishment for our separateness, or where we have become inflated in our *hubris*. In extreme cases, these kinds of feelings and fantasies can take over, and the person dwells in a night-world full of threat and horror.

Post-natal depression

Audience: Is post-natal depression linked with them?

Liz: Perhaps. There may also be a link with Hera, who is a symbol of the earthly responsibilities and structures of family life. Post-natal depression sometimes reflects the horror of discovering that one is mortal and will grow old. For many women – especially those who are strongly identified with the *puella*, the "eternal girl" – the birth of a child, even if it is longed for, is a dreadful shock, because they now have to engage with the responsibilities of ordinary, everyday earth-life. They realise that they won't live forever. They are not immortal and they can no longer be father's divine princess-anima. They are women just like their mothers, and they must take their place in the continuity of generations. Often these realisations result in a psychological crash. But post-natal depression does not usually involve the kind of paranoia which I associate with the mythic image of the Erinyes.

Post-natal depression can also be linked with a sense of being trapped, which may be particularly acute if the relationship with the partner is not viable. As long as there are no children, there is a chance to escape, but once a child is born, it is a lot harder. Sometimes the relationship is viable but not perfect, and becoming a mother involves accepting compromises which are anathema to the Uranian or Jupiterian woman. Saturn is usually more in evidence than Pluto in these cases, and we may see a transit of Saturn making a conjunction or hard aspect to Venus, the Sun or the Moon, reflecting the sense of imprisonment and depression that comes with increased worldly responsibilities. Whatever the conventional medical definition of post-natal depression, I believe that, in most cases, its archetypal core is a painful rite of passage into an acceptance of mortality. If it is sufficiently severe, the depression can result in a breakdown, and in extreme cases it is a true form of madness which may endanger the newborn child. But equally, post-natal depression can lead to a breakthrough and a more solid and more mature personality.

The madness of Saturn

Saturn doesn't afflict humans with madness, but he himself is a mad god. What kind of god swallows his own children, just because somebody says to him, "One day, one of your children will grow up and take your place as ruler of the universe?" That is what happens in the natural order of things. As we grow older, we must relinquish our place in the world, and the next generation takes over from us. We all have to accept the inevitable passage of time and the decline of our powers. It is simply a fact of life: the King is dead, long live the King. But Saturn cannot accept this inevitable reality. What kind of madness is this?

Audience: It's a denial of creativity.

Howard Hughes: in the grip of Saturn's madness

Liz: Yes, it is denial of creativity, taken to a pathological extreme of envy, negativity and rigidity. Think about Howard Hughes, for example. Although quite brilliant, he was an obsessively secretive and self-destructive man. As a teenager he was interested in mathematics, flying, and all things mechanical, but he was an indifferent student and never took a university degree. At the age of eighteen he inherited his father's wealth, after which he never looked back. As an aviator he held every speed record of consequence, and was hailed as the world's greatest flyer. He founded an international airline, two regional airlines, a major motion picture studio, mining properties, a tool company, gambling casinos and hotels, and a medical research institute. Many of the companies he founded are still flourishing today: Hughes Space and Communications, for example, is the world's largest manufacturer of commercial satellites. By the time of his death he had accrued enormous wealth and power. But throughout most of his adult life he was mad.

By the time Hughes was in his late thirties, he had achieved more than most people could ever dream of. But at the same time, his phobia about germs, which had begun in childhood, suddenly increased to alarming proportions. He had also become dependent on medication, which included both codeine and vallium – the first originally prescribed for pain from injuries suffered in a plane crash years earlier, and the second prescribed for his chronic anxiety state. This led to a complete breakdown, just as transiting Uranus reached his MC and opposed his natal Moon-Mercury conjunction in Sagittarius, and transiting Saturn opposed his natal Sun-Uranus conjunction in Capricorn. Even after he had reclaimed some semblance of sanity, he required the wearing of white gloves by everyone who came in contact with any object he touched. His servants had to handle everything with tissues. Fourteen years later, at the age of fifty-three, when transiting Pluto opposed his natal Mars-Saturn conjunction and transiting Saturn opposed his natal Pluto, he had a second complete breakdown. He spent most of his time sitting naked in a chair in the middle of the living room of his hotel suite, an area which he called the "germ-free zone", watching one film after another on a motion picture screen.

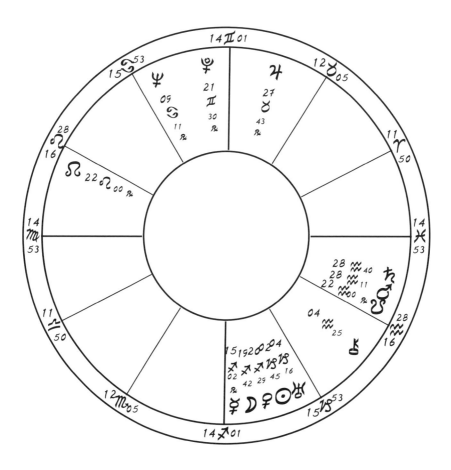

Howard Hughes
24 December 1905, 11.00 pm, Houston, Texas, USA

Hughes' behaviour deteriorated steadily after this second psychological collapse. Although he still managed his companies, he became a hermit who would not leave his bed. He kept changing his residence, from the Bahamas to England and from Mexico to Las Vegas, taking elaborate precautions at each new destination to ensure absolute privacy in a luxury hotel. No one ever saw him except a few male aides. He worked for days without sleep in a black-curtained room, and became so emaciated that a doctor who examined him compared his condition to that of the inmates of Japanese prison camps during the Second World War. He ended his days in Mexico, a mad recluse, emaciated, incoherent, and utterly alone except for his doctors and bodyguards. He died of heart failure at the age of seventy-one. X-rays taken during the subsequent autopsy revealed fragments of hypodermic needles broken off in his arms.

The phobic tyrant

Of course a strong Saturn is not the only factor involved in Hughes' madness. We will look at other possible contributors in due course, but it is worth noting the dominant Pluto at the MC, opposing the Moon and the chart ruler, Mercury. The madness of the Erinyes is here too, and parental complexes of an enormously powerful kind are suggested by the stellium in the 4th house and the oppositions between these planets and the two outer planets in the 10th. But Hughes was a Capricorn, and his life and personality are, in many ways, typical of this sign. Shrewd and worldly, introverted yet deeply ambitious, he lived most of the classic attributes of his Sun-sign to the full. Saturnian themes also coloured the direction which his mental deterioration took as he grew older. Saturn is in the 6th house, exactly conjunct Mars, and this conjunction, aligned with the Moon's nodal axis, makes a statement not only about his obsession with work and his need to prove his potency in the face of deep-rooted insecurities, but also about his obsession with his body and the belief that he was always under threat from disease and infection.

Hughes' mother is described by that wonderful euphemism, "overprotective", which probably means that she herself was hardly a paragon of psychological health. Pluto presiding at the MC and opposing the Moon hints at the mother as one of the main factors in the complex reflected by his phobia. Hughes inherited his wealth and position from his father, and the stellium of five planets in the 4th house, including the chart ruler, the Moon, and the Sun-Uranus conjunction in Capricorn, emphasises how extremely powerful this father must have been. But the dominance of outer planets – Sun conjunct Uranus and opposition Neptune, and that angular Pluto opposition the Moon – also suggests that both Hughes' genius and his illness were connected with an extreme receptivity to the collective psyche. He sensed where the collective needed to go, and made his contribution through characterically Uranian channels – engineering and aviation – and the characteristically Neptunian channel of the film industry. Born into the generation with Uranus opposition Neptune, he was also attuned, for both good and ill, to a deep split in the collective psyche which culminated in the outbreak of the First World War.

Obsessive-compulsive neurosis

The Sun-Uranus conjunction opposite Neptune is no doubt linked to Hughes' madness, and so is Pluto. Moreover, the amount of drugs he pumped into his body damaged his brain, so there are physical factors as well. But the form his madness took was peculiarly Saturnian and deeply symbolic. Hughes' madness manifested as extreme paranoid defensiveness, and he could keep going only by walling himself in behind rituals and structures which gave him absolute control over his environment. When Saturn's natural defence mechanisms get mixed up with a damaged ego and with Neptune, Pluto or Uranus – and Hughes had all of the above – the collective forces which threaten to overwhelm the personality can only be held at bay by obsessive rituals. These protective rituals regularly break down in the face of a psychotic episode, but they are re-established as the madness ebbs. In psychiatry, the symptom picture is known as obsessive-compulsive neurosis.

Obsessive-compulsive neurosis is often expressed through the repetitive washing of hands, doorknobs or money, or the urgent need to return to the house two, three or even four times to make sure all the lamps have been unplugged so that a fire doesn't break out. Such symptoms are commoner than one might think, and they may appear in otherwise well-adapted personalities at times of great anxiety. This kind of compulsive behaviour is also characteristic of certain kinds of autism. The rituals are a kind of magical defence, a protection against the obsessive terror of uncontrollable forces that might invade and destroy. This is Saturn's kind of madness, when the ego feels threatened by those vast collective forces which astrologers symbolise by the outer planets.

Obsessive-compulsive rituals of a mild kind are common to all of us when we feel threatened. Many people maintain their rituals throughout a lifetime without ever tipping over into psychosis. Repetitive, compulsive thoughts are another aspect of this Saturnian form of defence, and they can be far more frightening. But it is only when the rituals or thoughts become so compulsive that they take over one's life that we might appropriately call this a state of madness. There are people whose lives are crippled by it. They cannot go outside because of the dirt in the gutter or the cracks in the pavement. They are so compulsive about their rituals that they cannot do anything else. Their thoughts circle around and around the same theme, like an animal pacing back and forth in a cage. They wander about the house looking for a speck of dust they might have missed, and washing their hands until the skin becomes raw and painful. Some of you might know a film starring Jack Nicholson, called *As Good As It Gets*. It is a remarkable film, blackly funny but also full of remarkable insight into this very special form of madness. Nicholson plays an obsessive-compulsive personality. He is not entirely crippled by it; he is a successful writer of romantic novels. But when the film begins, he brings his own knife and fork to the local restaurant because he fears being contaminated by their cutlery, and is incapable of forming a relationship with anyone at all.

Audience: What kind of help is there for somebody like that?

Liz: Quite a lot, if there is enough understanding on the part of the helper. Go and see the film, or get it on a video or DVD. With states such as this, help ultimately lies in the strengthening of the ego. The same might be said about many states of madness. And the strengthening of the ego only becomes possible when a relationship is available which can gradually allow the person to build a sense of personal worth and inner safety. Obsessive-compulsive rituals are a defence system which protects the personality from the potential disintegration caused by the eruption of terrifying unconscious forces. These forces, which usually involve collective as well as personal factors, can be safely channelled into creative outlets only if the ego is solid enough to contain them.

The madness of Zeus

Like Saturn, Zeus does not afflict humans with madness, but he himself often behaves in a mad fashion. His violent tempers, profound sulks and florid self-aggrandisement hint at what we now know as manic depression. Although there are many factors involved with this particular symptom picture, as there are with all the others, a powerful Jupiter seems to be one of the most relevant.

Toppling from heaven

In Greek myth, the rage of Zeus is usually invoked by any god or mortal who dares to challenge his position as ruler of the universe. His punishments generally involve eternal suffering of some kind, or blasting the offender to oblivion with a thunderbolt. Fire is Zeus' usual implement: Ixion, who presumes to attempt the seduction of Hera, is bound to a flaming wheel, and Aesclepius, who presumes to raise the dead, is burned to a cinder with a thunderbolt. But the most famous punishment that Zeus inflicts does not involve fire. This is the punishment visited on Prometheus, and this mythic image can tell us a lot about the kind of madness which Jupiter reflects. Prometheus is guilty of stealing divine fire to give to mortals, against the explicit will of Zeus, so he is chained to a rock in the mountains and subjected to having his liver eaten by Zeus' eagle every day. Every night the liver regenerates, and the next day the torment begins all over again.

This cyclical suffering followed by respite is characteristic of the alternating states of manic depression, which is now understood in psychiatry as a "mood disorder" rather than an illness. The individual can hold the middle ground for a while, but slowly the manic state begins to build up. This involves a very high energy and activity level, extreme restlessness, euphoria, decreased need for sleep, and inflated self-esteem.. The extreme end of this manic state may terminate abruptly with a severe depression, often accompanied by thoughts of – and sometimes attempts at – suicide. One of the difficulties with manic depression is that, although more florid examples follow a well-documented symptomatology, the problem often begins in youth with quite gentle fluctuations of mood. At present, the frequent diagnosis of bipolar disorder in young people is a real danger in America, because those who are inherently predisposed to such fluctuations in mood without any suggestion of madness may be labelled and medicated.

Jupiterian qualities are evident in the manic episodes of the bipolar cycle. But many Jupiterian people are like this all the time, and they are not mad. They take risks, they are ebullient and self-confident, they trust their intuition and their luck without any apparent concrete basis, and their restlessness and enthusiastic pursuit of pleasure reflect the essential nature of the great mythic king of the gods. And they often fall into depression for a time if their dreams are unachievable or they are forced to wait for results. Saturnian qualities are also evident in the depressive episodes of manic depression. But many Saturnian people are by nature melancholic, mistrusting life and always expecting "worst case scenarios" in order to avoid being disappointed. This does not make them mad.

Mood swings are not always an indication of manic depression. Aspects such as hard Jupiter-Saturn contacts, a powerful angular Jupiter cohabiting with a powerful Saturn in the same birth chart, or an emphasis in both Capricorn and Sagittarius, can be reflected in cyclical episodes of "highs" and "lows". Reconciling these opposites may take the individual many years, and mood swings are both normal and inevitable. But severe manic depression moves into the realm of madness, and both the individual and those close to him or her suffer deeply. We need to explore why a "normal" degree of emotional lability, reflecting a particular kind of dichotomy in the natal chart, would become so extreme that both ends of the mood spectrum run out of control and swamp the conscious ego. There is no agreement among psychiatrists about the causes of manic depression, although it is generally thought to arise from a combination of factors, including inherent temperament, genetic inheritance and early environment. The organic end of the psychiatric spectrum naturally places the emphasis on biochemical instability, which is thought to interfere with the transmission of nerve impulses in the brain.

"Milligoon"

I thought we might look briefly at the chart of a famous person diagnosed with manic depression, from which he has suffered virtually all his adult life. His illness, if that is what it is, may be viewed as the source of both his suffering and his creative gift. Although he has been diagnosed with bipolar disorder, we need to look at the individual rather than the symptoms. We might also consider the possibility that his state of madness, like that of Howard Hughes, is an extreme form of the individual himself, rather than something "different" which erupts and distorts the personality.

Audience: Could you say that again?

Liz: Certainly. We might also consider the possibility that his state of madness, like that of Howard Hughes, is an extreme form of the individual himself, rather than something "different" which erupts and distorts the personality. I will try rephrasing it, if I have not expressed myself clearly enough. All the different symptom pictures we have been looking at are, from the medical point of view, classifiable into groups which form the definition of particular kinds of mental illness. But when we look at the birth chart, we can see that these symptom pictures are exaggerated versions of the individual's inherent temperament, pushed to an extreme because the ego has lost, or never had, the capacity to hold its ground.

Howard Hughes was not mad because he was a Capricorn, and we have seen how the dominance of the outer planets in his chart may be related to his madness. But the form the madness took was peculiarly Capricornian, and the isolated, phobic recluse is a caricature of a Capricorn on a very bad day. Likewise, Michael Jackson, who is not deemed clinically mad but who is certainly compulsively self-destructive, expresses his obsession in a peculiarly Virgoan way. Here, too, the outer planets are dominant, and he has not pursued his self-destructive course simply because he is a Virgo. But his determination to eradicate every tiny imperfection in his physical appearance is a caricature of a Virgo on a very bad day.

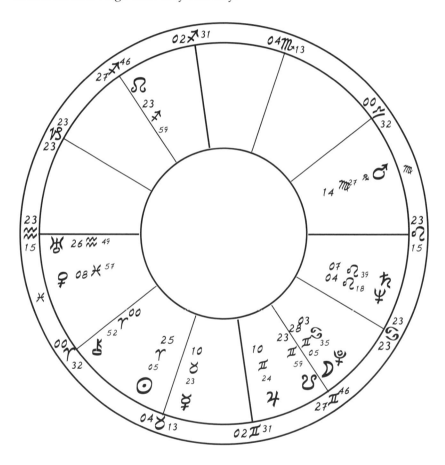

Spike Milligan
16 April 1918, 3.00 am, Ahmadnagar., India

Spike Milligan is also fondly known as "Milligoon" because he created *The Goon Show*. We should keep Thomas Szasz in mind as we explore this chart, since it could be argued that Spike Milligan does not suffer from madness; he simply suffers, and creates, from being Spike Milligan.[5] I would like you to look at this chart, not from the perspective of "spotting" where the manic depression shows up, but from the point of view of what kind of man this is, and what fuels his bizarre and hilarious sense of the absurd.

This chart contains a deep dichotomy. A picture of a very quick-thinking, positive, witty, sharp and eccentric individual emerges from placements such as the rising Uranus in its own sign, sextile the Sun in Aries and trine the Moon in Gemini, and Mercury in the 3rd trine Mars in Virgo, Mercury's own sign. Jupiter is powerful because it is angular, emphasising those Mercurial qualities by its placement in Gemini, and it sits at the peg of a T-cross involving Venus and Mars. The retrograde Mars stands alone in the southern hemisphere of the chart, a singleton which reflects the somewhat aggressive and edgy way he expresses himself to the outside world. All these placements are cool and cerebral, witty and inventive, but they are not predisposed to introspection or a well-developed feeling function. The other Spike is represented by Mercury square Saturn-Neptune, the Sun square Neptune, and the Moon-Pluto conjunction, which squares Chiron. None of these configurations will tell us about Spike's madness. But they point to a deep split between a highly rational nature and a powerful and disturbing connection with the realm of the irrational, represented by Neptune and Pluto. This dichotomy describes the quality of both his humour and his bouts of mania and subsequent dark depressions. Both reflect fundamental aspects of his nature.

The introverted extravert

We need to consider Spike's background in relation to his chart, since it is always the chemical mix between environment and inherent

---

[5] Although he was very much alive at the time this seminar was given, Spike Milligan died of kidney failure on 27 February 2002.

temperament which channels astrological configurations into particular forms of expression. Despite the wonderful lunacy of his humour, Spike's personality is and always has been a painfully sensitive one. We might not expect this from an Aries with an Aquarian Ascendant and a Gemini Moon, but the rising Venus in Pisces, the squares from Neptune to Sun and Mercury, and the Moon-Pluto conjunction squaring Chiron do describe this much more vulnerable and sensitive side of his personality. It is not uncommon for deeply introverted personalities to become actors and comedians. It is as though the conflict between their extreme sensitivity and their overpowering need to communicate can find no resolution except in front of an audience.

Spike was born in India. His father was a sergeant-major in the British army, and he was schooled in Roman Catholic convents. He did not return to England with his family until he was sixteen, and only a few years later he entered the Second World War as a gunner. His war experiences were transformed into laughter fodder in books such as *Adolf Hitler: My Part in his Downfall*, but we can only imagine what horror he must have experienced on the battlefield, and what it did to his inner life. Spike himself has stated that his experiences during the war began the gradual deterioration of his mental stability, and they were no doubt the trigger, although the seeds were probably sown much earlier.

Audience: Would there be a conflict between the Moon in Gemini and Pluto in Cancer? That is an out-of-sign conjunction.

Liz: The conjunction of Moon and Pluto is difficult in any sign, because the personal security needs are constantly being invaded by a sense of the often destructive survival instincts of the collective. The Moon in Gemini does not cope well with Pluto's realm even at the best of times, and easily feels overwhelmed by all that darkness. Air is an idealistic element, and Spike's emphasis in air suggests a finely tuned, aesthetically inclined and deeply idealistic nature. This man has a very strong sense of justice and fairness, as befits the Aquarian Ascendant. I am sure he was repelled by the inequalities and injustices imposed on the local population by the British Raj of which his father was a part, and it is also possible that his Catholic schooling did not help matters either. The war must have put the final nail in the coffin of his faith in life and in humanity. When we view his life in this way, it seems that his wild mood swings are actually a sane and appropriate response to a mad world. In 1987, Spike remarked in an interview, "You'd have to be a total idiot to be happy today. I would never have had four children if I'd known what I know now."

In addition to the dilemma of Moon-Pluto, there is also the dilemma of Saturn-Neptune. Saturn is co-ruler of Aquarius, Spike's Ascendant. The conjunction is placed in his 6th, and it is interesting to note that he is acutely sensitive to noise and regularly complains about the sound of planes and lawnmowers. This is a faint echo of Howard Hughes, with his exact Saturn-Mars conjunction in the 6th and his horror of infection. The 6th house is concerned with the integration of body and psyche, and where there is conflict or difficulty in adapting to everyday reality, symptoms may appear which reflect an acute physical and psychic sensitivity. Saturn-Neptune aspects, which are often associated with creative talent, reflect an ongoing friction between the ego-skin and the chaotic waters of the collective psyche. These contacts can be immensely creative when Saturn gives form to Neptune's imaginative realm, but they can be terrifying when Neptune seems to be eroding the solid walls of Saturn's reality structures. Enormous free-floating anxiety is a characteristic of Saturn-Neptune, and these aspects are often connected with phobias and hypochondria, both of which reflect a terror of the invasion of unknown invisible powers. Spike's obsession with noise may be part of this astrological picture, and the aspect may also be connected with the wild, ecstatic leaps and dark plunges which have characterised his emotional life for so long. Spike began receiving psychiatric treatment in 1956, when transiting Uranus in Leo moved over this conjunction and squared natal Mercury in the 3rd.

The traditional association of the 3rd house with "mental attitudes" seems relevant here. Where Mercury-Neptune submerges itself in the waters of Dionysian ecstasy, Mercury-Saturn closes down and views life through darkly tinted windows. The square of Mercury in the 3rd to Saturn-Neptune in the 6th seems to reflect Spike's volatile mental state. But a great many people were born under this generational aspect of Saturn-Neptune, and a great many of these were born with Mercury in hard aspect to the conjunction. They are not all manic depressives. Although this aspect is important, it is not the "cause" of Spike's difficulties. It does, however, describe a way of coping with intolerable pressure: swinging violently back and forth from Neptune's world to Saturn's, attempting to process his emotional experiences first through wild, absurd fantasies and then through a black and cynical vision of life. The Jupiterian mania into which he sometimes flies is a kind of escape from the intolerable pressure of that dichotomy. And we should not forget that Saturn as well as Uranus rules Aquarius. The split in his nature seems to have erupted not only with immense creativity, but also with immense personal suffering.

Madness and the ego

The damaged or unformed ego

Audience: Is the strength of the ego related to the element of earth?

Liz: A vulnerable ego is sometimes related to a missing element, but it may also be related to particular planets. As we have seen, Howard Hughes had plenty of earth in his chart, but nevertheless the ego was clearly fragile from a very young age. The ego as the centre of consciousness is partly symbolised by the Sun in the natal chart, but Saturn is also an extremely important factor, connected with the ego's ability to contain powerful emotions. The inner planets also have relevance to the ego, especially the Moon, which roots us in our bodies and in relationship to each other. Emotional disconnection or isolation is a repeating theme in states of madness, and healing, when it is possible, is usually connected with the forming of a stable relationship, most often with a therapist. Healing seems to involve the slow building up of something that has been undermined in early life, or that has simply remained too open and porous. It is like building up a muscle which has never been used, or which has been injured in some way and then atrophied. As with all psychological difficulties, the reasons for an insufficiently developed ego cannot be entirely explained by a "bad" family background, nor do they reflect some innate and unchanging incapability – unless the damage is organic. There is always a chemical mix between inherent temperament and early environment.

When we work with an undeveloped or damaged ego-structure, it is as though we have to start from scratch, building up a function that most of us take for granted. But in the mad person, a solid ego cannot be taken for granted. Sometimes the environmental issues are obvious. But it is never that simple, and the response of the individual, reflected in the birth chart configurations, is also a contributing factor. When the ego cannot serve its mediating function, it must be built up from scratch. This often needs long, intense psychotherapy, which is available only for the fortunate few.

Audience: If they want it.

Liz: Yes, if they want it. And they may not be in a state to recognise that they need it, let alone actively pursue it. And if they do know that they need it, they may be too frightened to embark on such a journey. We have students applying for the CPA Diploma Course who know our requirement of at least one year of psychotherapy during the course, yet they have all kinds of reasons why they feel they should be exempt from this requirement. This is usually because of fear, although the rationalisations often sound very impressive. Yet these people believe they are psychologically aware. If they are frightened to explore the inner world, can you imagine how much more terrifying it must seem to someone in a mad state?

Audience: A lot of the crimes committed in Greek myth are due to a state of inflation, and a state of inflation is caused by the weakness of the ego, not its strength. What appears to be an insult to the gods is actually due to weakness, and is not necessarily an act of hubris.

Liz: Hubris is not due to a strong ego. It is due to a rigid one, and rigidity is usually a defence against vulnerability. This is certainly the case with Euripides' Pentheus. He is terrified of the primal energies of the Dionysian realm. Because he cannot find a way to balance these energies with Hera's social codes, he can only repress them. If the ego cannot handle the conflict between opposing psychic forces, the individual is flung like a football between them. Some people in this position seek to bolster their sanity with a collective doctrine which is meant to substitute for the individual ego. This is what many religious and political systems do: they provide a moral and perceptual structure which removes individual responsibility and conceals the individual's inability to make his or her own value judgements.

A person who identifies completely with such a rigid system may seem sane if they are in accord with the prevailing collective perspective. But this is a questionable sanity, because no individual perceptions or choices are involved. The ego remains as unformed as the ego of an obviously mad person. This opens the door to many important and disturbing questions about collective psychoses and why they occur. It could be argued that episodes of collective madness such as the Nazi death camps and the genocides in Bosnia and Kosovo could never occur without the participation of large numbers of individuals whose ego-consciousness is undeveloped, and who are therefore dependent on a doctrine or ideology. There is then no defence against the eruption of unconscious collective forces of a destructive kind.

Is there a choice?

Audience: I wonder about things like heroin addiction. I'm troubled by that word "choice". Drug addiction is not usually seen as madness, but it *is* a sort of madness. There is self-destruction involved, and the ego is weak. It isn't really a question of the person choosing to become an addict. They are overwhelmed by something they can't control.

Liz: Destructive addictions are usually connected with a damaged or unformed ego. They are a form of compulsion. The individual feels helpless in the grip of something uncontrollable which rises up and overwhelms consciousness. This is not madness in the usual sense of the word. But I am not using the word choice in the usual sense either. There is often a choice to reject help, and to justify the addiction through rationalisation. This is especially obvious with compulsive eating disorders, which have lately been politicised. Obesity is currently reaching epidemic proportions in both America and Britain. But one must not suggest that such a condition is not only dangerous to one's own health and costly for the taxpayer, but also dangerous to others in situations such as an emergency on an aircraft, train or bus. Speaking the truth results in accusations of discrimination against "big people", the threat of lawsuits, and a virulent denial that there is a problem of any kind. It is the obese individual's choice to deny the magnitude of the problem and refuse available help, although the compulsion itself is not voluntarily chosen. We would not ordinarily view compulsive eating disorders as states of madness, but they are a partial kind of madness, as is any compulsion which the ego cannot contain.

Sometimes, like Pentheus, the ego makes a choice to rigidly defend its ground, and the resulting madness is a direct outgrowth of that choice. As we have seen, such a choice does not imply ego-strength, because rigidity is a compensation for the lack of ego-strength. But there is a choice involved. And even with addictions, the element of choice is sometimes clearly present. Michael Jackson had a choice about whether or not to mutilate his body. It could be argued that self-loathing and the compulsion to fulfil a parental fantasy lay behind his choice. But it is still a choice. If, through that choice, he has unleashed forces within his body which are now destroying him, his own decision is obviously implicated. Mad people do not make a rational decision to go mad. They are the victims of a collision between inherent temperament and early environment, or, if one takes the organic point of view, the unwilling recipients of a problematic genetic inheritance or a brain chemistry gone awry. They were never given the opportunity to choose a different environment, a different set of genes or a different brain. It is hard to understand how choice could be a factor in such cases. Yet the inherent temperament responds to the difficulty in particular ways which often involve subtle choices. There is a difference between a conscious decision and choice in the sense I am using the word.

Choice doesn't imply blame. We can easily understand Michael Jackson in the context of the culture in which he lives. He grew up in a world where being black meant being physically inferior. This is deeply ingrained in America, where the image of beauty is very stereotyped. Despite the efforts of the black community and those white people who are genuinely concerned, it is still very deeply entrenched. And Michael Jackson is not that young. He was shaped by the values of an earlier generation, when they were still having to transport black children to white schools amidst considerable violence and hatred. The civil rights movement in America did not happen that long ago; it was a product of the 1960s, like so many other major shifts in social values in the 20th century. Michael Jackson is a child of the 1960s. We can understand why his decision was a compulsion, rooted not only in his personal history but also in a collective problem. He doesn't want to look black because he believes that black is ugly, and he feels he has a chance of being beautiful in collective eyes if he has bits removed or changed. Collective eyes are important to him because his Sun is at the MC, and he identifies himself with his public image. And he has a Venus-Uranus conjunction, which demands perfection, and a Venus-Chiron opposition, which feels intrinsically damaged and flawed. We cannot blame him for either his choice or his compulsion. Sometimes there really seems to be no choice at all. Quite understandably, we may experience a sense of moral outrage when we hear about some of these situations. We live in a mad world, and if we expect consistent sanity from the collective, then we are quite mad ourselves.

Phobias

Animals as symbols of psychic energies

Audience: Can you see phobias in the chart?

Liz: Phobias are little pockets of madness. They occur in people who otherwise might be extremely well adapted, but the moment they see a spider or a mouse, they enter a mad state. The object of the phobia is symbolic. It is a trigger which unleashes fear of an overwhelming kind. Of course the real source is not the spider, unless it happens to be eight feet long. But the spider is the recipient of projections which reflect powerful unconscious emotional issues. These are usually related to factors in the birth chart which have been excluded from ego-consciousness. For example, a person may have nothing in fire except Mars in Aries, which sits by itself and is disconnected from the rest of the chart. This singleton Mars is a kind of "loose cannon", connected with deeply unconscious aggressive impulses bubbling away in a person who doesn't usually show anger or aggression and is normally civilised and restrained. A particular animal or insect can become the hook for a phobia because it symbolises aggression to that person. Of course this is not a rational process. The phobic object becomes the focus of one's terror because it acts as a catalyst for a piece of oneself that one cannot bear to face or deal with.

Usually there are parental issues around phobias. Otherwise, why should something in the chart be so horrific that a person entirely suppresses it? All charts have splits and dichotomies, but usually we can recognise these, even if we dislike or do not wish to express them. When a fundamental part of the personality is so utterly unacceptable to ego-consciousness, there is usually some early experience around it which has generated great fear. The phobia may also be associated with the parent as the source of aggression. If we go back to our singleton Mars in Aries, a father's violence may exacerbate the fear of one's own aggressive instinct to the point where the person cannot bear any sign of aggression, inner or outer. The phobic object is the carrier of an unconscious complex. If one begins to explore one's fantasies around this phobic object, one can get an enormous amount of insight.

For example, what is it about spiders that invokes so many people's fears? They tend to sit quietly, and then suddenly creep out from under a book or a piece of wood. They appear to be very slow, but they can suddenly drop on one's head from an invisible thread, or scuttle maniacally across one's hand. The way they move reflects a certain kind of energy. Spiders spin webs, and destroy the insects that get caught in the web. That is a powerful symbolic image. An innocent fly blunders along minding its own business, and suddenly it is poisoned into paralysis and is wrapped up, ready to be eaten. That image might describe a certain emotional dynamic in the family. Usually phobias fix on creatures that are linked in myth with particular deities. This collective mythology underlines their ability to convey archetypal meaning.

In the same way, astrological symbolism incorporates animals like the ram or the bull to describe fundamental life patterns. These animals encapsulate specific archetypal qualities in a symbolic way.

National collectives also use animals as emblems of the qualities they believe their nation possesses: the American eagle, for example, or the British lion and unicorn. A phobia reflects precisely the same projection of archetypal qualities and patterns onto an animal, albeit a negative rather than a positive projection, but phobias operate on a personal level and are unique to an individual's psychology because the archetypal meaning is combined with personal experience. With all states of madness, the personal component is combined with an archetypal element. Phobias are true states of madness, but they are contained by an otherwise well-adapted ego. When the phobic object appears, the person rushes out of the room screaming. Then some brave individual says, "Don't worry, I'll step on it," and that is the end of the spider. Afterward the incident is forgotten. But while one is in that state, one is quite mad. The fear is totally overwhelming.

Audience: So we would look for something disconnected or suppressed in the birth chart.

Liz: Yes. But there is no nice, tidy formula. A planet or configuration may be suppressed, not because it is disconnected through lack of aspects, but because it conflicts with other chart factors. And sometimes a planet or configuration is well integrated in the chart but was deemed utterly unacceptable to the family. Whatever the reason for the dissociation, that unconscious component of the personality will, sooner or later, find some kind of outlet in the individual's life.

Audience: Are phobias linked with Mars in some way?

Liz: Phobias are often linked with unconscious aggression. In myth, the Greek god Ares, whom we know as Mars, had two sons, who were called Phobos – from whom the word "phobia" derives – and Demos. Their names mean, respectively, fear and terror. A phobia is a dreadful fear, and the object of the phobia has acquired the threatening powers of a god. The spider, snake, mouse or bird has become a deity, and it seems life-threatening behind the humble form of its physical disguise. It is not that the actual spider is perceived as a god. It is a symbol of the god, and part of the fear is due to the fact that we do not know what is lurking behind. We only know that it could annihilate us. When we are unconscious of deep rage, we may experience it as overwhelmingly powerful and project it outward, and the spider becomes the hook for the projection. How many of you have a phobia?

The manifestation of a complex

Audience: I am working on one now! Can you say a bit about wasps?

Liz: Do you know what you fear about them?

Audience: My sister is allergic to them.

Liz: An allergy is not the same thing as a phobia. Fear of wasps is realistic, if one is allergic to them. There may be psychological issues connected with the allergy, but the physical response to the venom can be fatal. A phobia is an irrational fear of a creature that is not capable of destroying a human being, unless one is silly enough to put one's head in a wasps' nest. Wasps are always around in the summer. We get used to them, and we learn that if we leave them alone, they usually go on their way. An allergy means there is a dangerous physical reaction, and your sister has good reason to fear them.

Audience: What is the archetype connected with wasps?

Liz: Use your imagination. What do wasps do?

Audience: They sting.

Liz: Yes, they sting, and the sting contains venom, which means the poison which has entered your system will hurt for a long time afterward. Other creatures, such as scorpions and snakes, also carry venom. These are cold-blooded creatures, very far removed from human life and consciousness, which can be extremely aggressive if they are disturbed or threatened. They belong to a realm which we do not understand and which we fear. Although not all of them live underground, they are the symbolic emissaries of the underworld. They are the primal face of nature. You will not be surprised to learn that bees and wasps were sacred to the Great Mother in ancient cultures. They belong to the Plutonian realm.

Bees can be domesticated, after a fashion. We can learn to relate to them, and we benefit from their honey and their ability to pollinate plants, which is necessary for the generation of fruit. Wasps are different. We cannot domesticate them. Bees will only sting if their lives are about to be snuffed out or if the hive is threatened, because bees die once they have released their sting. But a wasp can sting as much as it likes, so it tends to be an aggressive insect. If annoyed, it will readily attack. It is connected with unpredictable aggression, and it also displays incredible speed and agility. The sting may be related to stinging, poisonous words which come out of nowhere and hurt us deeply. Can you think of anyone who behaves like that? Is there someone in your family who has a venomous, stinging tongue?

Audience: Yes. Me.

Liz: You are very honest, but I suspect you are not the only family member with that propensity. Phobias about wasps are often connected with a very early fear of someone attacking out of nowhere with a poisonous verbal sting. It happens very quickly, and the child has done nothing to deserve it, but it hurts, and the memory of the fear and hurt remains even if the specific incident is forgotten. Very often it is the mother who behaves like this – although it can also be a sibling – or there is unconscious aggression building up in the family psyche, and the child fears it could be turned on him or her unpredictably at any time. When we start exploring our fantasies about these insects, we can begin to understand what they might symbolise. Most species of wasp are benign, but some are quite vicious and will attack with little provocation. We even use the word in colloquial speech, and describe a person as being waspish. This tells us what kind of feelings are involved in the phobia. Astrologically, there is no specific configuration which states, "Wasp phobia!", but I would not be surprised to find a hard Moon-Mars or Moon-Pluto aspect, or Mars or Pluto in the 10th.

Audience: My sister is very cautious, but she still attracts them. It seems as though a fate is at work. She picks up a dead leaf and there is a wasp underneath. It goes beyond allergies.

Liz: Well, allergies sometimes go beyond allergies, if you see what I mean. I don't want to spend a lot of time on this subject, fascinating though it is, but this kind of allergy may be linked to an unconscious complex, and complexes work on the psychoid level.[6] They are physical as well as psychological. A complex may be highly charged and contain an enormous amount of energy, and this energy, if it has no other outlet, can break down the personality and precipitate a psychotic episode. It floods the ego and destroys the individual's relationship with external reality. Many states of madness are connected with the eruption of a complex. But sometimes the energy of the complex does not blow through the ego structure in such a dramatic way. It can also exteriorise in a strangely synchronous and frighteningly solid fashion. In such a case, the phobia seems to constantly attract the object of the fear. This might be the case with your sister.

I do know what you are talking about, because I have seen it at work. I once did a chart reading for a lady who had a wasp phobia – this particular phobia is fairly common – and, as it was summer, I had the window open. A wasp came in, flew straight at her and stung her in the leg. It ignored me completely, and then flew away. My client was wearing a short skirt and a pair of tights, and the sting punctured the tights and laddered them. She went completely hysterical, because she had been talking about her phobia at that moment and it had materialised, and I witnessed it. This lady, fortunately, was not allergic to wasps, but she was terrified of the way in which they seemed to hunt her. When an unconscious complex has reached boiling point, this kind of manifestation often occurs. Then it is time to do some inner work.

Of course there is a more pragmatic explanation as well, and the two are not mutually exclusive. Insects and animals can sense human fear. A frightened person gives off a certain kind of energy, and animals

---

[6] See Liz Greene, "Complexes and Projection", Part One of *The Horoscope in Manifestation*, CPA Press, 2001, for an exploration of the psychoid nature of complexes.

respond to it. There may also be a secretion which we release when frightened, which insects and animals pick up with their highly acute sense of smell. Wasps are intelligent creatures, as are bees. Bees know when someone likes them. They will come to a beekeeper who can communicate with them. Wasps also know when someone hates and fears them. It is an energy dynamic The creature becomes the focus for the person's unconscious energy and reacts, just as a dog will bark at someone who has a dog phobia. Unerringly, every neighbour's dog knows that person and begins to bark, because they pick up the person's fear and the unconscious aggression underneath.

Madness could be described as a complex which has erupted and taken over the personality. But if the ego is strong enough and the complex is not all-consuming, the suppressed energy of the complex can externalise. Then it begins to attract material situations which reflect exactly the same psychological dynamics as a psychotic state. When this kind of thing happens, we do not call the person mad, but there is a little pocket of madness somewhere which has manifested on the material plane. The archetypal components of an unconscious complex do seem to have a capacity to attract physical objects and events. It is as though there are energy lines that connect all the different levels of reality through symbolic meaning, and this includes such humble forms of life as insects. The idea is rooted in the ancient concept of *sympatheia*, on which astrology is based. Because everything in life is part of a unity, everything is interconnected through chains of meaning. Thus, for example, we have the idea in astrology that the colour red, the metal iron, the planet Mars, the human adrenal glands, and the emotion of aggression are all part of the same chain of meaning. A wasp, too, can be part of that chain.

Madness externalised in relationship

Our own madness may externalise itself through the people with whom we become involved. This is extremely common, and allows us to feel sane because it is clearly the other person who is mad. We may marry someone who is already mad, or who goes mad later. Or a child will act out the madness of the parents. It is a dreadful black joke in the psychiatric profession that, when a family brings in a mad child, spouse or parent for treatment, something very strange happens. If the mad person starts getting better, the family will often pull them out of treatment. This is because there is an unconscious investment on the part of the family to have that person acting out the madness. If that individual weren't acting it out, it would come out through all the other people who are unconsciously contributing to it. Our own madness can be expressed through other people. If one has a propensity for getting involved with people who are in severely disturbed states, it is probably a good idea to look at what is going on inside. The presence of a mad person in one's life doesn't necessarily mean that one is on the edge of going mad oneself. But it is possible that the same enraged deity that is expressing itself through the mad person also belongs to oneself, and needs to be brought into consciousness.

It is likely that many people who work in the psychiatric profession are drawn to their work because of precisely this dynamic. They need mad people, just as policemen need criminals. It may be margnally better to be a psychiatrist than to be the inmate of a psychiatric ward, just as it may be marginally better to be a policeman than to be a criminal. But there is always a reason why any individual chooses to commit themselves to spending their days with severely disturbed patients. Compassion and the wish to be of service may, of course, be a large part of it. But the efficacy of psychiatry would undoubtedly be very much improved if more psychiatrists could recognise their own secret madness. If they could grasp this, they would be far more effective in treating the people with whom they work, and they would probably have fewer suicides among their ranks as well.

The suffering of the schizophrenic

Here is our first example from the group. Anthea, would you like to tell us about this chart? I gather it isn't yours.

Anthea: This is the chart of my brother. His name is Roger. He had a breakdown before he finished studying at Oxford. He is extremely clever. He was also an artist; he did drawings, etchings, that kind of thing. He basically stopped talking for two years. He didn't finish his exams. He became catatonic, and went through the stages which were later classified as schizophrenic. For twelve years he has been subject to hallucinations. But he still keeps going.

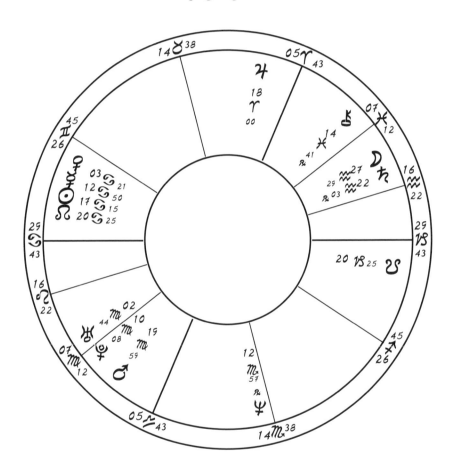

Roger
Birth data withheld for reasons of confidentiality

Liz: Can you tell us what kind of hallucinations?

Anthea: He has been through most things in the world, actually. There are a lot of religious questions, and a lot about social issues and the experience of being confined, being in a locked ward several times. Last time he managed to escape by running cross-country. There are also questions to do with hallucinations, and questions about imprisonment and freedom.

Liz: I doubt that we will be able to answer all these questions, but we may get some insights. One of the first things we need to look at is what gods are at war here. We also need to think about what has happened to the ego structure that has made it so difficult for Roger to contain and process his conflict. Clearly, he can't; the conflict keeps taking him over. One of the characteristic patterns of schizophrenia is that there are periods of relative lucidity, and then the personality disintegrates again. It is as if the ego struggles to form, reaches a certain point, fails and then breaks apart. Then the process starts all over again. Much of the suffering of the schizophrenic is not during the episodes of complete madness. It is during the period when the person is struggling to become lucid. That is when it is so terrifying, because there is an awareness that one is breaking apart. Roger knows when this is happening. He knows when he is going to slide back into madness again, and that is probably when he is in the greatest pain. Suffering is bound up with consciousness, and when he is able to get a bit of consciousness, that is when he suffers. What is happening in this chart?

Audience: Jupiter is square Mars.

Liz: Let's start with the Sun. I said earlier that the Sun is critical in terms of our understanding of the ego. Here it is in the 12th house in Cancer. It is square Jupiter and sextile Mars, and it is part of a grand water trine with Neptune in Scorpio and Chiron in Pisces. This grand trine dominates the chart, and we should think carefully about it.

Audience: There is a longing to merge with something much greater. There is a lot of imagination, a very fertile imagination. He would prefer to lay back and daydream all day, rather than going out into the world.

A grand water trine: over the hills and far away

Liz: Yes, the grand water trine, which involves both Neptune and Neptune's natural house, reflects a longing for fusion and a natural openness to the collective unconscious. It is Roger's line of least resistance. It reflects enormous imaginative gifts, but if he is thrust out of that womblike place, the world will seem unbearably cold and frightening. Something in him doesn't want to be born. He wants to stay in the uterine waters of the 12th house. Paradoxically, this is both an aspect of his creativity and an aspect of his madness. He doesn't really want to be here. Being incarnated is very threatening, not because he has been horribly treated, but because this is how he is made. In an earlier epoch, he might have gone into a monastery and lived a very rich spiritual life in a world where he felt protected and safe.

Roger has probably always had an enormous reluctance to incarnate. This is an ego issue, and the grand water trine tells us something about an ego structure which is, by nature, rather porous. It is not weak, but it is fluid and easily invaded. In order for him to make real use of his creative gifts, there needs to be something else in the chart that gives him the impetus to want to incarnate. It is difficult to find that impetus. Jupiter is the only planet in fire; it is a singleton and it squares the Sun. Rather than helping matters, this Jupiter exacerbates the problem by making him feel so special that he believes he should be exempt from worldly responsibilities. Jupiter in Aries in the 10th square the Sun suggests a certain amount of inflation and grandiosity, and this may be linked to his religious hallucinations. It may also be linked to his relationship with his mother, who might have perceived him as a kind of saviour, thus adding to – although not the cause of – his problems. The powerful Jupiter compensates for the loneliness of Moon-Saturn by saying, "I don't care if they reject me. I am a vessel for the godhead." This Jupiter contributes to the ego's difficulties in getting grounded.

Audience: But Liz, the Sun is sextile Mars, and Mars is in Virgo, which is a very active position for it.

Liz: Yes. But apart from that sextile, look at the other planetary aspects to Mars. Mars is the key to any individual's survival, and it might be the key to Roger's capacity to maintain his ego-consciousness for more than only brief periods. But Mars is opposition Chiron, conjunct Pluto and quincunx Saturn. Mars is really getting walloped. Yes, it is an earthy Mars and, in the 3rd house, full of mental energy. That may be part of the problem: Mars expends itself in the mind but does not act. And because of the Mars-Pluto and Mars-Chiron, when he wants to get really angry, he can't.

Anthea: He very, very rarely expresses any anger at all.

Audience: With Mars conjunct Pluto, there must be a fear of self-expression.

Liz: Yes, there is a great fear of expressing aggression and anger. Mars feels overwhelmed by Pluto, and the sense of impotence is compounded by the opposition from Chiron. There is great anger and frustration in Roger, but he is terrified of expressing it because he feels he will be annihilated, or he might annihilate everyone else. The sense of impotence adds to his reluctance to incarnate. Try thinking of it simplistically. If you were this about-to-be-born infant, and you looked out at life through the lens of this horoscope and asked, "What's out there for me? Is it worth leaving these lovely warm waters?" the answer would come back, "Sorry, mate, nothing but loneliness and frustration. I shouldn't bother." The Moon conjuncts Saturn in the 8th, and there is a perception of human relationships as being disappointing and restrictive. There is an expectation of being unwanted. There is also a sense that whatever he wants, he will be denied it. Where such perceptions come from is a complicated issue. Some of it may have to do with the early environment, and some of it may have to do with something in Roger that doesn't relate well on a feeling level but which is projected onto other people.

Anthea: I remember my mother saying that, when he was born, he was so lovely. She was so in love with him, and she made an enormous effort not to alienate my older brother, who was so difficult.

Moon-Saturn and the perception of rejection

Liz: Yet despite her attachment to him, it seems from the chart that Roger experienced feelings of rejection. That does not necessarily mean there *was* rejection. But that is how he felt. Moon-Saturn tends to perceive rejection in situations where other people are not actually rejecting them. The parent may be trying to be fair, which seems to be the case with your mother, or there are burdens or responsibilities which take her time and energy. Or she simply has something else to do at the moment the child wants attention. Although there is often some objective reality described by parental significators in the chart, the real meaning is subjective: that is how the child perceives the environment, and we need to understand the nature and teleology of that perception to make sense of the behaviour patterns which follow. Saturn always requires us to find our nourishment within, and when it aspects the Moon, this requirement makes it difficult for the Moon to register any nourishment given by others. Whatever we give a Moon-Saturn child, it is never enough. I am thinking of the younger son of a friend of mine. This boy has Moon conjunct Saturn. He has an older brother, born four years earlier. Whenever this brother gets to do anything exciting, the younger boy doesn't merely feel envious, which would be natural enough. He feels that his mother has deliberately ignored or overlooked him. He interprets any disappointment or frustration as a personal rejection, however justified or accidental it might be.

There may also have been conflict between your parents, which Roger sensed from a very early age and found threatening. He may have felt overwhelmed, and walled himself off from too much emotional contact. The Moon in Aquarius is not wildly enamoured of powerful emotional undercurrents, and feels easily inundated if the family psyche is heating up. Whatever the roots of these feelings of rejection, his perception of relationship is coloured by the assumption that he cannot expect anything from anyone, and that he is going to be let down. Some people can cope with Moon-Saturn's demand for self-sufficiency, but we need to view Roger's Moon-Saturn in the context of a grand trine in water, a 12th house Sun, and a Mars that has a very hard time expressing anger and desire. Of course this is not a signature of schizophrenia. But it is a signature of someone who isn't terribly happy about being incarnate and separate.

Anthea: Can I say something about rejection? I don't know if it's true, but I think it might have something to do with his watery trine. What I used to feel as his sister, before he got ill, was that his emotional neediness was too great. I didn't see myself as an unsympathetic person. But I around him I felt very rejecting and guilty, because I just couldn't cope with the demands. They were overwhelming.

Audience: I think there is a very important thing about the age when he had this breakdown, which the age of twenty-one. That is the time of transiting Saturn square natal Saturn.

Liz: And the time of transiting Uranus square natal Uranus, and transiting Neptune semisquare Neptune, and progressed Moon square natal Moon. And?

Audience: That is a time when there is a crisis of emancipation. You have to move out into life on your own. Perhaps there is a lack of identity as a male. Perhaps he didn't get a model of manhood from his father.

Liz: The sense of an inaccessible father is undoubtedly a factor in Roger's inability to feel confidence in his masculinity, not only on the sexual level but also in terms of moving away from mother and becoming an independent and self-sufficient individual. There is a very interesting book called *The Basic Fault* by a psychoanalyst called Michael Balint.[7] He writes from a psychoanalytic perspective, and he does not speak about gods and archetypes. But he is very sound. He puts

---

[7] Michael Balint, *The Basic Fault: Therapeutic Aspects of Regression*, Tavistock Publications, 1984.

forward the idea that, underlying not only physical illnesses but also states of madness, there is a fundamental split or conflict, of a kind that seems irreconcilable to the individual.

The world of the unborn

There is a fundamental dichotomy in this chart. Water, with its fear of loneliness and its need for emotional merging, is strongly emphasised by house, by sign and by powerful Neptune aspects. But then there is a Moon-Saturn conjunction, isolated in the 8th house. On the positive side, Moon-Saturn describes a detached, self-contained, cool and independent personality. It has a "grownup" quality, reflecting the capacity – and the need – to take responsibility for one's own emotional life. If this aspect could be expressed in a constructive way, it could provide an excellent balance for the diffuse longings of the watery side of his nature. But the two seem to be in a terrible battle. That is what Balint means by a basic split or conflict. Uranian issues are also relevant here, because the Moon is in opposition to Uranus and the Moon-Saturn conjunction is in Aquarius, Uranus' sign. There is a great need for distancing and separateness. Roger is both an unformed embryo in the womb, in touch with the *unus mundus*, and a sharply defined, intellectual, rational creature who needs plenty of breathing space and clear emotional boundaries. But he can't get these two sides of his personality to work together, so other people play the part of Moon-Saturn. They restrict him, they imprison him, they reject him, they confine him, they don't understand him. He, in turn, identifies with the grand water trine, and finds the world a cold, hostile, unfeeling place.

Audience: I'm not sure I understand the title of the book you mentioned earlier. What is the "fault" in *The Basic Fault*?

Liz: Balint is using the word as a *double entendre*. Fault usually means culpability, as in, "It's all your fault!" But here it is not just the sense of sin and guilt that comes from an apparently irreconcilable inner conflict. It is also a fault in the sense of the San Andreas Fault in California: a fissure in the underlying geological structure of the earth, where two plates moving against each other create earthquakes. Both meanings of the word are relevant to Balint's theme. You can also see how both meanings are relevant to this chart. The sense of sin comes from the horror of being "selfish", which results in being shut out by others. The geological fault comes from the dichotomy in the personality which I have just described, and the conflict between the two sides creates psychological earthquakes.

Audience: I have the fantasy that he could be a scientist or a researcher – somebody who breaks the conventional boundaries of knowledge. But then he would be completely alone. He wouldn't be able to cope with that, because that Sun in the 12th wants to feel connected all the time. I was also looking at Mars in the 3rd sextile the Sun, and his need to communicate ideas, but it's the same problem. I can understand that he doesn't want to be pushed into the responsibilities that his abilities would require.

Liz: On some profound unconscious level, he has found a way out of those responsibilities by choosing to be mad. To put it brutally, he has opted not to incarnate into an ego that can function in the world according to the world's – and his own – expectations. He just won't do it. He might have been able to exist as a 15th century monk, but he can't do that now, so he is a schizophrenic instead. He has made his alliance with Dionysus against Saturn and Ouranos. The only problem is that the rest of his family have to pay for it.

Anthea: He is very bright, and he wants to learn.

Liz: Yes. But then he would have to leave the womb.

Anthea: And he would lose the magical world he lives in.

Liz: There is an enormous challenge facing him. He must find a way to serve both gods, to honour both his longing for fusion and his need to share ideas and pursue knowledge in the outside world. This would require an acceptance of mortality, which is hard for him. As long as he remains in the womb, he is immortal. The only time that one is immortal is after death, in paradise, or before birth, in the uterine waters where one is fused with the creator of life. The child in the womb shares in the mother's life-generating power. Leaving the womb and developing Moon-Saturn and Moon-Uranus means Roger would have to give up his sense of immortality, and learn to bear the cold pain of separateness and the inevitability of death.

Audience: If he wants to stay a child, why shouldn't he stay a child and be looked after?

Liz: He would have to make a sacrifice, of a kind which would be extremely painful for him. But apropos your question, you might do better to ask Anthea how his condition affects the rest of the family. One might equally well ask, "Why should others suffer because this young man doesn't want to take up the challenge of getting a life?" It is not wise to idealise the mad.

Audience: There would have to be something promising out there to lure him out.

Liz: Ah, yes. And there, as Hamlet says, lies the rub. Do you know Hamlet's lines? They are highly appropriate:

> To be, or not to be: that is the question:
> Whether 'tis nobler in the mind to suffer
> The slings and arrows of outrageous fortune,
> Or to take arms against a sea of troubles,
> And by opposing end them? To die: to sleep;
> No more; and, by a sleep to say we end
> The heart-ache and the thousand natural shocks
> That flesh is heir to, 'tis a consummation
> Devoutly to be wish'd.

It seems that both Roger and Hamlet have a Neptune problem. Roger wants the guarantee of "something promising out there" before he will make the choice to incarnate. Of course there are no such guarantees. Yet all of us here have found something that gives us sufficient reason to try, and to hope. We have all opted, one way or another, to live our lives, even if we go to bed every night cursing life and wake up in the morning doing the same. On some level, we have made the decision to be here. Many people in this seminar have a difficult Moon-Saturn contact, and many have a full 12th house. However hard the aspects, we are trying. Why is Roger unwilling or unable to try?

Audience: He is doing what artists do, but no creative work comes out.

Liz: The artist enters a state of fusion when he or she enters and communes with the world of the imagination. But the process of giving those images form is a Saturn process, and then fusion ends. That is what Roger is avoiding. He is immensely creative, but the Saturnian effort to give his inner world concrete shape is evidently not possible.

Anthea: Would artistic work help him?

Liz: I don't know. It is sadly ironic that, despite his efforts to avoid it, he experiences Moon-Saturn anyway, in the form of incarceration in a psychiatric ward and rejection by society. The unlived, split-off part of the chart comes back at him from the outer world in concrete form. The community does not want a schizophrenic in their midst, the family feel he's a burden, and he gets locked away.

Anthea: I realise that a lot of his thoughts and inner dialogue are about organising his feelings. It is a never-ending process. I suppose that's the Moon-Saturn.

Liz: Mars seems to be important for any kind of progress. Roger needs to unleash the rage that has built up inside him. That rage really comes from having to be incarnated. His rage and his longing for fusion remain split, and the ego will not form properly. There is very interesting work being done with schizophrenics in therapeutic communities, but there are very few of these around of a standard which could give people like Roger the kind of support they need. The problem is that few people want to put that amount of time and energy into a single individual who might or might not come through. There is a very interesting book by John Weir Perry called *The Far Side of*

Madness.[8] Perry worked with schizophrenics in this type of therapeutic community. The patients receive constant therapy. No medication is given, but there is someone with them all the time. When the rage starts to come out, they are not subdued with drugs, but are put in a room without any objects that they might destroy or use to harm themselves or others. And they are constantly accompanied. What Perry found was that the apparently incurable condition of schizophrenia is sometimes curable. But the kind of commitment required from the therapist is, understandably, hard to find, and there are many more schizophrenics than there are therapists who will do this kind of work. The origins of schizophrenia are very deeply rooted, but it is not always an intractable condition. The basic conflict may go back in the family for quite a few generations. Anthea, could you tell us something about your father?

Anthea: He had a lot of trouble with feelings, and was very quiet. He was often ill, and had problems with his bile duct. So there was no firm, strong male model.

Liz: There may have been an extremely angry male model lurking in the family unconscious, because there is something about that Mars-Pluto which suggests that Roger felt a sense of great threat in his early environment. It is possible that your father's illness may have been linked with unexpressed Martial energy. The Greeks believed that bile was related to the element of fire, and perhaps your father's problems with his bile duct are synchronous with some difficulty in expressing fiery impulses. If there was a great deal of silent rage floating about, it would have been very difficult for Roger to trust his own Mars. When an inflamed Mars is picked up on the unconscious level in the family psyche, it can feel terrifying to a sensitive child. Then the whole Martial world is rejected, and the child's sense of potency is lost in the process.

Anthea: I have an older brother who was violent. So it was around.

[8] John Perry, *The Far Side of Madness*, Jungian Classics, 12, Spring Publications, December 1989.

Madness and Martial rage

Liz: The rage may have been there long before, and your brother acted it out, probably because he has a more aggressive, extraverted chart and therefore a more aggressive, extraverted nature. But Roger could not act it out, because of the gentle and withdrawn qualities which are so pronounced in the chart. He has a very sweet nature, and when presented with rage, he would retreat and disconnect rather than react with rage of his own. It seems clear that Roger is the "identified patient", enacting the hidden madness for generations of people, because his own temperament makes him the perfect vessel for it.

Anger is necessary for the formation of the ego. Children must be able to be furious. They need to pit their will against the will of the parent and shout, "I won't eat those mushy peas!" Sometimes physical demonstrations of anger are also necessary: the mushy peas may need to end up on the floor without the threat of a violent beating from father or a mother who dissolves in tears. Anger is the means by which the child defines boundaries and separates himself or herself from the parental psychic matrix. If anger is not allowed, the ego can't develop properly. The fighting arm of the emerging Sun is damaged. In Roger's case it is much harder because there is so much in him that recoils against aggression anyway. A child who has an emphasis in Aries or Scorpio, or an angular Mars in a fiery sign, would have a tougher nature and would be able to break through this kind of suppression, even though there might be other kinds of problems later. And we should remember Ronnie Laing's insights, too: Roger is deeply receptive to the larger collective, and may also be acting out its hidden madness. We might learn something from the kind of community he lived in, and the kind of school he attended as a child.

There is a often a powerful will at work in madness. Sometimes we overlook this in our efforts to understand and be sympathetic. We run up against something inside the mad person which says, "I am not going to be sane just because you are telling me to be." Mars shows itself in covert ways when it cannot be expressed in overt ones.

Anthea: He went out naked a lot. It outraged the neighbours. We lived in a small street, and everybody would look out of the window and whisper to each other.

Liz: I do get a whiff of an incredibly strong will in this chart. The Mars-Pluto-Chiron configuration cannot be expressed through direct action and overt anger, but it can be expressed through stubborn resistance and a delight in winding people up. This is one of the reasons why other people sometimes feel so very angry around schizophrenics. There is enormous anger, but the anger is not coming out in an open way. Apart from wandering the neighbourhood naked, Roger is expressing his rage merely by being mad. However much his family or his doctors insist, he *will not* get better. He will thwart them. He will continue to be a problem to everybody around him. This seems the only way his Mars can express itself. There is enormous strength there. He may be gentle, but he is not a weak character. But that strength is being used against his sanity, and against the people who want him to be sane. If he lived in a society where it was acceptable for him to wander about hallucinating, he would have to find some other way of exhibiting his rage.

Audience: Doesn't that make it sound logical, when it is actually irrational?

Liz: The unconscious has its own logic. Roger's behaviour is extremely logical, although it is not worked out beforehand by a rational ego.

Audience: I can see why you are drawing these conclusions, but I keep thinking about the ego that didn't get formed. What makes these decisions, if not the ego?

Liz: Decisions can be made on the emotional and instinctual level. A conscious ego is not required. Think of your cat or dog. These animals do not seem to possess an ego in the sense humans do, yet they make decisions and exhibit the same kind of stubborn anger as Roger if they are forced by their owners to do things which are against their nature. Even plants can behave like this. I am sure you will all be utterly fascinated to know that the Chinese wisteria grows in a clockwise direction, while the Japanese wisteria grows counterclockwise. If one tries to force a Japanese wisteria to grow clockwise, that branch will die off and it will send up a new shoot from the base which grows counterclockwise. Although they may be sentient living things, it is highly unlikely that wisterias possess an ego.

It is appropriate to say that Roger has an unformed ego. But the essential ingredients which define the personality are there in an unconscious form. Roger's Mars-Chiron-Pluto is still alive and kicking, even though his ego is not sufficiently cohesive to mediate it in any conscious way. If you are planning to make a loaf of bread, you must begin with dough. The dough has the same ingredients as the loaf which comes out of the oven. An unformed ego has the same personality components that it has when it is formed. But they are expressed unconsciously. Roger's ego may be unformed, but nevertheless he has a powerful will.

Anthea: Roger has not gone into the oven yet.

Liz: Probably not. But there is still enormous raw energy there, and if one eats the dough before it is cooked, one will still get a big chunk of Mars in one's teeth. The ego is unformed, but it has a lot of Mars in it, and even in its unformed state it will do no favours for any one.

Choosing to be born

Audience: I don't like the words, "choose to be mad". I don't think that anybody actually chooses.

Liz: It's fine if you don't like the words. However, I do, so I shall continue to use them. On the rational level, of course you are right: no one in their right mind would choose to be mad. Roger is overwhelmed by forces that are much larger than he is, and he cannot help himself. But it is more complex than that. Have you ever worked with psychotic people? Every now and then, one makes real contact, and there is something looking out of their eyes which quietly says, "Oh, no. Not on your nelly. I'm not joining *that* world." The ego does not make such a choice. But somewhere, on some level, something does.

Audience: You talked about people being in a therapeutic community, where the ego starts to form bit by bit. This seems to be the way to go forward.

Liz: Yes, it does. Can you understand why?

Audience: Because the person is getting what they didn't have in the first place.

Liz: Yes and no. Certainly, if parental issues are a factor, these can be addressed. The helpers in such therapeutic communities are highly trained, and they are able to deal with their patients' anger and terror in a way that a parent could not possibly do. But they are dealing with adults, not babies, and although we have been speaking about unformed egos, in fact something has partially formed in Roger. Like many schizophrenics, he has periods of clarity. This makes it possible for a relationship to be built between the therapist and the patient, and the person may eventually choose to take the risk of emerging into life.

Audience: So a Cancer who gets the twenty-four-hour love and care and attention they always wanted might eventually say, "All right, maybe I'll join life now." Is that how it works?

Liz: No, that isn't how it works. Your annoyance seems strangely excessive, but I will not probe you to find out why this discussion appears to be pushing so many buttons. It is not as simple as just giving endless psychological milk to a hungry baby. There is the little matter of handling Roger's global rage, and his potential for real destructiveness – or self-destructiveness – if that rage begins to rise to the surface. And it would have to, if he wishes to emerge as a whole person, because, as I said, Martial anger is one of the building blocks of the ego. I have never suggested that Roger *should* make the effort to "join life" and become a "normal" member of society. There is no moral issue involved here.

There is a strange kind of rightness in what he is doing, when we look at his nature and at the nature of life. His first schizophrenic episode occurred when he was at Oxford. That is not at all surprising. For many sensitive people, Oxford is not a fun place. It can be extremely restrictive and lonely, and tutors are expected to adopt what is known as the "adversarial" approach. That basically means unsympathetic, challenging and tough. Students who can stand up to it do well, but those who can't often have breakdowns. Oxford has a higher than average suicide rate among students. For centuries it has demonstrated the archaic British cold-water-baths-in-the-morning ethos: nothing should be made easy. Given the pressure of the transits he was experiencing at the time, I am sure we can all sympathise with Roger's retreat into madness.

Anthea, I would like to thank you for allowing us to discuss Roger's chart and situation in such depth. It can't have been pleasant.

Anthea: No. But it has been very, very helpful.

Breakdowns and breakthroughs

Astrological timing

I would like to look now at the issue of what are called "breakdowns". We have time for one more chart from the group, which Geraldine has kindly offered in relation to this theme. We do not normally call breakdown states mad. But they are mad states if we define madness as the overwhelming of the ego by the unconscious. However, breakdowns are temporary rather than permanent, although they can repeat. Clinically, a breakdown is referred to as a "psychotic break" or a "fugue state". Breakdowns can occur as the herald of, or an ongoing part of, a broader picture of mental disintegration, but they can also occur in someone who is quite well adapted. Many people experience a breakdown at characteristic points reflected by particular astrological cycles: at around twenty-one, when Saturn squares its own place and Uranus squares *its* own place; at twenty-nine, when Saturn returns to its own place; and at mid-life, when Uranus opposes its own place and Saturn subsequently opposes *its* own place. The role of Saturn will become apparent as we look more deeply at what these states involve. Often the individual emerges much stronger and more integrated than they were before the breakdown occurred. This is why, in transpersonal psychology, breakdowns are often viewed as potential breakthroughs with a positive teleology, rather than as a reflection of mental "illness". I want to look at this theme more carefully, particularly in relation to transits. We saw the importance of transits as triggers when we looked at Roger's chart. When did his schizophrenia begin? In a sense this is an impossible question, because it could be argued that the fundamental split in his psychic structure was part of his essential character when he was born, and that it actually began several generations ago. But many people are born with such splits and manage to preserve the integrity of the ego. When did Roger's symptoms first appear? Not surprisingly, at the time of transiting Saturn's second square to its natal place, coincident with progressed Moon square natal Moon and transiting Uranus square natal Uranus.

Audience: What about the Chiron cycle?

Liz: Chiron can certainly be involved in breakdowns as a triggering transit, either making aspects to its own place or to other planets, or as a natal planet triggered by a powerful transit. Everyone has a Chiron return at around fifty. But the transiting squares and oppositions to its natal place don't occur at the same time for everyone because of the planet's elliptical orbit.

Audience: What about the Pluto cycle?

Liz: The same. None of us lives long enough to see an entire Pluto cycle through, and it is most unlikely that we will experience a Pluto opposition to its own place. Pluto's outgoing square to its natal place occurs at different ages in different people because of its elliptical orbit. But it is often involved by transit when a breakdown occurs, in addition to other factors. In Roger's chart, Pluto was opposite Jupiter at the time he experienced his first real psychotic break. But I would understand this as an added factor, rather than the main theme. The age of twenty-one, when Uranus squares Uranus and Saturn squares Saturn, seems to be critical for the development of the ego. There is also a square from the progressed Moon to its own place at this time. As I said, a great many breakdowns seem to happen then. Universities are bedevilled by students dropping like flies at the time of final exams, and the nature of the transits tells us what kind of challenges may crack a fragile ego structure and unleash pressures that have been building up for a long time and go back a long way into childhood. Exams are the catalyst rather than the cause.

As astrologers, we will meet many clients who are on the edge of a breakdown, in the middle of one, or on the way out of one, or who are living with or involved with someone who is in the middle of one. Sometimes breakdowns take the form of severe depression: the individual is incapacitated by the depression and can no longer function in the world. There may be a suicide attempt, or there may be extreme apathy, and they simply will not get out of bed. Sometimes the breakdown is a more severe state involving extreme rage, screaming, uncontrollable weeping or hallucinating. Whatever the form, ego consciousness is fragmented by the eruption of unconscious emotions which can no longer be contained. If the breakdown is a one-off rather than part of a broader problem such as schizophrenia, it may be possible to come out the other side through the activation of internal resources. The individual may need asylum, containment and someone who will listen, rather than medication. Medication can be useful in the short term if there are successive attempts at suicide, or if the person is so agitated and frightened that some calm must be induced before any therapeutic intervention can be made. Orthodox psychiatry often ignores the importance of containment, and relies too heavily on medication. This may make things worse rather than better, as some people are very sensitive to medication and become even more depressed because they feel so physically wretched. Unfortunately at present it is rather like a lottery, and one may be lucky or unlucky in terms of the psychiatric consultant into whose hands one falls.

Breaking through

A breakdown is often an attempt on the part of the psyche to dismantle a personality structure that is not viable. This usually happens when a "false self" has developed instead of an authentic, solid ego structure. The individual has been forced into becoming someone else, because of family or environmental pressures which violate the real personality. An intolerable fissure then builds up between the deeper levels of the psyche and the "false self" which presents itself to the world. Eventually, the unconscious rises up and smashes the false structure, not because the individual is "ill", but because something healthy and real demands to be expressed. We have looked at this in the context of the Greek gods, who are symbols of the deeper patterns which belong to the individual's destiny. Unfortunately, the family may be the last to understand this, since it is often their expectations which have led to the building of the "false self". Sadly, they may attempt to oppose or undermine therapeutic treatment if it means facing their own conflicts more honestly. We are back in Ronnie Laing land again. Usually there are intense and violent emotions involved which, once they can be expressed, allow the beginning of healing and integration. If one has not been over-medicated or trapped in the fetters of a rigid diagnosis, many vitally important realisations can arise out of the breakdown, most of which have to do with recognising one's real identity and needs. Breakdowns can lead to transformation and healing, although they are a wretched and miserable experience at the time.

Audience: Could you explain what you mean by a breakdown?

Liz: I thought I just did. Would you like to see a demonstration?

Audience: I understand the principle. But I still don't have a clear picture of what happens.

Liz: What happens is very individual, and depends on both the basic temperament and what is erupting from the unconscious. Earlier, I talked about the way in which madness takes the shape of the essential character of the person. Whatever the symptoms, the individual can no longer cope with everyday life. The symptoms themselves, in a milder form, are characteristic of the individual. In a breakdown state, they become extreme and make it impossible for the individual to function. A person with a strong earth emphasis or a powerful Saturn may be inclined to the depressive type of breakdown, or they become obsessive-compulsive like Howard Hughes and attempt to ward off imminent disintegration through ritualistic behaviour. A fiery person may become highly agitated and violent, or experience hallucinations or delusions that they are God or have been chosen to save the planet. A watery temperament may disintegrate into a state of extreme emotional lability that simply doesn't stop, and they may go on crying for weeks. An airy or strongly Uranian temperament may become obsessed with an idea which overwhelms everything. Equally, an airy temperament may be overwhelmed by violent emotions, and an earthy temperament may be overwhelmed by fantasies which have been denied all expression for many years because they are deemed "unreal". We all go into such states for brief periods. But if one is still in bed sobbing after six weeks, one cannot function. In a breakdown state, the ego is no longer serving its mediating function between external reality and the deeper levels of the psyche. It has collapsed like a building with poor foundations at the least sign of an earth tremor, because it was badly built to begin with.

Audience: Is it possible to be in the middle of a breakdown and still partially function?

Liz: Yes, it is possible. There are degrees of breakdown, and sometimes the "false self" is very brittle and tenacious. A person can be in a breakdown state and still go to work, provided they can rely on a well-adapted function of consciousness to get them through the day, and provided nothing more is required of them. But if any pressure is placed on the weak points, the whole structure collapses. In some work environments, people don't have to communicate with each other. One can be in a dreadful state and feel totally disorientated, but as long as one is able to get one's body to the factory and fit the machine part in place, no one notices. One may function in a limited way, especially if one lives alone and there isn't anyone to see the state one is in. This is horribly common with people who live on their own. No one knows about these breakdowns except the individuals themselves, and sometimes even they do not know what they are going through.

When a client comes in that kind of state, we can feel their fear, because they know something is starting to fragment. These people know they are not coping, and they are very frightened. Sometimes there is great anger as well as great fear. We can pick these things up without difficulty if we are at all sensitive, and usually the transits corroborate it. Often the real reason they have come for a consultation is that they are afraid they are going to go mad. And the brutal truth is that they may have to, for a while. I am not sure I would put it quite so baldly to the client, but I would certainly point out that a difficult and psychologically unstable period may be coming up which requires the right kind of help, and I would talk about the possible reasons for it and the creative potentials it might yield.

Audience: What about someone who never breaks? I am thinking of people who ought to break down, but they just don't. They carry on, and sometimes they get physically sick instead.

Liz: Yes, there are people who are deeply disturbed but whose defences are so rock-like that they continue to cope and seem sane, provided one does not come too close. Usually their partners or children act out the madness, or, as you say, they become physically ill because the conflict has somatised. It is a common problem in families where the family psyche is full of deep fissures and splits. Sometimes I feel there is a deep explosive potential of this kind in the American collective, where everyone claims to be happy. Of course there are people who are relatively well balanced, and who will never need to go on these journeys into the dark. They are not necessarily the most intelligent, creative or sensitive people, but then, life is not always fair.

A psychotic break of this is a state of madness, but it is a state which contains its own form of self-healing. The unconscious erupts because the individual's psychological situation is intolerable and the real personality has no chance to develop. Then there is a breakdown. That twenty-one-year-old point is favoured one for this kind of experience because it is a juncture where the individual has to leave the family behind and move out into life. One of you pointed this out in relation to Roger's breakdown. If there are unhealed issues in the family, or if one has not really developed as a separate individual and has merely created a kind of false independence, the defences of the ego may prove too fragile, and something snaps. Midlife is another favoured time, because by that time we have cemented ourselves into structures which may block further development, and it can be nearly impossible to extricate ourselves without something cracking. Sometimes the dichotomy between what one has made of oneself and what one needs to become is too great, and the tension proves intolerable. The basic "fault" or fissure is too wide, and the structure collapses. The intent is not destruction, if there such is a thing as intent in these things, which I believe there is.

Audience: What about the Saturn return?

Liz: And the Saturn return. The same aspect that pitched Roger into his chronic state of madness can also pitch someone into a temporary state from which they might emerge, with a bit of luck and a bit of understanding from the people around them, much stronger, flexible and authentic. It isn't only the age-linked planetary cycles which can act as triggers. It is also outer planet configurations, such as Uranus-Pluto in Virgo opposite Saturn-Chiron in Pisces, which occurred in the mid-1960s, or Saturn-Uranus-Neptune in Capricorn opposite Jupiter-Chiron in Cancer, which occurred in the late 1980s and early 1990s. When such configurations trigger the charts of individuals with planets in the relevant signs, there are a lot of casualties. Any point in the chart which is unconscious can precipitate this kind of breakdown, because powerful archetypal energies are trying to come through and the individual ego simply can't deal with it.

      Entire nations went into psychosis under the Saturn-Uranus-Neptune configuration. Nations, like individuals, have a birth chart and operate according to the same psychological principles. Nations can have breakdowns and breakthroughs, and they can descend into madness. The disintegration that sometimes occurs under these powerful outer planet transits reflects old structures breaking down. As with an individual, we do not know whether there will be a breakthrough resulting in a stronger entity, or whether it marks the beginning of a chronic, repetitive cycle of madness.

Breakdowns and the Saturn cycle

I don't know whether any of this is in any way relevant to you, Geraldine. Do you want to tell us something about the timing, nature and circumstances of your breakdown?

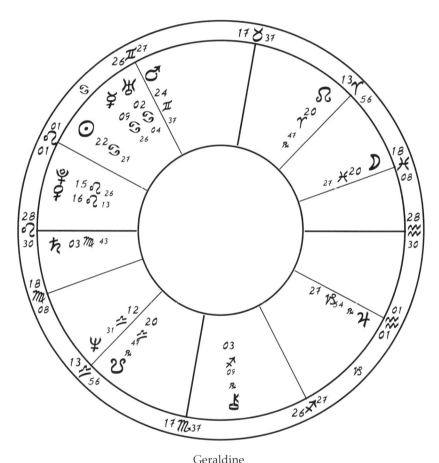

Geraldine
Birth data withheld for reasons of confidentiality

Geraldine: The timing was my Saturn return.

Liz: Would you be willing to tell us about it?

Geraldine: Yes, I would. I had been depressed for some time, although I didn't know it and had to be told that I was depressed. I was drinking a lot and taking valium. My husband finally couldn't stand it any more, and left. I tried to kill myself. That in itself was madness: I was saying, "Please get out," but I was also saying, "If you leave, I'll kill myself." He came back, but once again he couldn't stand it, and he left a second time. I tried to kill myself again, more seriously. I then ended up in a nursing home, on and off for about a year. I got the whole works: anti-depressants, anti-psychotic drugs and so on.

Liz: Did you have psychotherapy during that time?

Geraldine: No. The consultant was not terribly enlightened. He started mentioning a lobotomy. Then I got better.

Liz: You are illustrating what I mean by "choice".

Geraldine: But it is interesting because only now, in the past couple of years, have I actually been able to do anything with it, or even know what it might have been about. At the time, although I came out of it, I didn't necessarily come out of it any better than I went in.

Liz: Did you divorce your husband in the end?

Geraldine: Yes, but I don't think that had anything to do with it.

Liz: No? Perhaps you didn't come out of it "better" in the sense of an immediate breakthrough because you evidently had some rather unenlightened treatment. Sadly, a lot depends on the hospital one lands in. But you got there in the end. Let's see what we can make of the chart. The timing of the breakdown was your Saturn return, and Saturn is in the 1st house at the beginning of Virgo, conjunct the Ascendant at the end of Leo. It is a powerful Saturn, exactly square Chiron in the 4th house, which is connected, among other things, to the relationship with the father. Saturn is also sextile Uranus, which is in 2° Cancer. Although this is a strong, angular Saturn, it is not well connected to the personal planets in the chart, and it is possible that Saturn – the archetypal symbol of separateness – was trying to establish itself in a conscious way through your breakdown.

That's why I believe the issue of your marriage had something to do with it, although you seem convinced it was irrelevant. The breakdown may be connected with being unable to stand alone. What you went through may have been an attempt on the part of the psyche to deal with that difficulty, because your lack of separateness was preventing you from growing and becoming fully yourself. Angular planets, even on the Ascendant, are not always accessible to consciousness if they are not well knitted with the rest of the chart. Your Sun is in Cancer, opposite Jupiter and trine a Pisces Moon. There is a lot of water here, with a very powerful need for emotional closeness. The Moon, as well as being trine the Sun, is square Mars, but is not otherwise engaged. Perhaps you felt, "Why should I become a separate individual when it is so cold and lonely out there?" I wonder whether there are childhood issues involved as well, because of Chiron in the 4th. This suggests a very lonely environment and possibly a lack of support in early life: a lack of the kind of emotional closeness that you needed.

Geraldine: Yes. My parents were refugees. They didn't know what a child would need.

Liz: Where were they fleeing from?

Geraldine: Germany.

Liz: So there is a collective psychosis working through the family psyche.

Geraldine: Yes. And I couldn't carry it.

Liz: Never underestimate the impact of collective horrors on a family psyche. The feelings of victimisation, terror, rage and guilt invariably pass down to the next generation, and even to the one after that. Although the children of refugees and concentration camp survivors have not directly experienced the horror, it continues to have repercussions because it has affected the parents so powerfully. The consequences of such collective psychoses echo down the generations. Pluto is in the 12th conjunct Venus, and that suggests something from the family past: powerful primal feelings which could not be expressed in the family environment.

You are by temperament a person who needs a great deal of emotional warmth. With Saturn rising, there is also the capability of considerable self-sufficiency, but without emotional support in childhood, you could not grow to the point where you could utilise Saturn's positive qualities. It sounds as if you had the emotional expectations of a young child when you married, but then the marriage turned out to fall short of the hoped-for fusion and the loneliness began to bite. The drinking and the valium may have been part of a desperate effort to stave off a dreadful sense of isolation and anxiety, and a gnawing feeling of being worthless. Then the Saturn return came along. The message was, "Grow up and learn to stand on your own." But this was not possible because you didn't have the confidence to cross the bridge. The breakdown may have been the only way in which you could get the nurturing you needed, and also release pent-up emotions that were too frightening to face.

Geraldine: It was like that. I returned to the womb, I suppose.

Liz: You needed to be looked after, in a way that you had not experienced in childhood. Your family had no idea how to do this. How could they, after what they had been through? On some level, your husband's exit may have been something you yourself unconsciously wanted, because you couldn't sort anything out as long as you were locked into the relationship in a symbiotic way.

Geraldine: Yes, I set him up. There was no point in his staying any longer.

Liz: Whatever you had hoped for from him, it must have become clear that you weren't going to get it.

Geraldine: Absolutely. He was like my father, incredibly self-opinionated and emotionally unexpressive.

Liz: I am sure your breakdown has given you something of immense value, even though it has taken you a long time to realise it.

Geraldine: I am sure it did. It has taken a while to work that one out.

Liz: That may be partly due to the rather hit-or-miss nature of the treatment you received. But it can also take a long time for any individual to process these experiences. They create changes, but we can't benefit from the changes until the ego has developed enough to integrate them. It is interesting that transiting Saturn in Pisces opposed your natal Saturn in the last couple of years. You said you have only just begun to be able to work through this experience. The opposition marks the ripening of a process which began with the conjunction.

Geraldine: My mother also died during that Saturn transit, and that unblocked a lot of things. Having started my own therapy, I am thinking in terms of training to be a therapist later on.

The Moon in the 8th house: communications from the deep

Audience: I see that Geraldine's Moon is in the 8th house. I lived with a man with the Moon in Leo in the 8th, and when Saturn opposed it, he went psychotic. He had already told me that he had psychotic fits.

Liz: "Psychotic fits"? There you are, Geraldine, you have a lot to look forward to. Why don't we look at this Moon in the 8th?

Geraldine: I think it is easy for me to catch psychic infections. Life is not safe. The Moon is a place of safety, but I can't imagine feeling safe.

Liz: In one sense it is not safe, because the experience of relationship is constantly being buffeted by the unconscious. An 8th house Moon feels safe if one is prepared to live with and work with the unconscious. This house describes what lies beneath the surface of life. The 2nd house is a material house, but the 8th lies hidden beneath or beyond the material level of reality. We know that the Moon tells us something about the experience of mother. With your Moon in the 8th, your mother did not feel safe because behind her was the Holocaust.

In your breakdown we are seeing the aftermath of collective madness. The Plutonian elements in life are always there under the surface, but many people manage to get through life without encountering them. 8th house planets, however, are finely attuned to them. But we are given no education in these things, and are not taught how past tragedies are passed down psychically from parent to child. Although there are self-help groups which address the problem of what the children and grandchildren of refugees and Holocaust survivors suffer, it is generally not acknowledged, and even analysts, who ought to know better, overlook or underrate the importance of such issues.

Here the Moon is in Pisces, so mother is experienced as a victim, a woman who suffers and sacrifices. The Moon is also square Mars, so there is rage as well, bubbling away under the surface. All those powerful, unacknowledged emotions were bound to break through sooner or later, but they are not just your own, Geraldine. They go back through your mother to the collective destruction which she endured. The Moon in the 8th can be a vulnerable point, a channel for inherited conflicts and disturbances. But it is important to understand the potential of this placement as well as its difficulties. If there is a willingness to look at the underworld realm, there is an enormous amount of serenity to be found in being able to make peace with it. Pluto has its own kind of safety, although this is not the sort that most people covet. It is the safety of knowledge of the invisible side of life, which can give an indestructible faith in the deeper levels of existence. If it is possible to explore the 8th house realm, then this Moon, with all its psychic vulnerability, can be an enormously valuable placement. But an individual who refuses to look within may experience severe depression or repeated emotional eruptions.

If the 8th house is strong in a chart, it is unhelpful to deny the reality of the unconscious psyche, because it has a propensity for erupting if unacknowledged. Remember what Euripides said. Like the 12th, the 8th seems to be important in connection with mad states, whether temporary or permanent – not because everyone who has planets there goes mad, but because it is a sphere of life related to the family psyche and must be worked with consciously. Consciousness is needed with any house tenanted by planets, but the consequences of unconsciousness are different with other houses. We find it easier to acknowledge the reality of the 1st, 2nd and 3rd houses; the 4th house is accessible up to a point; and the 5th 6th and 7th are visible enough in outer life. But the 8th, in our current society, is ignored. We leap over it into the 9th, 10th and 11th. And we pretend that there is no 12th house, either.

These houses have a relationship with mad states, not because planets tenanting them "cause" madness, but because we are so utterly ignorant of what these planets carry. We are taught that this hidden realm doesn't exist, and yet we are interacting with it all the time, and the pressure can become intolerable. Geraldine, you must have known from a very early age that there was something dark operating beneath the surface of your family. The tragedy and grief were palpable to you, but your mother kept trying to be "normal" and pretending everything was fine. This does not mean it is her "fault" that you had a breakdown. Your own nature colluded with this split between surface reality and emotional depths. But in an ideal world, as soon as you were old enough your mother would have communicated with you more honestly. If she had faced her own inner conflicts, she could have helped you to understand and come to terms with what you were experiencing. When the family environment denies the reality of what the child perceives, it creates a split in the child which will have future consequences. It is most important that you learn as much as you can about the hidden side of life, and also learn to trust your own intuitions. Then the 8th house planets can become a great strength. But there was always a likelihood that, sooner or later, the unconscious would erupt.

Audience: Transiting Pluto has just come to Geraldine's 4th house Chiron, and she has started therapy and feels better. So the work of

Pluto is the understanding of the unconscious and this big wound in the 12th house.

Liz: The transits are very interesting, Geraldine, both at the time you experienced the breakdown and at the time you felt you gained something from the experience. It has taken a while, but I think that in the long term, going through this will prove to be an enormous asset.

Geraldine: Is it relevant that Venus and Pluto are the rulers of the IC and the MC?

Liz: Yes, it is relevant, because your parental inheritance is bound up with something that goes back into the collective past. There is a tragic experience there involving both parents, although it goes back historically beyond the parents. The parents are the carriers of a much older ancestral inheritance. We are back to the Greek mythic image of an angry deity inflicting madness on a whole collective. As I said early in the day, this is often a far better metaphor for the origins and nature of madness than the most sophisticated psychiatric definitions of our modern age.

I am afraid we have come to the end of the seminar. As usual, we have run out of time when there is still so much more to discuss. Thank you all very much for participating.

Part Three: The Scapegoat

This seminar was given on 26 April 1999 at Regents College, London as part of the Spring Term of the seminar programme of the Centre for Psychological Astrology.

Introduction

You are all very kind to give up this exceptionally beautiful Sunday to attend the seminar. I am surprised that so many of you have abandoned the sunshine to dwell in the murky realms we will be exploring today. I chose this theme last year during the late summer or early autumn, without any idea of how disturbingly pertinent it would become. When NATO began intervening in Yugoslavia, I realised this might turn out to be an uncomfortably relevant seminar.[1] I arrived in London on Friday night just in time to hear about the bomb in Soho, which, as you all know, was directed by one lone madman at the gay population of the West End.[2] It is obvious that the theme of the scapegoat is extremely important at the moment. Many of you will be carrying quite a lot of very strong feelings right now, because of what is going on "out there". I suspect there may be a lot of emotional intensity in the group today as we deal with the various dimensions of this ancient and eternal theme.

Now I'd like to tell you how we are going to proceed during the course of the day. Some seminars, as you know, are focused on a

---

[1] This seminar coincided with NATO's bombing of Belgrade in an effort to dislodge Slobodan Milosevic, following his persecution of the Kosovo Muslim population. His chart is discussed in detail on pp. 251ff, and also in Part One, pp. 72-76.

[2] This was the "nail bomb" that exploded in a gay pub in Brick Street in London's Soho on 24 April 1999, killing three people and injuring twenty-nine others. David Copeland, the twenty-three-year-old killer and a self-proclaimed Nazi, had, exactly one week earlier, set off a similar nail bomb in Brixton, the heart of the black community. He was caught before he could target further groups.

specific astrological symbol such as Saturn, or hard aspects, or the houses of the horoscope. In that type of seminar, we look at the astrological symbol and explore the different mythic and psychological levels that are related to it. In other words, we try to understand the astrology more deeply by looking at the mythic background and the behavioural patterns that are described by the symbol. With today's subject, we are starting with an archetypal pattern rather than a planet, and we will look at possible astrological significators afterward to see how they might relate to the pattern, rather than the other way around. Scapegoating is not unique in this society in this epoch. It is not unique in any particular society or historical period. It is universal. When we look at it in a cultural context, we can see that it is part of the mythology of every culture. There are scapegoat images in all myths, and there are rituals of scapegoating in all so-called primitive societies. This term "primitive" is a great joke, of course, as it is difficult to call some of our present-day antics anything other than primitive. Be that as it may, in so-called primitive societies the scapegoating ritual is part of the context of a collective religious framework, concerned with the cyclical renewal of the community through the ritualistic cleansing of its "sins".

We need to understand the archetypal meaning of scapegoating, rather than defining it only as we recognise it now: a pathology which is incredibly destructive, both internally and externally. It might be useful, after we have explored some of the mythic images of the scapegoat, to examine briefly some of the historical episodes where scapegoating has been rampant. As we work from the general to the specific, it will become apparent that the scapegoat image is a complex which can exercise enormous unconscious power in both individuals and collectives. It may be that we all have some elements of this pattern within us, but some people are more identified with it than others, and some enact the pattern compulsively. Some individuals, and some groups, seem to be more aligned with this particular mythic story than with another mythic story. Once we have some idea of the mythic and historical background, and how this pattern is enacted in individuals, we can begin asking the question, "Is there something we can recognise in the horoscope relating to this theme?" As astrologers, can we identify or get some glimpse of a pattern in the birth chart that might help us to understand why any individual – or any national collective – becomes a scapegoat or a persecutor?

The myth of the scapegoat

Let's start with some of the mythic images related to the theme of the scapegoat. It might be appropriate to begin with Leviticus, which is our chief Old Testament reference describing the ancient Hebrew ritual of the scapegoat. It is from this reference that we derive the word itself. Along with this Hebraic myth, we will also look briefly at some other mythic scapegoat figures: Jesus, Orpheus, Orestes and Oedipus. Just in case you might think the scapegoat is a purely Western theme, you might also keep in mind Tlazolteutl, the Aztec goddess of childbirth and "eater of filth". There are many more, but each of these images can give us some insight into what the figure of the scapegoat might symbolise.

The goat who escapes

The Hebraic image of the scapegoat is connected with the ritual of atonement. This extremely ancient ritual involved two goats. Every year on the Day of Atonement, one goat was dedicated to Yahweh and was killed as a sin-offering, so that its blood might cleanse and make sacred the sanctuary, tabernacle and altar. In Leviticus 16:16 we are told that the blood of this goat placated the angry god and atoned for the "uncleanness" of the people, "for their transgressions and for all their sins". The goat's remains were treated as unclean and were burned outside the boundaries of the community. The other goat was expelled from the community, and was dedicated to Azazel, a chthonic god who was later considered to be a fallen angel. Over this goat's head the high priest confessed all the transgressions of the people, laying them to the goat's charge. The living goat was then taken away and sent out into the wilderness. Leviticus 16:22 tells us, "And the goat will bear all their faults away with it to a desert place." The blood of the sacrificed goat thus atones and purifies, while the wandering exiled goat removes the taint of guilt. As a sin-bearer, it carries the confessed evils away from the community – or, in psychological terms, away from collective consciousness. The "scape" in "scapegoat", by the way, is a contraction of the word "escape": the goat who escapes.

This ritual, in which I am sure you can already see obvious psychological implications, reflects a cyclical recognition that there is something within us not entirely fit to be at one with the deity we worship. Albeit unconsciously, we recognise our human flaws and, as a collective, we ritually atone for these flaws on a regular basis by choosing a symbolic vessel which personifies what we feel to be the "sin" that alienates us from the deity. The sacrificial goat – whether killed or driven into the wilderness – is not just a dirty animal on which all the communal psychic rubbish is dumped. It is holy. The goat is something which, in ancient Greek, is called a *pharmakon*: a healing agent. This vessel for collective sin is the means by which the community reconnects with its gods. In the ancient world, the ritual scapegoat was sacred, and was perceived as the agent through which atonement could take place. Although we lost touch with this deeper archetypal meaning long ago, it is profoundly relevant for those individuals who are compulsively identified with the role of the scapegoat but do not understand why. We will look at this more carefully later.

Wandering in the wilderness is itself an archetypal motif which we can find in the myths of every culture. Adam and Eve are expelled from Eden and must wander in the wilderness, and it is the image *par excellence* of expulsion from the paradise of the womb and the sense of unity with the greater whole. The wilderness is the place where we become separate, first from mother and then from the collective. The wilderness is an image of the loneliness of becoming an individual, and reflects the existential experience of alienation and exile which we all feel at some point in our lives, and which those who are identified with the scapegoat experience at all times everywhere. We will look at this also more deeply later.

In this Old Testament presentation we can see something quite surprising about the image of the scapegoat. In myth and in ritual, the scapegoat is not perceived as innately inferior or tainted. The goat is chosen to carry something for the community, and it is therefore accorded a very high value. The goat belongs to God, so it is both the sin-carrier and the vessel for healing. This is a very difficult idea to digest, especially if we are connected with the archetype of the scapegoat personally and feel persecuted because of inferiority. Because most historical and personal enactments of scapegoating involve shadow-projection, the suffering of the scapegoat now seems very far from anything to do with sacredness. The archetypal core of the myth has been lost to us. But it is extremely important to keep this idea in mind, so that we can remember throughout the day what this archetypal pattern once meant. If we are going to make sense of the scapegoat complex, or heal any of the suffering that we carry because of it, or work with our own experiences in any creative way, it is essential to remember what this ritual originally meant.

The goat of Leviticus is interchangeable with many other symbolic sin-carriers. And, of course, what constitutes "sin" varies from one culture to another and from one individual to another. We will have to look very carefully at this, too, during the course of the day. The sacred carrier of sin in some ancient societies is human rather than animal – the Aztecs are a good example – and it is inevitable that we will find this repellent because of our particular modern consciousness and our valuing of individual life. But we do need to remember that, in the context of cultures such as the Aztec, the scapegoat was never a downtrodden, tyrannised victim. These human beings were sanctified by being chosen, and they accepted it because it offered a means of going directly to the embrace of the gods. When considering the meaning of the scapegoat ritual in such cultures, we need to put aside our modern thinking and remember the context in which the ritual was performed and the very different way in which individual life was perceived. In tribal communities, the individual is not the thing of greatest value; it is the tribe. In modern Western culture, individuality is at the centre of everything we do and everything to which we aspire. I am not suggesting that this is either the "right" or the "wrong" way to be. It is simply how we are. We in the West are solar-centred, and this is how we have developed over many centuries. Presumably there is some inner imperative that has made us develop in that way. But when we look at scapegoating rituals in tribal cultures, individuality is not even a concept. One is a member of a tribe or a community. To be chosen as the scapegoat is therefore an honour, because one is the healing agent for the community and is rewarded by immediate union with the deity.

The mythic images of scapegoats are enormously varied, and each reveals a different facet of the central theme of sacrifice for the collective or the group. Some scapegoat figures, like Jesus, are voluntary. Some, like Orestes, are involuntary. Some, like Oedipus, have actually committed a sin. Some, like Orpheus, have committed no sin. Some, like the Aztec goddess Tlazolteutl, are deities who voluntary take on the painful task out of compassion for human beings. Some are chosen as part of a cyclical collective cleansing ritual, and some are chosen because a special crisis such as a plague plunges the community into self-questioning. It is worth looking at several of these figures more carefully, because it can help us to grasp not only what sins the community is seeking to purge, but also what qualifications are needed to become a scapegoat.

The royal scapegoat

In myth, scapegoat figures are often royal. Oedipus is a good example: he is the son of the king of Thebes, even though he doesn't know it. Orestes is the son of the king of Mycenae. Jesus is also a royal figure: you can't get much higher than being the son of God. Orpheus is also fathered by a god. How is royalty represented astrologically?

Audience: The Sun.

Liz: Yes, royalty is solar. We know what it means on a literal level, but what does it mean psychologically, and what is its symbolic significance for the ordinary individual? If we have a dream that we marry into royalty, what might it suggest? Dreams about the Queen and Prince Charles are extremely common, and I would guess that virtually everyone here today has dreamed of one of them at some time.

Audience: Does it have to do with power?

Liz: Royalty is solar, so it is more connected with sovereignty than with power. It is also connected with being special. If we are royal, we are different from ordinary people. We are unique individuals with a special destiny. We carry the archetypal motif of the divine child. Mythically, royalty is always descended from the divine. Every Greek king claimed descent from a deity, and so did every Roman Emperor. The king is the vessel of the godhead on earth, the vehicle through which the divine will is enacted. In individual terms, this is related to the individual ego being a vessel for what Jung means by "Self" with a capital S. It is a sense of connection with the divine, a feeling of being special, a feeling of having a unique destiny.

Royal figures who are scapegoated are qualified to be scapegoats because they are special. They have something individual about them, something which separates them from the collective. They are both honoured and punished for this, and as redeemer-figures they carry the sins of the collective because they are the link between the collective and the divine. In archaic Greek culture, the king was sacrificed at regular intervals, sometimes yearly and sometimes according to the eclipse cycle of nine or eighteen years. He was sent back to the solar deity whose child he was, in order to ensure the fertility of the land and the protection of the people. I suggest that you read Mary Renault's wonderful novel, *The King Must Die,* which conveys this deep-rooted belief in the sacredness and healing power of the royal scapegoat far better than any anthropological study.

The maimed scapegoat

Another symbolic feature connected with many mythic scapegoat figures is deformity or maiming. Oedipus has deformed feet – the name in Greek actually means "swollen foot" – because as a child he was exposed on a hillside and nailed to the earth with a spike through his feet. In the case of Jesus, the maiming is inflicted through crucifixion. Dionysus, another mythic scapegoat, is torn to pieces, and so is Orpheus. Some mythic scapegoats, like Hephaistos, are born ugly or deformed. They are scapegoated because they are ugly, although they are often both ugly and royal. When we allow intuition and imagination to play with these motifs, we confront something deeply paradoxical. That which is divine may appear shining and beautiful, but at the same time it may also appear deformed or ugly because it is different or special in the eyes of the collective. We will look at this paradox more carefully later.

The foreign scapegoat

Differentness may also be expressed through the symbol of the foreigner. Foreignness is a scapegoat qualification. We fear the foreigner because we fear that the stable structures of our own collective will be undermined and changed by those who come from "outside". This may be interpreted literally: the "outsiders" will take our jobs and our homes, and "dilute" the "purity" of our bloodstock. But on a deeper level it is the fear of one's ego-defences being broken down and transformed through exposure to the alien, "foreign" world of the unconscious psyche. Dionysus, the agent of transformation and reconnection with the divine, is referred to in Euripides' play, *The Bacchai,* as a foreigner. We scapegoat the foreigner, the person in the community who comes from somewhere "other". Throughout the period of the witch-hunts, the scapegoats were not only people who were physically different in some way. They were also those who did not have their roots in the community. They were often handicapped, blind, mentally defective, or had a prominent wart or a deformed limb. But equally often they were simply from somewhere else.

Over many centuries the Jews have been persecuted because they are perceived as foreign and different. They are not "integrated" into the Christian collective or, in the case of the Middle East, into the Muslim collective because they are neither Christians nor Muslims, and so they are perceived as both ugly and dangerous. Blacks in the American south have also been persecuted, because their skin colour and their African origins make them appear foreign and different. From the point of view of the collective, the scapegoat is ugly because he or she is different. That which is different and special may appear to us as ugly if we identify with the collective norm. You can all see how profoundly paradoxical this is. From one perspective the different person is royal, beautiful and special. Foreigners too may seem exotically beautiful, as the film and fashion industries know very well. But from another perspective, the different person is ugly and threatening. Solar individuality may be perceived as either or both. "Superiority" and "inferiority" are deeply connected with solar issues. So is envy. When there is an insufficient sense of real individuality and specialness, the resulting feelings of inferiority may be projected outside. The scapegoat thus carries not only the projected inferiority of the collective, but also its unconscious and undeveloped solar specialness.

The scapegoat with magical powers

Another attribute often expressed by mythic scapegoats is the possession of some special or magical gift. Orpheus' music is so exquisite and enchanting that he can make the trees and stones weep, and he can even charm Hades, the lord of the underworld. Jesus can perform miracles and can even raise the dead. A special and mysterious talent can be seen as either a gift or a threat, and it is an important element of the scapegoat image. The association of the scapegoat with magical powers is also relevant when we look at historical episodes of scapegoating. In the 14th century, the Black Death decimated the populations of Europe. It is the kind of collective crisis which often triggers the need to find a scapegoat. We can find this theme in the Oedipus myth, in which an outbreak of plague in Thebes invokes a collective hunt for the culprit who offended the gods. During the time of the plague in the 14th century, a French poet called Guillaume de Machaut wrote about how the Jews were accused of poisoning the water; this was believed to have caused the plague.[3] In itself, this collective reaction is not surprising, as their "differentness" ensured that the Jews, in medieval society, were usually the favourite scapegoats for any misfortune that occurred. What is interesting is that, in the medieval mind, the Jews were credited with incredible power. They were

---

[3] The reference can be found in Guillaume de Machaut, *Oeuvres*, Société des anciens textes français, Vol. 1, Paris, 1908, pp. 144-145.

believed to be capable of destroying a third of the world's population. When we start thinking about such an accusation, we begin to realise that the scapegoat is perceived as a powerful threat. The same principle applies to the witch-hunts of the 17th century. The women who were singled out for persecution seemed terrifying and threatening because they were believed to have magical powers. It would appear that one of the qualifications for scapegoathood is special powers, gifts or abilities which can be used against the community. The scapegoat is not merely an inferior creature in the eyes of the collective. He or she is perceived as possessing the power to do great harm as well as great good.

When scapegoating occurs historically, it is usually at a time when the community is in crisis. When there is no crisis, there is no urgent need to find a scapegoat. The ritual of the Day of Atonement was an annual event, serving as a cyclical reminder of the community's ever-present risk of becoming alienated from God through greed, selfishness and corruption. The nearest Christian equivalent to the Day of Atonement is the period of Lent preceding Easter, and the nearest Christian equivalent to the sacrificial goat is Jesus, but the focus of Lent is on individual spiritual redemption and it does not carry the same significance in terms of shared social responsibility. Instead of guilt being shared by the community, any disaster is perceived as the fault of a specific individual or group. It is never a collective problem, but always someone else's sin which has invoked the god's anger. Consequently, the collective need to find a scapegoat has usually coincided with something like the Black Death, or the Thirty Years War which preceded the worst excesses of the witch-hunts, or the kind of breakdown of order within society that occurred in Germany after the First World War. Then the urge for reconnecting with this ancient archetypal ritual arises, but it is utterly devoid of understanding. There is no comprehension of what it means and, like all collective unconscious eruptions, it is contaminated with human shadow elements such as envy and spite. Then those whose gifts or powers were previously utilised for the benefit of the community are suddenly blamed for the disintegration of the community, and are hunted down and destroyed.

The mad scapegoat

Psychological handicaps are often part of the scapegoat image. Not only those who show visible physical differentness are suspect. So too are those who are mentally different, and the most different kind of mental differentness we can find is the mad. Although they are no different physically, they are perceived as different psychically – although, as any psychologically sophisticated person knows, they are not as different as we would like to believe. In history and myth, the mad are scapegoated because they are perceived not only as dangerous, but also as holy. The holy fool is a scapegoat because madness was understood as an affliction imposed by a deity. To the ancient mind, the mad had a special relationship with the gods. They were chosen. Even epilepsy, which we in the modern world do not understand as madness, was perceived as a divine visitation, often connected with greatness, as was the case with Julius Caesar. In the myth of the House of Atreus, Orestes has a special relationship with the gods. He is chosen by Apollo to visit vengeance on his father's murderer, and this in turn violates the law of the Erinyes, who drive him mad. Dionysus is struck mad by Hera: a god afflicted with madness by another god. The holiness or sacredness of god-inflicted madness is another qualification for scapegoathood, since these special individuals chosen by the gods are perceived as best suited to cleanse the sins of the ordinary people.

Today we have many rational explanations for madness. We believe we know all about it, what causes it and how to treat it, and we have diagnoses which are based on a very concrete approach to human nature. In orthodox psychiatric circles, madness is understood as genetic, hormonal, linked with brain damage or altered brain chemistry or, even if viewed as the result of family or social pressures, always attributed to a specific cause. Madness is not understood as a visitation by deity, and any psychiatrist who thought it was would, of course, be deemed mad. But somewhere deep down, we are not all that modern. The psyche has many layers which reach back into prehistory. There is still something in us which reacts quite irrationally to those who inhabit a different psychic world from ours, and we perceive something mysterious, powerful and threatening in them. This is clearly evidenced by children, who are not burdened by adult ego-knowledge and ego-defences, and who will fear and scapegoat any child who seems "funny in the head". This very ancient perception of madness is still with us despite all our rational explanations, our political correctness and our modern pharmacological arsenal. And the boundaries can easily become blurred between those who are genuinely mad and those who appear mad because their world-view is different from ours. The holy fool who must carry the sins of the community is not always clinically insane. He or she may be culpable merely of seeing a different vision, hearing a different music, or perceiving a different reality.

The outlaw scapegoat

The scapegoat in myth may also be an outlaw whose crime has turned the wrath of the gods against the community. The scapegoat is the one who has committed, or is believed to have committed, the murder, the theft, the rape, the breach of social taboos. But the motive behind these mythic crimes is never simple. The committed sin in Oedipus' case is patricide, leading to incest. He murders his father and mates with his mother, thus breaking two of the most fundamental taboos of the ancient world. Unlike the Jews in 14th century Paris or 20th century Germany, or the blacks in the American south, Oedipus does indeed do the thing he is accused of. Yet he does not commit his sin out of malice. He does it because the gods demand it, and thus he is the chosen one, fated from birth to expiate the sins of his own father Laius. The sin he commits is a divine imperative. He is a sacred outlaw, afflicted, like the mad, by a god's will. His incest and patricide, although crimes, originate with the gods. There are many other figures in myth who are scapegoated because of a divinely impelled crime. Orestes, too, must commit the crime of matricide at the insistence of a god.

Prometheus is another mythic outlaw who is scapegoated, although by gods rather than by humans. He is an outlaw because he flouts the authority of Zeus and steals fire to give to humans, and he is punished severely for his crime. He is a scapegoat because his punishment expiates the sin which human beings feel they have committed by using fire and thus becoming godlike. Like Jesus, Prometheus carries the collective sense of sin for the community, and his bitter agony releases humans from the need to suffer in the same way. The crimes of this kind of scapegoat figure are different from ordinary garden variety crime. These crimes challenge some universal authority, breaking collective law yet at the same time fulfilling a secret collective need. The scapegoat enacts the crime which all of us long to commit, which on the most profound level is the crime of individuality. The mythic outlaw is often an individual who defies the stagnant or unjust rules of society or the gods, and he or she is punished by those laws at the same time as being secretly admired and envied by the very people who have invoked the punishment. We need only to look at the kind of figure which Clint Eastwood plays in so many films – from *The Outlaw Josie Wales* to *High Plains Drifter* – to see this mechanism at work. Eastwood's characters are always scapegoats, although they usually triumph and ride off into the sunset at the end of the film. Martyred heroes such as Che Guevara also fulfil this kind of scapegoat myth.

The universality of the scapegoat pattern

All the mythic images I have mentioned have relevance on the personal as well as the collective level. These mythic figures are universal and timeless, and they can give us insight not only into the scapegoating mechanism in the collective, but also into why many individuals identify with the scapegoat archetype, despite the suffering this causes. The next thing we need to look at is how these scapegoat myths are expressed in everyday human life. There is no single group which has the prerogative of always being the scapegoat. Every group in society has been scapegoated at one time or another. Each of us, according to our own individual psychology and horoscope, will sympathise more strongly with one collective scapegoat than another, and feel rage and hatred toward one persecutor more than another. We project our own unconscious feelings of being scapegoated onto the scapegoats we perceive in the outside world, and we also project our inner persecutor onto those we perceive as persecutors "out there".

For example, many people are quite unresponsive to a report of genocide in Rwanda or Kosovo, or the murder of a black or Asian youth in London or Bradford, yet they will become deeply upset and even violent when they hear reports of animals being maltreated. This is particularly common in Britain. Animal activists project their own personal sense of victimisation on animals, and are sometimes quite happy to injure or even murder – in other words, scapegoat – other people on the basis of this identification with the animal as scapegoat. Anti-abortion activists project their sense of personal victimisation on the unwanted human foetus, and may likewise be quite happy to scapegoat other people on the basis of that identification. People who feel no outrage about many terrible and tragic situations in the world may nevertheless react violently because sheep are being transported across the Channel in brutal conditions, or whales are being exterminated. I am not suggesting that we should not involve ourselves in movements which seek to protect the persecuted, animal or human. But it is important to understand that, when we are roused by the plight of a particular scapegoat in the world outside, we are roused because there is a scapegoat within. And the persecutor, like the scapegoat, may be found in the same psychological back yard.

Race is an obvious sphere where the archetypal scapegoat theme is rife, on both personal and collective levels. Depending on our own experience and background, we may personally identify with the black or Asian scapegoat in a white culture. Equally, we may identify with the white community which feels persecuted by a flood of Asian immigrants. Religion is another favourite scapegoat playground. Again depending on our own experience and background, we may perceive either the Palestinians or the Israelis as the scapegoat. We may identify with the Catholic minority in a Protestant neighbourhood in Northern Ireland, or the Muslim minority in a Hindu neighbourhood in Delhi, or the Christian minority in Muslim Beirut. Class is another area where we may experience powerful emotional reactions. We may personally identify with the poor, the unemployed and the exploited. Equally, we may personally identify with the middle-class victims of a rabidly left-wing local council, and become enraged when our hard-earned money is used to prop up the indigent.

Sexuality is another sphere where scapegoats are commonly found. Homosexuals are regularly scapegoated in every Western society. The bomb in Soho on Friday night demonstrated this kind of sexual scapegoating in a particularly horrible way. Yet equally, the gay activist movement has been known to scapegoat those gays who choose not to broadcast their sexual preferences, by forcing them to publicly "come out". Women have often carried the scapegoat role in society as well as in their own families. Not every woman perceives herself as a scapegoat. But many women experience the scapegoat archetype most powerfully in their own biology – although it might be argued that some of the more extreme elements in the feminist movement actively scapegoat men, on the grounds that they are persecutors.

The scapegoat, like beauty, is in the eyes of the beholder. The pattern is archetypal and the phenomenon has occurred in every society in every epoch of history. And it invariably involves shadow projection. But our individual ways of enacting and responding to it are highly personal. If each of us here today were to describe those groups or individuals whom we feel to be the most unfairly scapegoated, we would never reach any objective truth about the world because we are in a hall of mirrors. By this I do not mean that there are no "real" scapegoats, now or historically. Of course there are, and if we care about life at all, we need to do what we can, on however small a scale, to stop the phenomenon of scapegoating wherever we find it. But we must begin where everything begins: within ourselves. In the end, our personal responses to the world's scapegoats and persecutors will tell us much more about ourselves and what we feel to be the scapegoat and the persecutor within. This is where the astrological chart can be of enormous value. The next thing we need to look at is how the scapegoat complex operates on a psychological level. Before we look at the psychology and then the astrology of this eternal human drama, are there any comments or questions?

An interlude for discussion

Audience: I have always associated the scapegoat with helplessness. A child or an animal is helpless. Those are the scapegoats who arouse the strongest response in me. Does that mean there is something in me that feels helpless, even though I don't feel it consciously?

Liz: Yes, that is very likely. Children and animals *are* usually helpless when they are victimised, but that does not mean it is less important for you as a personal inner theme. There are many other kinds of scapegoats, but you feel most strongly about those who cannot fight back. Many people feel as you do about children and animals, but your strong response probably does reflect some inner issue around power and powerlessness. The feeling of being a helpless victim in the face of something overwhelmingly powerful is an important theme in the scapegoat story, but both characters in this story are part of an inner dynamic. I would like to look at this theme more carefully a bit later, if that is all right, because the astrological significators are sometimes quite clear. As you might expect, Neptune usually looms large when feelings of helplessness, conscious or unconscious, are an issue. We will see later that Neptune, with its theme of the victim-redeemer, is one of the most important planets relevant to the scapegoat pattern, although it is not the only one.

Audience: You mentioned that the British are particularly prone to see animals as the scapegoat. Do you have a view on why that is so? I agree with you, but I don't know why.

Liz: I don't know why, either. There may be clues in the national chart, because countries have psychological structures just like individuals, and these psychological structures are symbolised in the national horoscope. A national chart – or a sequence of them, in the case of countries which have had many different incarnations over the centuries – can give us some idea of the archetypal patterns which are most relevant to that culture. The people who live within that culture, even if they don't personally identify with the patterns, will still feel them to a greater or lesser extent.

Animals may be the favoured symbol for the scapegoat in Britain because both the 1066 chart for the crowning of William the Conqueror and the 1801 chart for the United Kingdom have the Sun in Capricorn. This is an earth sign, and the natural world may therefore provide us with many of our most important symbols. Gardening is another famous British obsession, perhaps because it also provides us with a symbolic expression of the national psyche's deep relationship with the earth. There may also be some connection with the famous restraint of the British, the proverbial "stiff upper lip", which is a Capricorn quality. We like to see ourselves as a self-controlled and civilised nation, and although we do not have an empire any more, we have never quite forgotten that we once did. Animals, especially benign ones such as donkeys and sheep, are an excellent metaphor for our collective shadow: the mute, helpless, instinctual side of ourselves which does not fit into our competent, worldly self-image.

Audience: Yet we have imposed a six-month quarantine on animals entering the country, which is a horribly cruel system. Before 1970, it was twelve months. Lots of dogs and cats have died in quarantine, and the ones which survive often go feral because they feel they've been abandoned. Every other European country has used a system of vaccinations for many years. We're only going to start next year. That's the other side of the coin..

Liz: Indeed, it is. As I said, we are in a hall of mirrors, and the scapegoat and the persecutor both live in the same back yard. An archetypal pattern is like a magnet. Perhaps some of you experimented with magnets when you were children. If one moves a magnet above a pile of metal filings, the filings attach themselves to the magnet according to its shape. An archetypal pattern, whether in an individual or a collective, magnetically attracts the substance of material reality, and the outer world begins to take the shape of the pattern. Human behaviour, actions, ideas and creations all take on the shape of the archetypal magnet hidden beneath. Although the pattern is invisible, we can discern its shape by observing the shape of outer reality.

It may be that the British have draconian quarantine laws as well as bizarre institutions such as homes for retired donkeys because the scapegoat pattern enacts itself so readily through animal symbols – after all, the original image is a goat. And we must not forget that the British social system, reflecting that Capricorn Sun-sign, is a hierarchy based on class. We have not abandoned this system. We have merely reversed it, so that the new aristocracy all speak with regional accents and have a working class background. The animal, as ever, is at the bottom of the hierarchy. But these are just speculations. As I said, I don't know the answer, I only know that it is so, and that other countries laugh at us because of it. Many Italians find it hilarious because they are so unsentimental about animals. They shoot songbirds and wonder why the British get upset and refuse to eat them.

Audience: I am very interested in the different attitudes we have toward criminals. Punishing a crime is not the same as scapegoating, but some criminals are scapegoated. And others are seen as scapegoats because they are sick. There seem to be a lot of confused attitudes here.

Will the real scapegoat please stand up?

Liz: Criminals who are scapegoated usually carry the shadow projection of the collective. They are outsiders, and their differentness is interpreted as the "cause" of their criminality. They often act as persecutors, yet they are also scapegoats. As you say, this is not the same as being sentenced for a crime. Think about Thomas Hamilton, the man who committed the Dunblane massacre in March 1996. He killed sixteen children and their teacher, and then shot himself. The press was full of comments about Hamilton being "different". He was a profoundly introverted loner, and his neighbours were very quick to proclaim that they had never liked him. They always thought there was something funny about him because he didn't "fit". Lots of people don't "fit", but they never commit crimes, and lots of sociopathic criminals are charming and interact well with other people, at least on a superficial level. In Hamilton's case, the nature of his crime was horrible enough, but reality became mixed with myth because his temperament was so aligned with the scapegoat archetype. He was obsessed with little boys, although no evidence was ever found that he had abused or even propositioned any of them. But his fascination made him sexually "different". He was not ensconced in a conventional family structure, and was therefore suspect. He was deeply embittered by the rejection of the collective: he had been asked to leave his position as a Scout master, and was then turned down as a voluntary worker for the primary school where he killed the children. People didn't like or trust him because he didn't fit into the community.

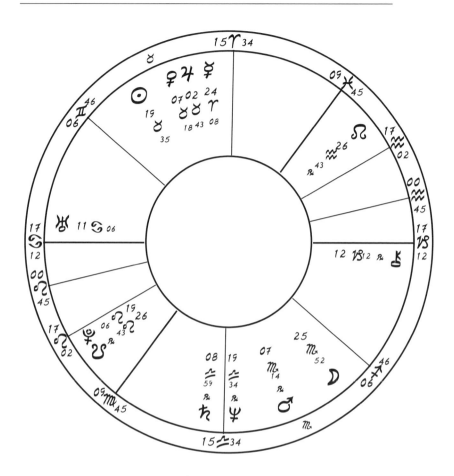

Thomas Hamilton
10 May 1952, 8.50 am, Glasgow

Hamilton's story raises many difficult questions about the mysterious secret identity between scapegoat and persecutor, and the ways in which the collective not only hunts scapegoats, but also turns them into persecutors. After Dunblane there was a great outcry about tightening the gun laws, which always happens when anyone goes on the rampage. That is a facile solution to an extremely complex problem. So is the accusation of differentness. As a collective, we always feel reassured when we can silence our uncomfortable questions with the observation that there was always something a bit funny about the person. We want to believe that the criminal is always distinguishable from the "normal" members of the community. It is a very short step from this belief to witch-hunts and genocide.

Audience: I understand what you are saying. But are you suggesting that if the "different" person doesn't commit the crime, then the normal one will?

Liz: No, I am saying that people cannot be classified as "different" or "normal". We each contain elements of both. Individuality is "different", while identification with the collective is "normal". And identification with a small collective may be "different" within the body of a larger, "normal" collective. Neither is intrinsically "good" or "bad", but there needs to be an inner recognition of both, and a conscious effort to maintain a relationship between them. Otherwise a split develops and the collective shadow of differentness gets projected onto those who do not "fit". The ancient scapegoat ritual was intended to encourage this relationship, with the religious dimension providing the deeper meaning of the process. When the religious dimension is lost, all that is left is collective shadow projection.

I don't want to spend too much time on Hamilton's chart, as we need to look more carefully at the psychological dimension of the scapegoat complex before we move on to the astrology. If there is time, perhaps we could come back to it later. But I would like to call your attention to one factor in this chart which we will meet again in other examples. That is the powerful Pluto, which forms a T-cross with the Sun in Taurus and the Moon in Scorpio. The square between Hamilton's Sun and Pluto is exact. Keep in mind the link between the mythic scapegoat and the outlaw, who serves deeper instinctual forces rather than the dictates of collective consciousness. In family dynamics, it is often the Plutonian child who is "different", the "black sheep" of the family, who carries the shadow projection of the family psyche and winds up being its potential victim, its potential healer and its potential destroyer.

Because Pluto is concerned with the most primitive expression of the collective survival instinct, it is often "outlawed" in cultures which attempt to exercise rigorous control over the darker and more intense human passions. It is not surprising, therefore, that a Plutonian should carry the shadow projection of a small Scottish community. No doubt he also carried the shadow projection of his family from a very early age. It is interesting to note that the Sun is in the 11th house, along with Venus, Jupiter and Mercury, so a place in the community was especially important to him. When the community rejected him so forcefully, the fixity and intensity of this man's personality reacted in the time-honoured Plutonian way, and he felt compelled to annihilate those who had injured him and, in the process, annihilate himself.

Of course there are many more things we could look at. Mars retrograde in Scorpio is not known for its forgiving nature. Then there is the generational T-cross involving the Saturn-Neptune conjunction square Uranus opposition Chiron across the Ascendant-Descendant axis. This angular Chiron-Uranus opposition is relevant, and Chiron, conjuncting the Descendant from the 6th house, is trine the Sun, emphasising Hamilton's sense of exclusion by others and his sensitivity to both his own and others' pain. Both Chiron and Uranus can be important planetary factors in the scapegoat pattern. But I would like to leave further discussion on these kinds of configurations until later, after we have gone more deeply into the psychological dynamic of the scapegoat pattern.

Audience: Could you say something about O. J. Simpson? Why was he not more scapegoated? He's black, after all.

Liz: Cultures can change in terms of the objects on which they hang their projections. Political and economic factors can contribute to this change, as well as increased understanding. The scapegoat of one decade can become the respectable collective representative of another. Think of the "Reds-under-the-bed" McCarthy era in America during the 1950s, when anyone suspected of left-wing political affiliations – usually artists and Jews – was scapegoated. Because the Soviet Union is no longer perceived as a threat, this particular projection has lost its head of steam, and other, quite different nations and groups are now seen as the enemy. In America, smokers are among the new scapegoats. There seems to be a general belief that stamping out smoking will somehow magically remove all of American society's problems with drug addiction, obesity, gun-related crimes, chronic depression, environmental pollution and religious intolerance. As long as O. J. Simpson doesn't smoke, he'll be all right. Political correctness is an incredibly powerful force, and it is shifting the objects of scapegoating. A case could be made that, in present-day Britain, the criminal is no longer the representative of society's evil as he or she was in Victorian times. It is now the robber and the rapist who are perceived as the real victims, because of an unhappy childhood or social and economic disadvantages. The criminal's victim is in fact more likely to go to prison if he or she exhibits too much liveliness in self-defence. The objects of collective scapegoating are not fixed.

Audience: Richard III is a lovely example of a collective changing its scapegoat projection. The deformities which Shakespeare attributed to him were invented, and he never murdered the Princes in the Tower. He was vilified only a long time after his death.

Liz: Yes, the deformities of Shakespeare's Richard III were invented, partly for political reasons. Shakespeare was writing under the rule of a Tudor Queen, and it was her grandfather, the Tudor Henry VII, who destroyed Richard and ended the rule of the Plantagenets. Making Richard into a monster was the politically expedient thing to do, and reflected a shift in collective perceptions. But Shakespeare's inventions are also mythic. He had a profound understanding of archetypal patterns, which is why his plays continue to be relevant century after century in every culture. Shakespeare's Richard, although historically inaccurate, is an archetypal scapegoat. He is royal and he is deformed.

Audience: And he does commit a crime.

Liz: Yes, in the play he murders his own nephews, so he fulfils most of the qualifications for scapegoathood. As you say, the real Richard probably didn't murder the princes, wasn't a hunchback, and was undoubtedly as decent a chap as was possible for a ruler to be at that time. He is still very highly regarded in Yorkshire, the seat of his rule. But the mythic Richard fits into the archetypal pattern. He is a scapegoat who becomes a persecutor. Some of the most powerful portrayals of the scapegoat myth can be found in literature. Another Shakespearean example is Shylock. It is an eternal theme, and it has always coloured the lives of particular individuals, but it tends to erupt as a collective phenomenon only when social cohesion begins to break down. That is when collectives begin to feel they have offended the gods in some way, and must expel or destroy the symbols on which they project their inferiority. We are in this kind of breakdown at the moment, in terms of our religious and social structures. Whether we see the scapegoat myth enacted in the form of school bullying, or in a flamboyant crime such as the Dunblane massacre, or in genocide such as Milosevic perpetrated, scapegoating is at present a large part of our daily collective diet.

The scapegoat as a psychological complex

Let's look now at the scapegoat complex from a psychological perspective. Who are the characters in the story, and how are they experienced within any particular individual? We need to think in these terms because all complexes are best expressed as a story involving a dynamic between two or more figures. If there is a scapegoat, there must be a persecutor.

The persecutor and the victim

The figure who inflicts or imposes punishment on the scapegoat is an essential character in the story. Who is this figure? In Leviticus, it is the high priest, who represents the authority of the collective. He also interprets God's law to the community, and so he symbolises the bridge between the two: the *pontifex maximus* or "great bridge-builder". The persecutor is usually identified with collective authority, collective values, collective morals and collective tastes. There is an interesting book on the scapegoat theme by a French academic called René Girard, in which he states laconically: "The best way not to be crucified, in the final analysis, is to do as everyone else and join in the crucifixion."[4]

In order to understand what values, morals and tastes this authority figure represents, we must understand what constitutes the highest values of a particular society. The same applies to an individual, in whom the ego's values have the highest authority. If we look at the story of the scapegoat not only as a social phenomenon but also as an inner story, there is a potential persecutor within us who speaks with the authoritative voice of what, on the conscious level, we believe we are supposed to be. Freud called the judgemental aspect of this inner voice the superego. This is our internal lawgiver, who passes judgement on our sins according to a stern and inflexible code. The values with which the conscious ego identifies are not always so crystallised or destructively judgemental, but these values are reflected in the natal chart. They are also influenced by the family background and by the values of the society in which one lives. All three of these factors have to be taken into account.

Audience: Is this Saturn?

Liz: Saturn seems to have a lot to do with what Freud called the superego. Saturn can also play the scapegoat, because it reflects those areas in which we feel inferior and excluded. Saturn the judge and persecutor easily transforms into Saturn the victim and scapegoat, and *vice versa*. We are peculiarly vulnerable to collective opinion wherever Saturn is placed in the birth chart because that is where we feel weak and unworthy and seek collective validation. And the less conscious we are of this dynamic, the more rigid and judgemental Saturn becomes.

All the characters within the dynamic of any complex are secretly interchangeable. They are all part of a unity, and are inseparable. A society or an individual, in order to preserve stability, must repress, exclude, limit or expel those elements which constitute a threat to that stability. The rebellious, outlaw, "different", inferior element – the scapegoat element – is part of the same entity as the

---

[4] René Girard, *The Scapegoat*, trans. Yvonne Freccero, Johns Hopkins University Press, 1986, p. 155.

persecutor. If we want to be good members of society and fit into its expectations, and if we want to be good members of our family and be appreciated, loved and wanted, we must therefore stifle big chunks of ourselves. The moment a definition of "normal" or "good" is formulated, there will always be components within the individual or society which don't fit that formulation, because every individual is paradoxical. There is no birth chart that doesn't contain conflicts and warring elements. As soon as an individual or a collective creates laws which establish order and stability, something will be sacrificed or suppressed. These laws are healthy, necessary and inevitable, but so too is the pain and anger of whatever is excluded. Everything then depends on the relationship between conscious and unconscious. If there is some fluidity and openness to change on the part of consciousness, the tension can be enormously creative. If the laws become too rigid and tyrannical, a disastrous split is created, and the shadow may be projected outside and persecuted.

The scapegoat complex always involves shadow projection. Whatever we deem to be sinful, wicked or inferior within ourselves or society, we tend to project on someone "outside". The religious context of the ancient scapegoat ritual required the community to be conscious of its shadow, and the sacrificial goat, rather than carrying the shadow projection of the group, was a consciously chosen symbol meant to enact in ritual form the need for collective expiation. But the scapegoat complex as we see it exhibited in ordinary life has lost this connection with communal responsibility to God. The scapegoat, whether an individual or a group, is not a consciously chosen symbol, but is perceived as sinful, wicked or inferior because he or she carries the projection of the unconscious and unacceptable aspects of the persecutor. And the persecutor, in turn, carries the unconscious aggression and power-drive of the individual who is identified with the scapegoat who feels unable to fight back. That is why, in individual terms, they always find each other.

The issue with all complexes is how much we identify with them. Everyone has complexes, and so does every collective. And it is possible that the scapegoat pattern, when it is not compulsive, may take quite a different form and generate many positive and creative expressions, not least in the helping and healing professions. But unconscious identification turns a complex into a compulsion and, in turn, into fate. Whether or not the scapegoat pattern dominates an individual life therefore depends on how much that individual is secretly identified with either the persecutor or the victim. To understand why any person might be locked into this kind of identification, we need to look, not only at inherent character, but also at the family background, and the way in which early experiences have coloured or distorted the natural responses of the inherent character described by the birth chart.

The scapegoat pattern usually begins early, and the dyad of persecutor and victim has been at work in the fabric of the family psyche for many generations. Once the pattern is set, many of the more powerful, aggressive elements in the individual will be projected onto an outside persecutor. Any individual habitually inclined to look for a scapegoat needs to confront their own shadow. And any individual who habitually feels scapegoated needs to look inside for the persecutor, because otherwise the pattern will keep repeating itself, and one will continue to attract persecutors or unconsciously invoke aggressive behaviour in others. Obviously this is only applicable to individuals. When scapegoating occurs on a collective level, it is absurd to talk about individual responsibility or individual identification with a psychological pattern. When great collective eruptions occur, the individual is subsumed, and may be scapegoated whether or not there is any individual predisposition for it. When a bomb goes off in a gay pub in Soho, we cannot point to any person and say that he or she was somehow unconsciously responsible for "attracting" the bomb. Such events, like the Holocaust, are part of the unleashing of a collective process of scapegoating, and we are not individually culpable. Yet ultimately, as a collective, we all carry the responsibility.

The family scapegoat

Now we need to explore the kinds of personal experience which flesh out the archetypal pattern – the iron filings which have been drawn to the magnet and have taken its shape, so that an individual is deeply identified with this complex. The first thing we need to look at is the family, because that is where it all begins on a personal level. A family is a mini-society, and the same psychic laws operate within the family as in society. In turn, the same psychic laws operate within the individual as in the family. From the universal to the personal, the basic energy dynamics of archetypal patterns are the same. A "black sheep" within the family carries the same stigma as a "black sheep" or "rogue state" within a community of nations. Scapegoating within families is one of the main places where we encounter this archetype. If an individual's inherent temperament is strongly aligned with the pattern – and this is where the birth chart may provide insight – then family scapegoating provides the "causal" basis for the scapegoat pattern in adult life, the flesh on the bones of the essential mythic pattern.

How many of you feel like family scapegoats? Most of you? Well, that is not really surprising, given the collective view of the "alternative" nature of astrology. Do those of you who put your hands up feel you understand the sins you had to carry for the family?

Audience: Yes, but I don't want to talk about it just yet.

Liz: That's fine. It is, after all, a rather painful subject. A family, like a society, bases its stability and coherence on certain values, structures and laws. This means that many components of the family psyche have to be suppressed in order to maintain equilibrium. The same applies to the larger collective: many fundamental elements of human nature must be suppressed if a coherent and civilised society is to be maintained. If any member of the family is, through inherent temperament, particularly receptive to those suppressed components and acts them out in an overt way, that individual will be experienced by the other family members as threatening, and the person will be scapegoated. What kinds of "sins" within the family are most likely to provoke such a response? Very often it is a sexual issue. That is partly because we have so many sexual taboos in our culture. In a great many families, the individual who appears to be more or less sexually motivated than the rest, or whose sexuality is orientated differently from the other members of the family, may wind up carrying the scapegoat archetype.

Audience: Scapegoating might also depend on what you look like. If you look like a grandmother or aunt who was seen as bad or sinful, then you may get scapegoated just for that reason. I was.

Liz: Yes, there are often physical reasons for family scapegoating. As in your case, the scapegoat may strongly resemble someone whom the family would prefer to forget. In such a case, we need to look at why that other family member was so threatening. You are evidently a stand-in for someone else who is also a family scapegoat. Sometimes the physical reasons for scapegoating have to do with family definitions of beauty and ugliness. There is usually a collective background to this. Scapegoating a child for such a reason hints at older family members themselves having experienced scapegoating because of their physical appearance, and these original scapegoats have turned into persecutors.

The stories people tell about their experiences of being scapegoated by the family are very painful and often tragic. Something about the individual was perceived as threatening to the family psyche. Sometimes it is sexual proclivities or sexual energy. Sometimes it is physical appearance. A physically or mentally handicapped child may be scapegoated by parents who cannot bear their own inner ugliness or stupidity. Equally, a highly intelligent or gifted child may be scapegoated by envious parents who cannot bear their own mediocrity. Sometimes scapegoating is connected with the child's personality. In a family in which the overriding values are extraverted and focused on the outer world, the introverted child may be scapegoated. In a family in which the overriding values are concerned with material success, the child who is not motivated by mundane achievement may be scapegoated. The imaginative child may be perceived as a threat. The child who has insight and sees through the proverbial emperor's new clothes may be perceived as a threat. In all these cases, we can gain insight from the synastry between the charts of the scapegoat and the persecutor. You can see why Neptune, Pluto, Saturn and Chiron so often figure strongly, both in the individual's chart and in the synastry with the charts of those family members who play the role of persecutor.

The reasons for scapegoating within families really depend on the psychological structure of that family. But behind the family patterns are the deeper, mythic issues which we looked at earlier. These include differentness, foreignness, royalty, deformity, and special gifts that could turn into secret powers for doing harm. These are the mythic roots underpinning a specific family's dislike of a child. Superficially, it might be because one has black hair instead of blond, or because one's features resemble those of an earlier family scapegoat. Whatever the apparent reason, the family scapegoat seems to threaten the family fabric through behaviour, personality or appearance. Sometimes the fact that a child is born at the wrong moment – for example, at a time when the family is experiencing suffering through financial hardship or war – is sufficient reason for scapegoating. Sometimes it is because the parents had to get married because the child was already on the way, or because one's mother had to give up a promising career, or because one's father went off and had an affair while his wife was pregnant. Bad timing is often an apparent reason for scapegoating, although it is never really as simple as that. But nursing such wounds and blaming the family that has inflicted them will not heal the problem, because the complex will recreate the original situation over and over again until the roots are made conscious and the archetypal pattern is recognised and channelled more creatively. Without consciousness, family scapegoats find themselves being scapegoated later, or they become persecutors of other scapegoats, who are often their own children.

Audience: If both figures are inside, how does the scapegoat react to other scapegoats?

Liz: Often with empathy. But equally often, the presence of someone apparently weaker arouses the inner persecutor, and the scapegoat may begin to scapegoat others to alleviate the sense of pain and victimisation.

Audience: That's what happened in my family. I am the youngest child, and I have three older brothers. There is a fourteen-year gap between me and the youngest of these three brothers. He is three years younger than my middle brother, and that brother is three years younger than my oldest brother. What I realised is that my youngest brother was scapegoated by my two older brothers. When I was born, I became *his* scapegoat. My two older brothers always gave me lots of affection, but this brother would always persecute me.

Liz: The pattern is not uncommon. Children who have been subjected to violence often exhibit violence toward their own children. Obviously this is not always the case, but it is frequent enough to be a recognised family dynamic. Not everyone who is victimised identifies with the scapegoat archetype. Probably there needs to be an inherent conflict, recognisable in the birth chart, between power and vulnerability. An example might be someone with the Moon opposite a Mars-Pluto conjunction, who also has a rising Neptune conjunct the Sun. Where there is identification with the scapegoat archetype, feelings of helplessness and powerlessness sit side by side with great rage and a will to power. One cannot express rage and power if one is weak and helpless, because any exhibition of anger might earn even more abuse, so the rage is buried deep. But equally, in adulthood, the person may not be able to bear the feelings of weakness and impotence, so the entire painful knot of conflicting emotions is buried. Deep down, the person may feel he or she is not worthy to live. But these feelings, like the rage, are unconscious. Then, as the person grows up, the sense of helplessness is projected onto a suitable hook outside, and the once-scapegoated adult suddenly begins to scapegoat others. The school bully is often abused at home, and can only cope with the pain and humiliation through abusing a weaker child at school.

The unconscious rage of the scapegoat may also be turned inward, resulting in psychological or literal self-destructiveness. Suicide is the extreme form of this identification with the sinful scapegoat who doesn't deserve to live, but there are subtler forms of physical self-destructiveness which do not result in death. Such people carry far more than a personal sense of sin. They are carrying the sins of the family and sometimes the larger collective. The feelings of unworthiness may be so vast that they go beyond any conceivable individual fault or shortcoming. This is an identification with the ancient sacrificial goat who bears the atonement of the whole community.

Audience: For many centuries, suicides could not be buried in churchyards. Maybe there was some kind of recognition that anyone who destroyed themselves was carrying the sins of the community.

The redeemer-victim

Liz: Another element in the scapegoat pattern is inflation: a sense of self-aggrandisement which is often of a religious kind. This is because the individual who is unconsciously identified with the scapegoat myth feels the sacredness of the role. As compensation for the pain of being an impotent and humiliated victim, the scapegoat secretly feels he or she is the chosen one, the saviour or healer-redeemer. When we are unconscious of these dynamics, we become locked into the archetypal pattern, which begins to dominate our life. Inflation sits side by side with self-loathing and self-victimisation.

Audience: Do you think the Kosovars unconsciously identify with this role?

Liz: I don't know whether they do as a collective. A group can certainly identify with the myth of the sacrificial victim at a given point in history, or even regularly, but I could not say whether the Kosovars identify with the myth or are simply helpless victims of a power they can do nothing against. We perceive them through mythic eyes, however, and for us they do carry an archetypal image. Whether they are really that helpless remains to be seen, and we will not know until they are out from under Milosevic's yoke and can express their own collective character. But at present, all of our own feelings of being scapegoated are projected onto them. Of course they are true scapegoats, as the Jews were for the Nazis, the Armenians were for Attaturk, and the Aborigines were for the Australians. But for many people they carry the archetypal image of the victim-redeemer, which is one of the reasons why we feel so deeply involved.

Audience: How do they redeem us?

Liz: If we can save them, we have rescued the scapegoated part of ourselves, and we have destroyed the persecutor. It is a hall of mirrors. By saying that, I am not implying that I know the right thing to do on the external level. But our own unconscious complexes are all mixed up with external events, and the more unconscious we are, the more compulsively we respond. We feel so much better by rescuing helpless victims in another country, because we can purge ourselves of our own persecuting tendencies.

In Western countries, we don't often get the chance to enjoy collective scapegoating rituals. The closest we have come recently was Princess Diana, who nicely fit the role. She was perceived as both a victim and a redeemer. Her ability to play this role so well resulted in the collective projection of the persecutor on both Prince Charles and the press. Whether she merited this projection as an individual is beside the point. Her adoring public perceived her as an archetypal figure and, perhaps because of her own personal insecurities, she identified with it a little too much. But since her death, we haven't had a really good collective scapegoat purge in Britain. As a collective, we have lost our connection with the deeper levels of the scapegoat myth, so it enacts itself politically and socially in ways that are completely out of our control. It is not that our efforts to help the Kosovars are false or hypocritical. Much of it, if not all of it, is very genuine. But there is a very convenient lapse of memory about the last time the British or the Americans scapegoated a minority collective, which allows us to claim the moral high ground in a very unreflective way. All the NATO countries have dirty hands, because there is no modern nation that has not scapegoated someone at some point in its history – and sometimes very recent history. When we only see the evil "out there", we are trying to purge ourselves of something inside. We unconsciously identify with the victim, and if we do that too blindly, we will make bad judgements on the external level.

Audience: It's swings and roundabouts.

Liz: If there is nothing else you take away from this seminar today, I hope you will all realise that it *is* swings and roundabouts. This archetype involves a polarity, and we cannot understand it if we identify with only one side. Milosevic has conjured up Serbian ferocity and strength by reminding them of their own victimisation at the hands of the Ottoman Turks. The fact that it was over six hundred years ago is beside the point.

Audience: That's very important, though.

Liz: Yes, it's very important, because history is much longer for a collective than it is for an individual. As individuals we cannot really grasp much beyond our grandparents, because we have no personal experience of anything further back. For a collective, six hundred years is a mere blink of the eye. The Serbs were themselves were once the victims of the Muslim Ottoman Turks. Then they were the victims of the Nazis during the Second World War. And then they were the victims of Tito's pro-Russian communist regime. The Serbs feel themselves to be historical scapegoats. If we begin to think more deeply, rather than just reacting emotionally, we wind up in a disturbing and disorientating hall of mirrors, which tends to erode a little bit of the ferocious self-righteousness which is so prevalent at the moment.

The astrology of the scapegoat

Now let's look at the chart of Slobodan Milosevic, the man who, at the moment, we all love to hate.

Will the real persecutor please stand up?

Audience: Milosevic's father was a suicide.

Audience: Both his parents were.

Liz: We can look at the family pattern more carefully in a few minutes. We know that Milosevic is playing the role of persecutor on the world stage. We also know that both persecutor and scapegoat are always within the individual. But could we can tell from the chart alone, without knowledge of his actions, whether he would play the role of the scapegoat or the persecutor?

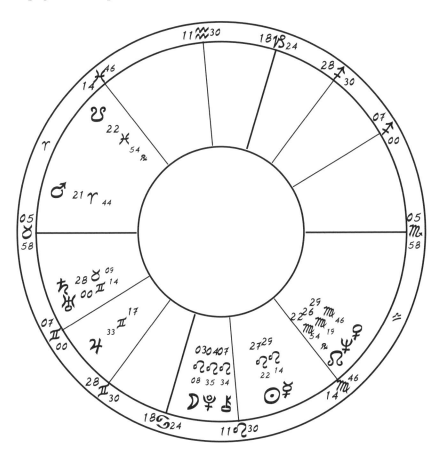

Slobodan Milosevic
20 August 1941, 10.00 pm, Pozarevac, Yugoslavia

Audience: He is a Leo with the Moon in Leo, and he has a Mars-Sun trine. That's a very powerful combination. From the chart, I think he would become a persecutor rather than a victim.

Liz: I agree. We will come back to this later. But although he is a persecutor, Milosevic is also our current scapegoat. He is the one who carries the evil for the community of Western nations. We all feel so much better knowing where the evil is. He is also a scapegoat on a more personal level. There are particular aspects which I would like to focus on, beginning with the Sun-Saturn square. No doubt there will be patterns very like these in your own chart. Keep these aspects in mind, because they will keep popping up in other charts throughout the day. And we will see particular planets in dominant positions: Saturn, Chiron and Pluto, as well as Uranus and Neptune.

Audience: There must be some relationship between Milosevic's chart and Bill Clinton's. In a way, Clinton is acting as the persecutor, and Milosevic is his scapegoat.

Liz: There is a relationship. This is usual when two individuals get locked into the pattern together. Both have the Sun in Leo, Milosevic at 27° 22' and Clinton at 26°. That in itself is interesting. Clinton's 10th house Saturn in 2° Leo sits on Milosevic's Moon-Chiron-Pluto conjunction. Milosevic's Mars at 21° 44' Aries opposes Clinton's Chiron at 19° Libra. As you can see, the usual suspects are activated: Saturn, Chiron and Pluto. When a complex is enacted in this way, the parties involved will invariably have close synastry connections involving the relevant planets. National charts can also be drawn into the picture. Neptune in the birth chart of the USA is at 22° Virgo, exactly conjunct Milosevic's north Node, and the north Node of the USA is at 6° Leo, right on Clinton's Saturn and Milosevic's Moon-Chiron-Pluto. We could spend hours just looking at these links and the mutual projections they describe. But that is getting us off the point at the moment. I would like you to try to get some sense of the polarity of scapegoat and persecutor, and where it lies in this chart.

The exiled goat

We also need to consider the different faces of the scapegoat archetype. Not all scapegoats are the same. Let's think again about the two goats in the ancient ritual of atonement. One of the goats is sacrificed. This is the helpless victim, always on the edge of extinction.

The other goat is sent into exile, and has to survive in the wilderness. There are feelings and perceptions connected with the exiled goat which are different from those of the sacrificed goat. Not all scapegoats feel like helpless victims. The exiled goat may compensate for the pain of being cut off from the community by attempting to win back approval through service. The exiled goat does not exist in a state of psychic paralysis like the helpless goat awaiting destruction. This goat is mobile and strong, but it must live carrying the burden of sin for a whole collective. The hunger for reuniting with the collective is intense. If we are exiled, we want to go home again.

Audience: It is a hunger to be reunited with God. It's the dark night of the soul.

Liz: Yes, on one level it is a hunger for reuniting with God, because the collective takes its imperative from God. The reason the goat is exiled is not because the community doesn't like goats. It is because the community has offended God, and the exile is carrying that which has caused offence. This goat bears not only the pain of alienation from the community, but also the pain of alienation from its spiritual source. The exiled goat within us may struggle very hard to win back the acceptance of the collective through serving others, and so we have one of the chief components in the psychology of the helper. It is also one of the chief components in the psychology of many political leaders, particularly those who see themselves as the saviours of their country. The scapegoat complex is often very important for those who seek to help and serve others as a means of reconnecting with the collective that has abandoned them and the god who has been offended.

But the exiled goat may also turn its back on the collective. The anger may be too great, and personal pride may also be involved. The exiled goat may say, "I don't need them anyway. In fact, I am going to do everything in my power to sabotage and destroy the collective which has rejected me." This is the mentality of Thomas Hamilton, the Dunblane killer. The exiled goat can become an anarchist and a revolutionary. It is the lone gunman, the social outcast who consciously chooses the role of the outlaw. In its most extreme form, it is Charles Manson, who gleefully accepts the projection of the collective shadow and says, "Since you will condemn me whatever I am or do, I may as well do what I have been accused of, and justify your condemnation of me."[5] That response provides a form of power and a feeling of being special, and this can compensate for the humiliation of rejection. Such exiled goats are necessary to a community which is unconscious of its own sins, because they carry the collective shadow.

Audience: What do you mean by "necessary to a community"? Do you mean that we create them?

Liz: Yes, I believe we do. Thomas Hamilton was as much a creation of his community as he was of his own pathology. If the exiled goat is treated with the honour it merits, as a sacred carrier of consciously acknowledged communal sin, it does not respond with rage. If it is treated with scorn and contempt, and is made to carry the projection of elements which others cannot bear to face in themselves, it may respond with deep destructiveness. The exiled goat who serves and suffers is very acceptable to the community, and it is acceptable to the scapegoat's self-image, too. Everyone feels better. But it is not so easy for the exiled goat to acknowledge its rage, which usually sits side by side with that compulsion to be a helper. The buried rage of the exiled goat is very active in the helping professions, but it is usually deeply unconscious. This is one of the reasons why many spiritually inclined therapists cannot cope with the raw primal anger of their patients, and prefer to spend time doing uplifting guided imagery exercises instead. It is also one of the reasons why many helpers are so self-destructive, ignoring their own needs and boundaries to the point where they become ill or burn themselves out.

The nationalist firebrand

Let's get back to Slobo, bearing all that in mind. We need to understand how an individual chart might suggest an affinity with this archetypal pattern. If there is an affinity, and it is exacerabated by

---

[5] See Part One, pp. 52ff for a discussion of Charles Manson's chart.

childhood experiences, can the chart tell us anything about how the components of this complex might be enacted?

Audience: Would the emphasis in fire be relevant?

Liz: Yes, it is very relevant in terms of which character in the myth he would identify with. As one of you has already pointed out, the Sun and Moon are both in Leo, and there is a strong trine from the Sun in the sign of its dignity to Mars in Aries, the sign of *its* dignity. This is a powerful nature which expresses the fighting spirit easily. The fact that Mars is in the 12th does not lessen this. It suggests that he expresses not only his own aggression and rage without difficulty, but also the fighting spirit of his collective. The basic temperament is not exactly that of a victim, is it? Double Leos don't tend to see themselves as victims. Nor does Sun trine Mars. The Sun is also in the 5th, its natural house. All this suggests that he would probably identify with strength and power, because these qualities are easily accessible to the conscious ego. If the scapegoat pattern is suggested by other configurations, it is likely that the helpless victim, the sacrificial goat, will be deeply unconscious and therefore projected. If the Sun and Moon were in Pisces and both were opposite Neptune, it would be more likely that he would identify with the scapegoat, and the inner persecutor would remain unconscious and would probably be projected.

Milosevic's conscious ideals are fiery and heroic. All Leos are prone to self-mythologising, and this Leo, with his powerful Mars, casts himself in the crusader's role. He will fight vigorously to defend an ideal or a cause. The internal scapegoat, which is suggested by both the Sun square Saturn-Uranus and the Moon conjunct Pluto-Chiron, cannot be acknowledged. His image of himself is heroic to an extreme degree. This is also a chart with no planets in water. Personal feelings of vulnerability and pain are not acceptable to consciousness. The whole feeling realm is very threatening. Of course many people have the Sun and Moon in Leo and the Sun trine Mars. That in itself is hardly malevolent. It can be enormously vital, generous, magnanimous and courageous. Many Serbs see Milosevic that way. He is a hero to them, a nationalist firebrand who can restore pride to his people. He is cut from the same cloth as Napoleon, who was also a Leo. In 1987, when he was speaking before a crowd of Kosovar Serbs who had been brutalised by Albanian police, Milosevic listened to them shouting, "They are beating us!" and replied, "No one shall ever beat you again!"

Audience: There is something about Moon-Chiron-Pluto which makes me think he always feels a sense of threat.

Liz: Yes, there is a great sense of threat suggested by that conjunction. I want to work my way up to this group of planets in the 4th house. But first I would like you to get a sense of what kind of person Milosevic is on a conscious level. We can recognise the fiery heroism and self-mythologising propensities in the Sun-Mars trine and the emphasis in Leo. It is not a reflective combination. This is not someone who would question his own motives and ask, "Why am I doing this?" And Mars in the 12th is carrying a collective need which goes back into the ancestral psyche. He expresses not only his own anger and aggression, but that of his family and his nation. He is driven not only by personal ambition, but by a heroic mission.

Sun-Saturn: the inner judge

We know that Milosevic is sensitive to the archetypal scapegoat pattern, but we also know that he doesn't want to be perceived as weak. Milosevic has a Sun-Saturn square. We need to look more closely at this aspect in relation to the scapegoat pattern. Any person with Sun-Saturn, particularly the hard aspects, tends to be very vulnerable to collective opinion. Saturn acts as an inner judge, a kind of Freudian superego, constantly criticising and setting standards which require enormous effort and struggle. There is often a gnawing inner feeling of failure, which is aggravated by any suggestion that one has not "made the grade" in the eyes of others. Now, that can work very creatively. A person who is so very sensitive to society's needs and expectations can create an immensely useful and dynamic life serving the world in some way. Sun-Saturn contacts can generate tremendous ambition and tenacity and, if they are lived out rather than avoided, they often lead to considerable worldly success. But the square in Milosevic's chart, although it has indeed resulted in tenacity and worldly success, also suggests that, deep down, he is a deeply insecure man.

Hard Sun-Saturn aspects can generate enormous anxiety and self-doubt. The inner judge says, "This is what you should be. This is what the world expects from you. This is what your family expects from you. If you fail, you have committed a great sin." The inner expectations are incredibly demanding, but they are projected outside. There is a great need for acceptance by the collective, which is why Sun-Saturn people often find fulfilment through some kind of service to the collective. They need a position of responsibility in order to make their mark on the world. We know from that Sun-Saturn square that Milosevic is particularly attuned to a major component of the scapegoat complex: the priest-king who is also a judge, who mediates between the gods and the collective and says, "This is what God wants from you." Sun-Saturn people often fear that they will not be good enough. And that is an important factor in the scapegoat complex.

Saturn-Uranus and ideological fanaticism

Uranus is also relevant to our archetypal theme, and it can play both the scapegoat and the persecutor. Because Uranus is connected with our collective vision of the perfect society, it can become a dogmatic and self-righteous critic, and in Milosevic's chart it allies with Saturn. Uranian people are often scapegoats because they identify with new ideas which have not yet become collectively acceptable. But when they are scapegoats, they are usually dogmatic scapegoats. Their claim to absolute truths, and their stubborn refusal to compromise with existing collective norms, can be as much of a problem as the intractable conservatism of the collective which persecutes them. When Saturn and Uranus conjunct, as they did during the Second World War, the vision of a perfect society can be very powerful, even to the point of fanaticism. We might view the conjunction which presided over this war as a reflection of the ideological fanaticism which fuelled the Nazi vision of racial purity and global power. Saturn-Uranus generation groups have an intensely idealistic view of society. They deeply desire a perfect world. Saturn wants stability, but it is prepared to accept warts. But

Uranus strives for perfection. The deeper collective energies which fuelled the Second World War are, in large part, described by this conjunction.

Milosevic was born under the conjunction, and it is particularly strong because it squares his natal Sun. His individual development and destiny are inextricably bound up with the collective events occurring at the time of his birth. He came into the world when the vision of a society purged of its imperfect elements was erupting everywhere. Squares and oppositions between Saturn and Uranus are also important, but they are not as powerful as the conjunction which kicks off a new cycle. The conjunction of 1941 began at the end of Taurus and continued into Gemini in 1942 and early 1943. This conjunction seeded a new cycle which culminated in the opposition from Pisces to Virgo in the mid-1960s. Uranus was joined at this time by Pluto, and Saturn was joined by Chiron. The next conjunction began at the end of Sagittarius in 1987 and moved into Capricorn in 1989, when it linked up with Neptune. At this time, Jupiter and Chiron opposed them from Cancer. The opposition which marks the culmination of this particular cycle will occur in 2008, when Saturn will be in mid-Virgo opposing Uranus in mid-Pisces.

You can all see how important this Saturn-Uranus cycle is from the point of view of collective institutions and ideologies,[6] and anyone born under a conjunction will enact the cycle in their individual life, parallel to the unfoldment of the cycle in the outer world. Critical times occur in the person's life when the two transiting planets form squares or oppositions in the heavens, even if they do not directly aspect the individual's birth chart, and the next conjunction, following the one presiding over the birth will be particularly important. For example, in 1989, under the conjunction which followed that at his birth, Milosevic took power in Yugoslavia.

When Saturn conjuncts an outer planet, there is a great openness to what is going on in the collective at the time of one's birth, and there is often a sense of being constantly buffeted by terrifyingly powerful collective energies. There may be little consciousness of this, but it can generate enormous anxiety, and anxiety can, in turn, generate

---

[6] See Charles Harvey, *Anima Mundi: The Astrology of the Individual and the Collective*, CPA Press, 2002, pp. 176ff for more on the Saturn-Uranus cycle.

fanaticism. Milosevic carries within him a kind of "racial memory" of what was happening in his homeland at the time of his birth, when Hitler's Croatian puppet Ustashi was targeting the Serbs for persecution. This experience of collective scapegoating is part of his psychology. The world, for Milosevic, is an unstable and unsafe place, where the vision of a perfect world can only be achieved through ruthless control. Saturn-Uranus contacts can be immensely creative, and they can contribute to revolutionary thinking in the best sense. But there is often an intractable fanaticism in this combination of planets, and it is connected to the scapegoat theme through the mythic image of the outlaw. It is a Promethean combination which may invoke a Promethean punishment. Sun-Uranus people, even without the added complication of Saturn, can feel like scapegoats because they see the shape of the future yet know that no one around them will understand.

The scapegoat dynamic is not as powerful in those who are not profoundly sensitive to the collective psyche. This is because the scapegoat is a symbol of collective expiation and atonement. This complex is always linked with the group in some way. It is not a purely personal theme. Sensitivity to the collective is an essential ingredient of the pattern, and the squares from Saturn and Uranus to the Sun, as well as the Moon's conjunctions with Pluto and Chiron, suggest that Milosevic is an excellent candidate for the complex. We have already looked at which part of the scapegoat dynamic he would be likely to identify with. A double Leo with a Sun-Mars trine is not likely to think of himself as a powerless victim. He will identify with the hero, the crusader who will create a perfect world. How will he achieve this? By purging his society of those carriers of sin which have caused so much collective suffering. Where are these sin-carriers in Milosevic himself?

Audience: In the family. In the Moon-Chiron-Pluto conjunction.

Moon-Chiron-Pluto: family secrets and racial memories

Liz: Yes, the Moon-Chiron-Pluto conjunction in the 4th suggests that there are many dark secrets in this family. Both parents are implicated, because both the Moon and the 4th house are involved. The progressed

Sun reached the exact square with Saturn when Milosevic was only six months old. When he was three, his father, an Orthodox theologian who became a Marxist, left the family home. At that time, the progressed Sun reached the exact square to natal Uranus. Perhaps he never felt he had a father, because the Sun was applying to the Saturn-Uranus conjunction throughout the early years of his life. In 1962, when Milosevic was twenty-one, his father committed suicide. Transiting Saturn at this time was in early Aquarius, opposing the natal Moon-Chiron-Pluto conjunction, and transiting Uranus was in Leo, conjuncting the natal Sun and squaring the natal Saturn-Uranus conjunction.

Ten years later, his mother, who was a teacher, also killed herself. The Moon reflects our most fundamental needs: to feel safe, secure, wanted and nourished. The conjunction of the Moon with Chiron and Pluto suggests that, as an infant, he felt unwanted, bad, and damaged. He probably also felt constantly threatened: a sense of imminent annihilation was there at the very beginning of life. Both parents were probably deeply depressed. The progressed Moon reached its exact conjunction with Pluto at only one month old, and its exact conjunction with Chiron at four months old. These inner experiences of loneliness, darkness and damage were locked in during the first year of life. Here is a helpless, isolated victim, perpetually threatened with extinction before he is even a year old. When his father committed suicide, the transit of Saturn opposition Moon-Chiron-Pluto suggests that he was plunged into the same place of isolation and darkness that he had experienced as a baby. And transiting Uranus on the Sun, triggering the natal Sun square Saturn-Uranus, must have activated the sense of imminent chaos and destruction which had permeated the world when he was born.

I don't know what destroyed Milosevic's parents. His father abandoned his former religious faith and became a dedicated communist. It does not take a degree in rocket science to work out that the suppression of the religious instinct which was practiced so consistently by communist regimes is deeply destructive to the human psyche. I don't know anything about the mother, other than that she was also a dedicated communist. But with a Moon-Pluto conjunction, Milosevic must have felt that whatever destroyed his parents could destroy him, too. Placed in the 4th house, there is a sense of some terrible destructive force at work within the family fabric. This sense of threat has been projected onto the Kosovars. They appear to him as the Plutonian carriers of imminent destruction. This projection has very little to do with the actual collective. While there may be individual Albanians who are destructive, Milosevic thinks in broad racial terms, just as Hitler did. His fantasy is both personal and mythic, and has amalgamated with his parents' history and the history of his land.

The echoes of the past are intensely important to Milosevic because of that group of planets in the 4th house. He has a long racial memory. His family history merges with the history of his land, and it becomes his personal history because he identifies so deeply with it. That in itself does not have to be destructive. If one feels that way about one's roots, one may wish to contribute one's creative gifts to the place of one's birth. It is possible to have a deep and passionate feeling for the history of one's land without persecuting anyone. For Milosevic, the history of his people is his history, but it is a history coloured by the suffering and persecution reflected by the Chiron-Pluto conjunction under which he was born. His perception of his nation's history is one of victimisation. His nation was humiliated and destroyed more than once, and when Milosevic looks at history, he can see nothing else.

Venus-Neptune and the quest for perfect beauty

I would now like to look at the body dimension of the scapegoat complex. Destructive feelings about the body may be a powerful expression of this complex. One feels ugly, deformed, sick or tainted in some way. We can see the link between this negative body image and compulsive behaviour patterns such as bulimia, anorexia and self-mutilation. The scapegoat is experienced in the body, which becomes the carrier of sin. Milosevic may carry these kinds of feelings about his own body, partly because of the Moon's aspects and partly because of the Venus-Neptune conjunction in the 6th house. But the feelings are projected onto the ethnic Albanians.

Audience: Why do you say that about Venus-Neptune in the 6th?

Liz: Because the 6th has a lot to do with how we feel about our bodies, and Venus is the ruler of the Taurus Ascendant. I am not suggesting that we should consider Venus-Neptune as pathological in itself. No aspect in itself is inherently "bad". Everything depends on how it is expressed. Venus-Neptune can describe extreme aesthetic sensitivity and romanticism. It is a longing for perfect beauty, particularly when it is in Virgo. It is an artist's aspect, deeply receptive to beauty in all its forms, and it equates love with suffering and sacrifice. But like any other chart configuration, this longing for the ineffable can become twisted and made to serve the complex. Everything in Milosevic's chart has been enlisted to serve the scapegoat complex. When a complex takes over the psyche, it appropriates the chart, and the expression of the signs, aspects and houses is coloured by the archetypal pattern. Rather than the individual being at the centre, it is the complex which runs the show. At that point, free will becomes meaningless, and destiny is dictated by unconscious compulsions.

Planetary configurations reflect an openness to certain archetypal patterns. We all have different myths, and the scapegoat myth is not everyone's myth. Many people don't feel scapegoated, even if they have been subjected to difficult experiences early in life, and they don't need to scapegoat anyone else either. In a group of astrologers, or any other group within the helping professions, the scapegoat complex is likely to be strong. Why do we become helpers? And why have we chosen a field of work within the helping professions which is itself considered to be fringe, abnormal or weird? The theme is very relevant to all of us here today.

The degree to which we are dominated by the complex depends on how conscious we are of all its components. If we are unconscious of either the persecutor or the victim, we will identify with one and project the other. Then the complex takes over and uses the whole chart, including benign aspects such as Venus-Neptune. The chart no longer reflects the development of a complete human being. It has been swallowed up by a hungry complex. When we are dominated by unconscious compulsions, our planets are not free to be what they could be. An unconscious complex can become like a huge vortex that sucks everything into itself, or a magnet which shapes the iron filings of the chart according to its own outlines. Venus-Neptune at its best is a wonderfully poetic and compassionate aspect. In Milosevic, it is not free to be what it might be.

Audience: Could it make him see himself as a saviour?

Liz: Ordinarily I would not associate that particular perception with Venus-Neptune, but I would with Jupiter-Neptune, an aspect which is often prone to fantasies of redeemership. Milosevic has them in square. This square supports the crusading propensities of the Sun-Mars trine, giving a mystical justification for his crusade. The Venus-Neptune conjunction may describe a particular relationship with his wife, and he may perceive her as a saviour. The press is constantly telling us that she is actually the power behind the throne. I would question this, because he is not a weak personality. But he may idealise her.

Audience: He might put her on a pedestal.

Liz: I am sure he puts her on a pedestal. That is what I mean by "idealise". But that does not mean she dominates him, or that the idea to exterminate the Kosovars was her idea. She may epitomise his ideal of beauty, and she may also embody something that he feels about his land and his roots. His longing for beauty and perfection may serve the complex by making him repelled by anyone who does not fit his fantasy of pure Serbian blood.

Audience: I was wondering if she provided the missing water.

Liz: Possibly. It is worth noting that he met Mira at secondary school. She was an orphan, so they had an immediate empathy with each other's childhood loneliness and abandonment. This is a literal case of marrying one's childhood sweetheart. Often, people who lack an element in the birth chart look for someone who can provide it. We tend to seek partners who can offer what we are not very good at providing ourselves.

Audience: Is she a Scorpio?

Liz: I don't know. I don't have her chart. Later on, I would like to look more carefully at how we can work creatively with the scapegoat complex. The first requirement, as I have said, is to be conscious of it. Moon-Pluto, for example, can be an enormously creative aspect because the sense of threat in the environment forces us to develop good survival instincts. We can discover something inside that is strong and independent because we are not fooled by the surface of people and situations. We learn to rely on an attunement to nature which can reveal great beauty and depth as well as a nose for danger. But for the creative dimension of such an aspect to be available, we need to be conscious of the complex and how it dominates us. Milosevic's Moon-Chiron-Pluto reflects the powerful rage of the exiled goat. He is the outsider, the loner, the outlaw. No doubt he is thriving on being the man everyone loves to hate. Something in him needs this, because he is identified with the exiled goat. Every nation in the world hates him. The more pressure they place on him, the stronger he feels, because he is thwarting the community which has exiled him.

Audience: It may also be Leonine pride.

Liz: In part, yes. Milosevic will not creep and crawl and beg America's forgiveness. But he also has the tenacity of the exiled goat, determined to survive in the teeth of life-threatening opposition. The exiled goat thrives on isolation. The combination of Leonine pride and the stubborn tenacity of the exiled goat makes Milosevic need to be a hunted outlaw whom everyone hates. It feeds the complex. And because of that Saturn-Uranus conjunction square the Sun, his destiny is involved with the collective, and he can't demonstrate his specialness except in the context of the collective. He also carries a sense of being damaged to the point of extinction. Something inside him is utterly twisted, and the likelihood is that this "something" is going to be projected outside. Why do you suppose he really wants to rid Yugoslavia of the ethnic Albanians?

Audience: He wants the wealth of their land.

Religious conflict and the scapegoat

Liz: That is a conscious reason, and certainly material gain is involved. But it is much more than that. Milosevic is a shrewd political leader. He could claim the wealth of the land in ways other than invoking the kind of holocaust he has generated. Public and private investment in the region would also result in wealth flowing back to Serbia, and he could take advantage of the generosity of other nations through grants and loans. Milosevic's persecution of the Albanians has made him international enemies who are now in process of destroying him. What is so threatening about these ethnic Albanians? They are not of a different race. The religious issue is a large part of the problem: they are Muslims and therefore they invoke the ancient enemy. In the eyes of the Christian Serbs, they are heretics. Persecuting heretics has been a favourite pastime of Christians for many centuries, and the victims have included the Jews within their own lands and the Muslims in the Holy Land during the Crusades. It has also been a favourite pastime of Muslims for many centuries, including the Christian Serbs when the Ottoman Turks invaded the Balkans. Religious conflict – and I include the Nazi definition of racial purity under that heading – has resulted in more bloodshed throughout history than any other form of scapegoating.

The issue of religious war is very interesting if we consider it from the perspective of the scapegoat complex. People who worship a different god often seem a threat to the community because there is a deep-rooted archetypal fear that they will anger one's own god and will bring down misfortune on everybody. The fear is that, unless they are driven out or destroyed, they will destroy the fabric of society. This is a primal terror, which goes back to the days when we believed that everything we did as a tribe could invoke either benefits or curses from the presiding supernatural powers. This primal fear is very easy to constellate in a collective which has lost its way, which is why both Hitler and Milosevic were so skilful at arousing it. It is most easily invoked when times are bad and the collective is seeking a redeemer who will restore the well-being of the community.

Planetary indications of collective scapegoating

Audience: Why is the scapegoat theme so strong at the moment?

Liz: Although all atrocities involve victims, not every victim is a scapegoat. But the smell of the scapegoat is quite pervasive at the moment. Within the space of the last few weeks, along with the war in Kosovo, there have been other incidents. Six days ago, exactly an hour after the Americans dropped a huge payload of bombs on the Serbs, two American high school students killed twelve other students and a teacher at Columbine High School in Littlewood, Illinois, and then killed themselves. And we have had the three nail-bombs in London targeting minority groups. Something seems to be breaking out in a big way. It is a bit like boiling pasta or soup at a high temperature when the lid of the pot is jammed on too tight. When there is no chance of release, the accumulation of steam blows the lid off, and the contents of the pot fly all over the kitchen. For a long time there has been a lid jammed down on our collective feelings of anger about the world we live in, and the scapegoat archetype is on the march at the moment. This tends to happen when we feel powerless as a collective, which inevitably occurs when our secure social, religious and economic structures start breaking down. We feel humiliated and ineffectual. Certain individuals who are open to the archetype but cannot mediate it with a strong enough ego may identify with it to the point where they hit back against their feelings of powerless – which are also *our* feelings – in violent ways. Although it is painful to acknowledge, they are our mouthpieces.

Audience: Are there particular configurations in the heavens which you would connect with this?

Liz: Certainly. Our old friends Chiron and Pluto are involved. They are presently conjuncting in Sagittarius, and the sixty-year Chiron-Pluto cycle has a profound connection with eruptions of collective scapegoating.[7] Milosevic was born under the last Chiron-Pluto conjunction in Leo. In Sagittarius, the conjunction raises the theme of the

---

[7] See Part One, pp. 73ff for more on the Chiron-Pluto cycle.

foreign scapegoat, and also of religious differences as a justification for scapegoating. There is also an exact Saturn-Neptune square in the heavens at the moment. Neptune has a great deal to do with the helpless victim, and Saturn has a great deal to do with the persecutor. Mars has turned retrograde in Scorpio, and it is linking up with the Saturn-Neptune square. The whole configuration has been activating Milosevic's chart very powerfully: Neptune is opposing his Moon-Chiron-Pluto conjunction, while transiting Saturn, which is on his Ascendant, is squaring the conjunction. Transiting Mars is retrograde at the Descendant. No doubt he cannot understand why America and its allies are behaving so aggressively toward him, and he feels victimised. The scapegoat theme in the heavens is triggering the same theme in Milosevic's birth chart.

We feel quite powerless as a collective at the moment. Can any of us do anything about Kosovo, besides donating a bit of money? Can we do anything about the bombs going off in London? We can look out for suspicious packages on the street, but since every London street is full of suspicious packages, that is not very effective. Can we do anything about two students going mad in America? All these incidents activate very deep feelings of impotence. Although we know more about everything that goes on in the outer world because of television and the internet, we feel we can do less about it. Such feelings become very acute under transits like Chiron-Pluto and Saturn-Neptune, and that inevitably unleashes Martial rage – especially when Mars is also involved in the transiting configuration. Mars is always activated when we feel helpless and threatened. So, in answer to your question, there are two transiting configurations in the heavens which are very deeply linked with the scapegoat complex. When such transits hit the charts of individuals who are also deeply linked with this complex, it is not surprising that they enact one of the characters in the story, either in their private lives or on the world stage.

Audience: With which character do people like the London bomber identify?

Liz: They are identifying with the exiled goat. The Columbine High School boys were loners like Thomas Hamilton. They carried deep feelings of inferiority and rejection by the collective. They were exiles in their community. They envied and hated the attractive, popular students. They felt themselves to be helpless scapegoats, and their Martial rage exploded and turned them into persecutors. Then they destroyed themselves like sacrificial victims. We may all be capable of such behaviour, albeit in much smaller ways. We may enact the scapegoat complex through spiteful behaviour toward those whom we envy, or those who we feel have excluded or rejected us. We may enact it by allowing ourselves to be victimised by people in our personal lives. We may enact it by scapegoating other people in order to avoid feeling like scapegoats ourselves, even if the cruelty is subtle and is directed toward our partner or our dog.

Audience: Do you have anything to say about the fact that almost everything in Milosevic's chart is below the horizon?

Liz: This is what is known as a bucket chart, with everything except Mars below the horizon. The emphasis in the so-called "subjective" houses suggests that, most of the time, Milosevic has very little objective perception of the outer world. His relationship to life is focused on his own development, and it isn't easy for him to step back and see his place in the larger picture. He only sees his own picture, projected onto the universal landscape. Mars is a singleton by hemisphere. It is the "handle" of the bucket. When he does relate to the larger collective, it is through Mars: aggression and anger.

The religious leader as scapegoat

Chiron as the wounded *pharmakon*

Here is another example chart. Before I give you the man's name, I would like you to think about whether he has acted out the persecutor or the scapegoat.

David Koresh
17 August 1959, 8.49 am, Houston, Texas, USA

Here is a Sun-Uranus conjunction in Leo, echoing Milosevic's Sun in Leo square Uranus. The Sun is also widely conjunct Pluto, and both are in the 11th house. And the Sun is in close opposition to Chiron. I would like you to think about Sun-Chiron; it is very relevant to the scapegoat and, like Sun-Saturn, reflects great sensitivity to the collective. But while Sun-Saturn says, "I'm not good enough, so I'll do something to make them approve of me," Sun-Chiron says, "I'm not good enough and I never will be. They will always hate me, whatever I do."

Audience: He's not helped by the fact that Saturn is angular, right on the IC.

Liz: No, and Saturn aspects the Sun with a wide, out-of-sign trine. It is a very powerful Saturn. The emphasis in the 11th house suggests a strong awareness of his place in the group and a deep need to contribute something special. We have the same ingredients here as we found in Milosevic's chart: openness to the collective, including its darker elements, yet with a feeling of not being good enough. The aspects are different, but the same planets are on stage again: Chiron, Pluto, Saturn, and Uranus.

Audience: I think this is the chart of a persecutor. He would identify with the Leo side. That's what he has in common with Milosevic. If the Sun were in Pisces, he might act out the victim.

Liz: Let's look at some other aspects before you come to any definite conclusions. We know that Sun-Chiron has elements of the exiled goat, the goat that carries collective sins and poisons.

Audience: Could you say more about the fact that the Sun is in the 11th, and Chiron is in the 5th?

Liz: The Sun in Leo in the 11th suggests that he needs to contribute something special to the collective. He wants to feel involved with collective progress, because this gives him a sense of meaning and purpose. There is intense sensitivity to the collective, and a powerful urge to influence the future of the group through his special efforts and talents. But he also feels that, whatever he offers, it won't be good enough. Chiron in the 5th in Aquarius reflects a sense that he will always be an outsider, and anything he creates will be flawed and unacceptable.

Moon-Neptune and the victim

As far as feelings of victimisation and martyrdom are concerned, we can see a suggestion of this in the Moon-Neptune square.

The Moon, like Chiron, is in Aquarius, and he finds his sense of emotional security in feeling that he belongs. But because Chiron is there too, he feels he will never belong, so the Moon's needs are doomed to frustration. When we start with an archetypal theme and then try to find chart configurations which might reflect it, we won't get one single, definitive formula. Every chart is different. But certain planets will keep coming up in certain kinds of patterns. Chiron is an obvious scapegoat significator, as is apparent in myth. A powerful Chiron connected with the Sun, Moon, Saturn or Pluto does give us some hints about the importance of the scapegoat archetype. We may see different arrangements of these components, but the same components will keep appearing. This man has Sun conjunct Pluto in Leo, opposite Chiron. Milosevic has Moon conjunct Chiron and Pluto in Leo. This man has Sun conjunct Uranus in Leo. Milosevic has Sun in Leo square Uranus. This chart has Moon and Chiron in the 5th. Milosevic has Sun in the 5th. These configurations cannot tell us that the individuals will act out the scapegoat pattern, nor in what way, but they do suggest that the individual is in some way aligned with the scapegoat myth.

The scapegoat myth does not have to be acted out destructively. Its dark side is most in evidence when the person is unconscious. The scapegoat as a sacred vessel, a *pharmakon* or healing agent, is an immensely positive image. But with deep unconsciousness and an overriding sense of personal grievance, the pattern can become very unpleasant. This man's Moon in 12° Aquarius not only squares Neptune but also opposes Uranus. Where can the Moon find comfort and nourishment? It forms hard aspects to two outer planets, and also opposes Mercury. It makes no harmonious aspects to any planet, and no aspects to any personal planets except for the opposition to Mercury, so he has enormous difficulty in communicating his feelings even if he understood what those feelings are. How are his instinctual needs going to be met? How can he feel like anything other than an exile?

The life of David Koresh

This, by the way, is the chart of David Koresh. This exiled goat found his compensation by becoming a religious saviour. He formed his own religious group in which he could feel important and valued. He was the ruler, the adored one; he didn't have to feel deformed or damaged any more. Although the collective was the persecutor, he created his own collective, in which he could act as both saviour and persecutor. I will give you a brief potted biography so that you can see how his early circumstances put flesh on the bones of the scapegoat pattern. Koresh was born to a fifteen-year-old single mother. He never knew his father, and was raised by his grandparents. We can see how Saturn exactly at the IC would describe certain feelings about this absent father and the society which made his illegitimacy so shameful. The theme of the missing or spiritually "sick" father is also an important component in the mythology surrounding Leo, because the quest for a spiritual or inner source is fundamental to Leo's creative drive. I have often mentioned the myth of Parsifal and the quest for the Grail as being relevant to Leo, and here the enactment is quite literal.

In his late-night conversations with the FBI during the Waco siege, Koresh described his childhood as lonely. He was scapegoated by other children. He was dyslexic and a bad student, and eventually he dropped out of high school. Here we can see the 11th house Pluto opposite Chiron already at work: Koresh carried the "group shadow" from a very young age. But he found solace in the Bible, and by the age of twelve he had memorised large parts of it. When he was twenty he became a member of the Seventh Day Adventist church, his mother's church, which we know as the Jehovah's Witnesses. But he was expelled because he was deemed to be a bad influence on other young people. In 1981, when he was twenty-two, he went to Waco and joined the Branch Davidians, a religious sect which had settled outside Waco in 1935 and which, by the time he joined it, had around 1400 members.

Koresh then had an affair with a woman in her late sixties called Lois Roden, the "prophetess" of the group. When she died, a power struggle ensued within the group between Koresh and Lois' son George. Koresh withdrew to east Texas with a handful of disciples. But in late 1987, when transiting Saturn and Uranus were conjuncting in Sagittarius and forming trines to his natal Sun-Uranus, he returned with seven followers, armed with rifles, shotguns and ammunition. There was a gunfight, and George Roden was killed. David and his followers then went on trial for attempted murder. They were all acquitted, and by 1990, when transiting Pluto in Scorpio was forming an exact square to natal Uranus in the 11th, Koresh had become the leader of the Branch Davidians. His real name was Vernon Wayne Howell, but he now changed it to David Koresh "for publicity and business purposes". The word *koresh*, just in case you wondered, is a Hebrew transliteration of Cyrus, the Persian king who allowed the Jews held captive in Babylon to return to Israel.

What happened next became world news. The FBI heard that the Branch Davidians were accumulating firearms, and in February 1993 they moved in to search the complex and arrest Koresh on illegal weapons charges. A battle ensued in which four agents and six Davidians were killed, with a lot more wounded on both sides, Koresh among them. A fifty-one-day siege ensued. Finally, in April, the FBI used tanks to launch incendiary tear gas into the buildings, and the complex burned to the ground. Nine Davidians survived; eighty died, including David Koresh. The Justice Department claimed that the cult members started the fire in a kind of apocalyptic mass suicide gesture, and accusations, convictions and lawsuits have been flying back and forth ever since. It is worth noting that, during the period of the siege, transiting Saturn was in Aquarius, lined up on Koresh's natal Sun-Chiron opposition, and transiting Pluto was retrograding in Scorpio, square the Sun-Chiron. And transiting Chiron was stationary in 17° Leo, exactly on natal Uranus. The Sun-Chiron opposition was powerfully activated, entrenching Koresh's paranoia and hatred of collective authority, and perhaps also impelling him to self-immolation and martyrdom. As early as 1989, he prophesied to his followers that they would have to suffer and submit to being persecuted, tortured and murdered. Whether he was killed by the FBI or by his own hand, his identification with the scapegoat archetype was complete.

Sun-Jupiter: the scapegoat as religious prophet

An article in *Time Magazine*, published in May 1993, comments that Koresh was "a type well known to students of cult practices: the charismatic leader with a pathological edge". He is referred to as a psychopath, "uncannily adept at manipulating and conning people".[8] We should note that the Sun is exactly square Jupiter in David Koresh's chart. That is not a planetary combination which we would readily associate with the scapegoat, but if there are feelings of being scapegoated, Sun-Jupiter contacts may be mobilised as a defence system in quite florid ways. One way in which the exiled goat may try to compensate for terrible feelings of inferiority and shame is through inflation. A sense of grandiosity and messianic fervour may flood in to fill the empty space created by loneliness and isolation. This is especially the case because the Sun is in Leo, and Jupiter allies itself with that fiery Sun to inflame the feelings of being superior to ordinary mortals.

If the Sun were not square Jupiter, Koresh might have enacted the scapegoat pattern in a different way. Milosovic has a Sun-Mars trine, which he mobilised to compensate for his feelings of exile, damage, isolation, impotence and badness. David Koresh's Sun-Jupiter was mobilised to compensate for similar feelings. Where Milosevic became a Martial leader and fighter, Koresh became a religious prophet. He then proceeded to turn himself into the very thing that he hated in the collective. The rules of his community were more stringent and cruel than anything he found in the outer world, and his disciples became his scapegoats. While the men were subjected to rules of celibacy, he took their wives and daughters as concubines, explaining that his seed was divine and that therefore only he had the right to procreate. He plucked sexual partners as he pleased from among his followers, rationed their food in unpredictable ways, beat them and relieved them of their bank accounts and personal possessions. When we are in the land of the scapegoat, it's always a hall of mirrors.

The 10th and 11th houses and the great "They"

In order to make sense of the astrological patterns connected with the scapegoat myth, we need to look not only at the planets, but

8 See Part One for an exploration of the astrology of the psychopath. Like Milosevic, Koresh's chart has many significators in common with other psychopathic personalities.

also at the houses. Sensitivity to the collective can be described by a powerful Saturn, but an emphasis in the 10th house can also suggest it. People with a strongly tenanted 10th house are often ambitious. This may not necessarily be ordinary garden variety ambition, but there is a need to be recognised as a useful and effective figure in the world's eyes. There is a deep need to be part of the social fabric and be seen as a person of importance. Even if the rest of the chart is saying, "I don't give a damn what anyone thinks," the person with a strong 10th house cares very much. The caring can turn into hate if one feels rejected by society, and this is sometimes the case when Pluto, Uranus, Neptune or Chiron is placed at the MC. We do not hate things that do not matter to us.

A strong Uranus may likewise be relevant to the scapegoat pattern, and so is an emphasis in the 11th. We might recall the chart of Thomas Hamilton, the Dunblane killer, who, like David Koresh, has the Sun in the 11th, along with Venus, Jupiter and Mercury. Although his 10th house is untenanted, David Koresh has Mercury, Uranus, the Sun and Pluto all lined up in the 11th, and this deep involvement with the collective is underlined by the Sun-Uranus conjunction. The 10th house is Saturn's house, and an emphasis there makes us sensitive to what society requires of us. The 11th, whose natural rulers are Uranus and Saturn, is concerned with the sense of belonging to the larger group. If either house is dominant, other people's opinions matter very much. It matters whether we have a role to play and something useful to contribute, and whether we are recognised and respected for our abilities and efforts. In one of his sermons, David Koresh himself puts it explicitly: "I was introduced to the Lord when I was seventeen...It came at a time when I was looking for acceptance from anyone. I had spent the previous four years in high school trying to gain acceptance. The Lord was the best decision I could have made."

The scapegoat and the Capricorn goat

The signs are also relevant. An emphasis in Capricorn – Sun, Moon, Ascendant or a group of planets – can reflect a sensitivity to the scapegoat theme. Koresh has an angular Saturn in Capricorn, right at the IC. Capricorn has an acute recognition of collective expectations, and a strong need to be useful to the world in some way and contribute to or change existing structures. If this sensitivity is combined with a feeling of victimisation and exile, the scapegoat pattern will probably be a dominant theme in the person's life. I never believe Capricorns who say, "I don't care what other people think." They may not care in the obvious way – not all Capricorns tow the collective line, and some are overt rebels and anarchists – but deep inside, there is a need to serve some kind of authority principle, even if the authority is inner. The rebel who spends his or her life battling against existing social structures is as dominated by those structures as the person who works to sustain them. In every Capricorn, conscious or unconscious, there is an acknowledgement of the importance of a higher law, whether that law is extroverted and perceived in society or in physical substance (which is the basis of what we call science), or whether it is introverted and perceived as a spiritual or psychological imperative.

The desire to obey the law runs deep in Capricorn, and because of this, there can be great guilt and unhappiness when one feels one has broken the law. Obviously, not all Capricorns are scapegoats, and not all scapegoats are Capricorns. But the archetype of the scapegoat may be relevant for many Capricorns, as well as for those who have Sun-Saturn or who have a strongly tenanted 10th house. There are many possible expressions of the Saturn principle, including its sign. If one is strongly Saturnian and happens to grow up in a privileged environment in which one belongs to the "right" class and social background, the scapegoat theme may not be relevant, and other archetypal themes may be more important in one's life. But when Saturnian themes are combined with feelings of differentness and exclusion by the collective, the mythic scapegoat will not be far away.

The scapegoat and the water houses

Audience: Would an emphasis in water houses also be important?

Liz: Yes, if other factors are also involved. David Koresh has a Venus-Mars conjunction in the 12th. Venus-Mars conjunctions are known for their passionate qualities, but in Virgo, and hidden away in the 12th, this passion may be hard to express through ordinary relationship channels. Moon opposite Uranus and Chiron in the 5th opposite the Sun also suggest difficulties in making relationships, so we have an intense individual, fiery and passionate, who has no outlet for those powerful feelings because he is so much an outsider and an alien. The conjunction in the 12th suggests that expressing emotional and sexual passion is a problematic issue in his family background. His illegitimacy, and his mother's pregnancy at such a young age, must be part of this difficult family pattern. It is interesting that Koresh turned his cult into a kind of sexual servicing centre, helping himself to any woman he chose but forbidding the other men to engage in sexual relationships.

In Milosevic's case, the water houses are also strong: the 4th house is emphasised and so is the 12th, although I would place more importance on the planetary aspects. But yes, water houses may be relevant if the bones of the pattern are reflected in other ways. Planets in the 12th are important because they act as mediators for ancestral memories. If there is a scapegoat pattern in one's life, one is usually carrying something more than one's own personal experience. A strongly tenanted 12th house does not, in itself, necessarily imply a scapegoat pattern. But it always points to issues which are much older than the individual.

We need to remember that the mythic scapegoat carries the sins of the group. It is not condemned merely for its own sins; it is condemned as a vessel of collective sin. The sin committed by Oedipus is not committed by choice. It is committed because the gods have required it of him as the fulfilment of a family curse. The same applies to Orestes. He is punished because he murders his mother. But he murders his mother not because he fancies it, but because he is required to by Apollo. He is charged with this task by the god because this, like Oedipus' crime, is the culmination of a long line of family sins which begins with a family curse. The burden of sin carried by the scapegoat is always larger than the individual. For anyone who feels victimised or locked into a scapegoat role, it can make a big difference to recognise that one is carrying more than one's personal share. Planets in the 12th house make this statement very clearly.

Milosevic's Mars in the 12th also works in this way. Even if we were not exploring the scapegoat theme, and were just trying to interpret a 12th house Mars in Aries trine a 5th house Sun in Leo, we might come to the conclusion that the heroic role Milosevic needs to play – the champion of an oppressed people – is not just an expression of his own Martial nature. He is Martial enough on a personal level, but he is also being fed by an underground stream that has its source in history. His own Martial drive is enhanced and inflamed by a collective psychic inheritance of war and struggle. His power is derived from this ancestral inheritance, and his natural aggression is exaggerated by it. It is interesting to observe how important the 12th house is in the charts of political leaders. Hitler had Uranus in the 12th, just like Thomas Hamilton. Tony Blair and George Bush both have the Sun there. A leader with integrity always knows that his or her charisma comes from something greater, and does not personally identify with the source of the power. But if we make the mistake of thinking that the power is ours alone, then we inflate, and a charismatic leader can become a persecutor like Milosevic.

Realising that one is carrying ancestral patterns can be an enormous relief. The sense of shame, guilt and badness which accompanies the exile and the victim can be deeply unconscious, and strong personality defences can be mobilised against such feelings. But the feelings, whether conscious or unconscious, are much larger than the individual. It is actually a kind of arrogance to imagine that one is really so globally, vastly bad that one deserves collective scapegoating. This is inflation of the same kind as the belief that one is a saviour. The scapegoat carries sin and shame for many generations. In order to stop identifying with such ancient ancestral issues, one has to disengage and recognise what one is carrying. Detachment can help to create breathing space between oneself as an individual and the mythic figure, allowing one to mediate it rather than be its victim.

The importance of consciousness

Audience: Is there one particular planet that indicates which side of the scapegoat theme will be conscious? Like, for example, Saturn?

Liz: Saturn, in an individual who has an earthy nature and is well related to the material plane of existence, is not necessarily unconscious. No specific planet indicates unconsciousness. It is the way the planet or configuration "sits" in the chart. Milosovic, with his strongly Leonine nature and Sun-Mars trine, is likely to identify with the exiled goat rather than the sacrificial one, as we have seen, because he can express energy, power and initiative. His self-image is strong and his weakness is unacceptable to consciousness. It is therefore suppressed and projected. An individual who aligns himself or herself in this way will either rush in to help victims or destroy victims. But the victim will always appear outside because it is unconscious.

There are many strong capable people who are deeply identified with the scapegoat complex yet who don't perceive themselves as victims. They are compelled to work with those who are weak and suffering because they unconsciously identify with the victim. But they don't know they are victims themselves. This happens frequently in the psychiatric profession. Psychiatric training in Britain does not involve personal psychotherapy. One can obtain one's qualifications and work with the seriously disturbed without ever having to confront one's own inner world. Thus there are many helpers who have never discovered that they are also victims. They perceive themselves as strong, yet psychiatrists have the highest suicide rate of all the professions. They may recognise the exiled goat, but the sacrificial goat is unconscious. When it is triggered by the people with whom they work, they are suddenly overwhelmed by feelings of impotence and despair. But no single planet can tell us this. We need to examine the overall chart, and we need to view it in the context of the individual's family and cultural background.

David Koresh did not perceive himself as a pathetic, powerless victim. He clearly felt persecuted, but his self-image, with the Sun-Uranus conjunction in Leo, the Sun-Jupiter square and the chart emphasis in fire and air, reflected the exiled rather than the sacrificial goat. Koresh saw himself as a misunderstood genius, a divinely chosen visionary whom society was too shallow, corrupt and stupid to recognise. The helpless sacrificial goat suggested by his Moon-Neptune square would have been far too painful and humiliating for him to acknowledge, so he projected it onto his followers. In this respect he was like Milosevic.

Victims can become healers. In fact, that is probably what they need to become in one form or another, in order to express the archetypal pattern creatively. But they need consciousness in order to avoid identifying with either the victim or the persecutor. Sadism is usually linked to the scapegoat complex. That should be obvious to you. The person who abuses or tortures humans or animals needs to assert power by injuring something weak and helpless. This compulsion emerges from a complete inability to recognise the helpless victim inside. It is interesting to see how often sadism and cruelty are expressions of a strong but unconscious Neptune. We often think of Neptunian people as victims, but if there are other factors in the chart which suggest strength and power, the Neptunian may become a persecutor and the inner figure of the helpless victim will be projected outside. The relationship such an individual makes with the carrier of the projection may contain enormous rage and hatred. If we feel weak and impotent but are unable to acknowledge these feelings, we may experience deeply destructive feelings toward people who remind us of this unconscious dimension of ourselves. Then we have to injure and humiliate them, or even stamp them out.

Astrologers often secretly identify with the exiled goat, and unconsciously invoke hostility from the collective. This may reflect the strongly Uranian element in astrology and the strongly Uranian emphasis in the charts of many astrologers. We also enact the scapegoat theme in another way: we perceive ourselves as the helpless victims of the planets. We want to know what dire thing is going to happen to us under the next difficult transit, particularly if the transit involves an outer planet and world events are involved. What will the heavens "do" to us? There is something about this kind of helpless fatalism which is very disturbing. It is not a helpful approach. The unconscious forces that move external events are collective, but the particular manifestation of these movements in the collective psyche is dependent on the channels each individual provides. If a nation is comprised of deeply unconscious individuals, that nation will enact the transits to its natal chart in very literal and compulsive ways. If a nation has a certain percentage of relatively conscious individuals, the outcome is not so predictable. None of us, as individuals, can instantly affect world events, and we may all become the victims of a collective eruption. But if our values, beliefs and actions are formulated from a place of individual consciousness rather than a place of mass unconsciousness, we do ultimately affect the future, and we can discover specific areas in our lives where we can do something constructive – even if our children and grandchildren, rather than we ourselves, are the beneficiaries of our efforts. Even Milosovic could suddenly wake up one morning and realise what he is doing. It is unlikely, but it is possible.

We would all love to understand why the world is as it is, and we would all love to know what we can do about it. Keeping ourselves informed about world events gives us the illusion that we have more control, which is why people become so addicted to television and the newspapers during times of collective crisis – even if the crisis is occurring many thousands of miles away. When something archetypal is being enacted out in the world, it can be very frightening. These archetypal patterns were once called gods, and we feel impotent in the face of such overwhelming forces. At present the enactment is particularly disturbing, because through the veneer of the various political and military issues, the ancient myth of the scapegoat is revealing itself. Because it is relevant to each of us personally, it brings up a sense of distress which goes beyond simple compassion for people who are being victimised, and pushes us into an awareness of both our own helpless inner victim and our own inner persecutor.

Working with the complex

Perhaps we could talk more about ways of working with the scapegoat complex so that we can restore the sacred meaning to this archetypal pattern. If the scapegoat theme is strongly emphasised in one's life, one cannot remove it, no matter how much consciousness one brings to bear on it, because the myth is a fundamental aspect of one's destiny. In the same way, one cannot send in and get a new birth chart, and if patterns involving Saturn, Chiron, Pluto, Neptune and Uranus are powerful in the chart, the task is about learning how to live the patterns creatively rather than being dominated by an unconscious scapegoat complex. Every society, like every individual, needs values in which to believe, goals and aspirations which make the future worthwhile, and a connection with the transpersonal realm which infuses life with meaning. The scapegoat myth reflects both our profound need for a relationship with deity and our aspiration toward fulfilling our human potential. The ritual of atonement symbolises the recognition that, whatever we have achieved, it could be more and better, and we have made mistakes along the way. As a collective, we must keep a sense of connection with something greater than ourselves.

When our religious instincts are suppressed, thwarted or disillusioned, we simply replace the usual image of God with surrogates, and continue to seek our meaning in those surrogates without realising the true nature of our devotion. And because we can sense our failure as a collective, we can never rest smugly in the belief that we have fulfilled all that we could become. Even if we try to ignore the need for atonement, the sense of failure gnaws at us, and then we begin to seek a scapegoat to alleviate the inner distress. Conscious atonement is fundamental to any kind of spiritual aspiration, but if we do not recognise our need for it, we force others into becoming sacrificial victims, and create yet another human tragedy and an even greater need for atonement later. This need accumulates in the collective psyche over time, and results in a cyclical purging of the scapegoat, which may be connected with the sixty-year Chiron-Pluto cycle.

When we view the scapegoat myth from an archetypal rather than a pathological perspective, we can see that it is a means for the collective to reconnect on a cyclical basis with a sense of its source. In order to reconnect, we must, as a collective, admit our flaws, own our failings, and acknowledge our sins. We are not yet the divine children that we know we could become. We are still flawed mortals. The symbolic ritual of the scapegoat involves recognising this, atoning for it, and consecrating it through some kind of effort to transform those elements in us which have alienated us from the source. The issue of serving the collective is fundamental to this dimension of the scapegoat myth. Anyone who is deeply connected with this pattern is connected with other people in a way that requires some kind of acknowledgement of the value of the group, and the need to offer something to the group as a healing agent. The only way we can avoid being either a scapegoat or a persecutor is to become a *pharmakon*. That does not necessarily mean we must become healers in the literal sense. An artist can be a *pharmakon*, and so can a textile designer, and so can a comedian: laughter is one of the most healing of all human expressions.

Extricating ourselves from the oppressive and destructive dimensions of this complex involves recognising its basic core, and accepting the responsibility it places on us while keeping a sense of humour and a firm grip on our human limits. Then it is possible to fulfil the archetypal role in a creative way. Differentness requires us to offer something back to the collective. Whether the differentness is a special talent, a high degree of sensitivity, an especially rich imagination, a particularly fine intellect, a deep capacity for compassion born out of suffering, or an unusual capacity for insight, being different does not only involve being scapegoated. It is also a gift which must be paid for. It is useless to hope that one can become "normal", and equally useless to resent the collective because the gift sometimes seems threatening to others or makes us feel isolated. And it is even more useless to imagine that, because of the gift, one is superior in some way. The gifts which define our differentness are borrowed from the collective. They are not our own creation, and we can claim no credit for them.

The goat cannot say, "Look, I don't want to be a goat any more. Can I please be a corgi, and then I won't get scapegoated?" If this archetypal pattern is fundamental to one's psyche, the object is not to "cure" it. That is not possible anyway. The individuals we have been looking at have mishandled this complex badly, and have injured and destroyed many people – including themselves – because of it. That does not mean the complex is pathological, but it says something about how clumsily we deal with it when we are unconscious. Throughout history, human beings have indulged in the most dreadful forms of scapegoating. There is no group that is not culpable of persecuting others, and no group which has not been scapegoated at one time or another. This is why, when we look at a chart like Milosevic's, we need to avoid jumping in blindly and declaring, "Of course he is a brutal psychopath, just like Hitler." That is undoubtedly true, but the chart alone cannot tell us so. The configurations in his chart will be very similar to configurations in our own charts, and somewhere within all of us is a capacity to turn our own inner scapegoat into a persecutor. Even if it is only a snide remark about someone whom we deem to be inferior to ourselves, we are displaying a little piece of Slobo or Adolf. We are all capable of it, and equally, we can all indulge in feelings of victimisation and poisonous rage when our needs are not met.

If our family background has made the archetypal pattern blossom as a wound, we are at great risk of identifying with the scapegoat myth. There is an enormous responsibility involved in working with this complex. It is much easier to be a scapegoat in the usual sense of the word, and feel dreadfully sorry for ourselves. We can identify with the victim or the exile, and we can always find a persecutor "out there" to blame for our misfortune, because persecutors really are out there. It is much harder to ask oneself, "Where is the persecutor inside? What do I scapegoat in myself, and why? Do I cultivate victimisation because being miserable makes me feel special?" These are hard questions, but unless we ask them, we won't get anywhere at all. Although we in Britain may not fall victim to someone like Milosevic – although we can never be certain – we may fall victim to a lover, a friend, an employer, an employee, or anyone else in our lives whom we cast in the necessary role in order to fulfil our complex.

Audience: Do important transits mean we can work more constructively with the pattern?

Liz: The opportunity is there. If a transit triggers a natal aspect like Sun-Chiron or Moon-Pluto, we might become more conscious of the pattern and work with it more creatively. Whenever a natal planet is transited, something new concerning that planet tries to emerge into consciousness. Very often we enact our transits before we realise what is going on. We experience them concretely in the world, and sometimes that is necessary because the experience serves as an awakener. We cannot force things into consciousness before they are ready through some kind of abstract intellectual process, and we cannot use our astrological or psychological knowledge to avoid life. But even if a painful external situation arises, a powerful transit can give us a chance to understand the deeper meaning of the pattern.

Paranoia and martyrdom

Audience: Could a transit also trigger paranoia?

Liz: When we speak of paranoia, we are describing the feeling that others are out to get us. Sometimes, of course, this may be true. Then it is not paranoia, but a sound survival instinct. An Albanian in Kosovo, or a Jew in Germany during the 1930s, could hardly be accused of paranoia. But sometimes the survival instinct loses its connection with reality, and becomes pervasive to a pathological degree. This is usually connected with a difficult Pluto, and it is rooted in an early sense of imminent danger in the environment. Even when the danger has passed, the individual persists in seeing it everywhere. This experience is often a feature of the scapegoat complex. Thomas Hamilton, with his exact Sun-Pluto square, is a good example. There is a sense that "they", whoever "they" might be, are out to destroy us. Sometimes the fear and rage become so unbearable that one becomes a destroyer oneself to preempt imminent destruction. In the clinical picture of paranoid schizophrenia, acts of destructive violence reflect the intolerable pressure which results from a constant sense of persecution.

A strong Pluto may indicate that we believe we have earned punishment because we are so bad. A strong Jupiter or Neptune combined with a strong Pluto may indicate that we believe we are being punished because we are so good. David Koresh, with his Moon battered by both Pluto and Neptune, is a good example of this combination. It contains a profound paradox, characteristic of the scapegoat complex when it turns messianic. The passive victim who feels full of shame and guilt may also secretly feel "chosen". The medieval saint personifies this paradox, and no one provokes as much anger as a martyr. By this I don't mean real victims like the Kosovars. I mean the professional victim who plays the role of the martyr to the hilt, and whose unexpressed rage can provoke great anger and even cruelty in other people. Helpless victims who persist in being saintly are usually split off from their rage. Then the rage comes out indirectly, or is projected and experienced vicariously.

Audience: Is it ever valid to get angry because of someone else's suffering, or is the anger always because of one's own complex?

Liz: Being scapegoated is not always the result of one's own complex. Individuals can be overwhelmed by collective conflicts, regardless of their own psychological patterns. Nor is a strong response to others' suffering always based on one's own complexes, although personal identification with others' pain is often where compassion begins. But ultimately the anger of the helpless victim needs to be expressed by the victim, not by a surrogate champion or saviour. It is necessary to learn to fight. When the scapegoat starts fighting back in an honest way, something has already begun to shift. It is when the scapegoat's rage is unconscious and indirect that it is so often lethal. Reciting an endless litany of woes is an expression of self-pity, not of honest anger. Part of the healing of the helpless victim begins with the acknowledgement that it is appropriate and healthy to be angry. The goat is not wise to stick its head on the block and say, "I am so unworthy and full of sin that I deserve to be destroyed." It might be wiser to say, "Who the hell do you think you are, judging me?" Anger, for the scapegoat, heralds the beginning of self-esteem. It does not stop there, however. The anger ultimately needs to be channelled creatively by consciousness, because a permanent state of anger goes nowhere. Anger which does not lead to constructive action will lock the individual into provoking more victimisation, because it is rooted in impotence. Or the victim may turn into a persecutor. But initially, anger is an appropriate and necessary response to being scapegoated. And even if one's victimisation is projected and one's anger is directed on behalf of other scapegoats, at least it is anger, and it can open the door which leads one to one's own inner story.

Audience: Would you consider Mother Theresa a scapegoat? She devoted her life to healing scapegoats.

Liz: I don't doubt that the scapegoat pattern is important in her psychological makeup. Otherwise she would not have been drawn to that kind of work. But she seems to have avoided identifying with it on the personal level. Perhaps it's because she had a spiritual life already, and this gave her a connection with the sacred dimension of the myth. This connection is necessary to make something creative out of the pattern. The scapegoat myth must be part of her pattern, but she consecrated it because of her spiritual ideals. It is when the sacred element is missing that problems start arising. This doesn't mean one has to be a Catholic nun. But consecrating one's life to something greater than oneself seems to be the way to work with this pattern without identifying with it.

Audience: You said that martyrs generate a lot of anger.

Liz: Yes. But Mother Theresa was not a martyr. Martyrdom is not simply religious dedication. Martyrs have a profound unconscious need to suffer, and this is often allied with inverted rage and a powerful unconscious will to power. Consecrating one's life to something sacred doesn't mean that one pursues either suffering or power. Consecration acknowledges that one's life is fuelled and given purpose by a commitment to something greater, whether the mask that "something" wears is music, healing, gardening or astrology. Consecration involves a recognition of the numinous in life. But it does not require misery or victimisation, and it is not a form of manipulation, which martyrdom often is. In the martyr, the religious element is often secondary. Martyrdom is a form of masochism. Mother Theresa didn't identify with the victim. She felt compassion for the victim, which is rather different.

Audience: And therefore she didn't attract anger.

Audience: But she got up the noses of a lot of journalists.

Liz: Journalists are very easy to wind up, and many of them seem to have exceedingly large nostrils. It doesn't seem to have bothered her much. Whoever one is, the moment a person attracts public attention, journalists will have a go. In early life, I am sure Mother Theresa was victimised, but she somehow found a way to avoid identifying with it. She seems to offer us a demonstration of how to disconnect from the compulsion of the complex. Her secret may lie in her religious ideals, but it may also lie in the ability to laugh at oneself and recognise the fundamental absurdity of life.

Pluto and the exiled goat

Audience: Would you include Sun-Pluto with aspects that reflect victimisation?

Liz: As we have seen, Pluto is often involved in the scapegoat pattern because it is prone to carrying the collective shadow. Different planets relate to different dimensions or facets of the scapegoat theme, and not all scapegoat complexes involve Plutonian issues. Plutonian people are particularly attuned to the darkness in the collective. They are aware of it from a very early age. They sense it and smell it, and their survival instincts tell them when the environment is potentially dangerous. Plutonian children are often scapegoated because they see too much. They sense everything which everyone else is busy concealing. The ruling Saturnian structures in both the individual ego and the collective require the suppression of the more primitive side of human nature. But the Plutonian person always knows when the psychic septic tank is leaking. For this reason the Plutonian child may be scapegoated by parents, siblings, teachers or peers who have a lot to hide.

But Pluto's response is not the same as Neptune's. Pluto is not really a victim. Occasionally one may see Plutonian people playing the victim role, but there is usually a strongly manipulative element in it. More often they nurse their grievances, and wait for the right moment to exact revenge. It is rare to see a pathetic Plutonian. More often we see blackly depressed or enraged ones. Thomas Hamilton, with his exact Sun-Pluto square, is a good example. So is David Koresh, with his Sun-Pluto conjunction. In Milosevic's case, it is Moon-Pluto. Pluto is a very important factor in the scapegoat pattern, but it is not a helpless victim. I have known a few people with Sun-Pluto or Moon-Pluto who give the impression of being powerless victims, but they are extremely strong people who carry a lot of poison underneath, and martyrdom gives them great power. Plutonians usually play the exiled goat, compelled to take vengeance on those who have injured them, and sometimes destroying themselves in the process.

The mythic scapegoat is a *pharmakon*, a healing agent for the community. This mythic pattern needs to be accepted without inflation and without identification with the victim. Conscious rage may be necessary and valid, because unconscious rage can be very dangerous and makes it almost impossible to loosen the grip of the complex. Sometimes feelings of helplessness may also need to be expressed, because many scapegoats don't know they carry this pattern. They believe they are strong and competent, yet they keep getting victimised. Dependency needs may have to be expressed rather than hidden beneath the isolated, angry pride that so often accompanies the scapegoat in exile. Many of the emotional dimensions of the pattern may have to be worked through in a therapeutic context. But in the end, dealing with the scapegoat creatively involves accepting a mythic pattern without identifying with any of the roles.

I would like to show you one more example chart. After that we can look at a couple of charts from the group.

The great American witch-hunt

Joe McCarthy is not as contemporary as Milosevic or David Koresh, and to our knowledge he did not actually have anyone exterminated, although he destroyed a great number of lives by other means. Unless any of you grew up in America during the 1950s, the impact of what later became known as McCarthyism might not seem relevant. But the means which McCarthy used to destroy his opponents and generate a climate of mass paranoia is a terrifying example of how, even in a so-called democracy, politicians can not only scapegoat the public, but can also incite members of the public to scapegoat each other. According to Richard H. Rovere, one of his biographers, "No bolder seditionist ever moved among us – nor any politician with a surer, swifter access to the dark places of the American mind."[9]

---

[9] Richard H. Rovere, *Senator Joe McCarthy*, University of California Press, 1996.

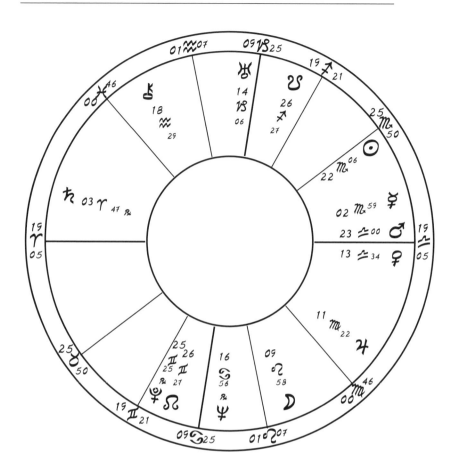

Senator Joe McCarthy
14 November 1908, 3.00 pm, Grand Chute, Wisconsin, USA

The farm boy from Wisconsin

As we might expect, McCarthy the persecutor grew from the fertile soil of McCarthy the scapegoat. He was never a helpless victim, but as a tough and tenacious exiled goat, he certainly got his own back on a collective which had excluded him because of his social and financial disadvantages. As a Senator, he targeted the wealthy, particularly wealthy Jews, which probably reflects the anti-Semitism endemic in his family background. His parents were devout Irish

Catholics, and he was the fifth of nine children. All nine were told that they had to live by the sweat of their brows, and Joe took the biblical injunction very seriously. He grew up in a farming community which was primarily populated by the children of Protestant Dutch immigrants; Irish Catholic families were rare in the area. He was an outsider because of both his religious background and his parents' extreme poverty. The family home was a white clapboard shack with no electricity and no indoor plumbing. He was a shy and awkward child who was teased and mocked by the other children. Later he became too aggressive to be bullied, which is not surprising in light of the powerful Martial energy in the chart: the Sun in Mars-ruled Scorpio, a Mars-ruled Aries Ascendant, and an angular Mars in a grand trine with Chiron and Pluto. Once he began to grow up, nobody messed with Joe McCarthy.

McCarthy left school at fourteen, and tried to establish a chicken farming business on some land borrowed from his father. But five years later he caught pneumonia, and at the same time, the chickens all died of disease. That might have made a lot of people feel like victims, but Joe just packed his bags and moved to another town, where he ran a grocery store for a while. He then decided he could only advance in life if he completed his education, so at the age of twenty he returned to high school and finished four years of schooling in only one year. He got up before dawn each day to study and attended classes for nine hours a day. He then went on to university, and graduated with a law degree at the age of twenty-seven. That was the beginning of his career in politics. By the time he had finished his Saturn return at the age of thirty, he was the youngest circuit judge ever elected in Wisconsin.

McCarthy's personality always provoked powerful reactions. Some people believed in him as though he were a kind of messiah, and others deeply mistrusted him. As a judge he was credited with being hard-working and fair, but he was also rebuked for abuse of judicial authority after destroying court records. He was also censured for violating the ethical code that prohibited sitting judges from running for non-judicial posts. As we shall see, a certain tendency to be economical with the truth eventually caused his downfall. During the Second World War he joined the Marines and, not surprisingly, served as an intelligence officer. After the war, at the age of thirty-eight, he became the youngest member of the United States Senate. For a long time he did his job quietly and assiduously, fighting for causes such as new housing legislation. But the political climate in America was changing, and the Cold War was generating a lot of paranoia. The biggest national issue at the time was the suspicion of communist infiltration of the US government, following a series of highly publicised espionage trials. McCarthy saw his chance. In February 1950, just as transiting Neptune in Libra stationed at his Descendant, he made a speech claiming that communists were secretly dominating the State Department. He called for an investigation.

Some of you may know Arthur Miller's remarkable play, *The Crucible*, which was made into an excellent film starring Daniel Day Lewis and Winona Ryder. I would recommend that you see this film. Miller's play, which is set at the time of the Salem witch-hunts, was a response to the mass hysteria which McCarthy's accusations generated in the minds of the American public, and the inevitable scapegoating which followed. McCarthy's power to stir fears of creeping communism were not entirely based on illusion, but McCarthy boiled down a complex global political situation into terms any illiterate American farmer could understand: China had "gone Red" under Mao, Russia was becoming increasingly threatening to American interests, Europe was leaning left – as exemplified by Italy, where the communist party was the largest outside Russia – and America too might soon be destroyed because the State Department, staffed under Democratic presidents, was full of treasonous pro-Soviet Jewish intellectuals.

McCarthy's star shone in the firmament for four years. During that time, the hunt for "Reds under the bed" was led by the House Committee on Un-American Activities, headed, of course, by Senator Joe McCarthy. Arthur Miller has commented that many of the practices of the House Committee were identical to the practices of the Salem witch trials. A very large number of people were investigated, initially those in government, but later, anyone in the arts who might be deemed unsympathetic to McCarthy's idea of American patriotism. The hunt inevitably reached Hollywood, and the film studios – many of which were run by Jewish immigrants from eastern Europe – were coerced into submitting artists' names to the House Committee for "clearing" before they could be employed. Writers, painters and playwrights also came under fire, especially if they were Jewish, and a large number of people lost their jobs and their reputations. Lies and smear campaigns were regularly utilised; McCarthy never let facts stand in the way of truth. He then moved on to target what he believed were anti-American books in libraries, and discovered some 30,000 books by "communists, pro-communists, former communists, and anti-anti-communists". These books were removed from the library shelves, in the time-honoured fashion of the great Nazi book-burning ceremonies. Ironically, a close friend of McCarthy, called Urban van Susteren, later commented that Joe had looked at only one book in his life: Hitler's *Mein Kampf*.

After the Jews, McCarthy's favourite targets were homosexuals, particularly in the theatre and film world. But for some time his opponents had been accumulating evidence concerning his own homosexual activities. In an attempt to stop the rumours, McCarthy married his secretary, and then adopted a five-week-old girl from a foundling home. He then began investigating communist infiltration into the American military. This enraged even the Republican administration headed by President Eisenhower, and McCarthy's career was doomed. His fall was as meteoric as his rise. The US Army passed information about him to journalists who were known to be opposed to him, and his tactics were exposed. In 1954, a censure motion was passed in the Senate condemning his conduct and accusing him of abusing his power as a Senator. Once he was disgraced, the media lost interest in his claims of a communist conspiracy. He had ruined the careers of hundreds of innocent men and women, yet he had never been able to directly convict a single suspected communist of a crime. Now he was discredited and isolated, just as transiting Saturn in Scorpio arrived on his natal Sun. He had always been a heavy drinker, but now his drinking increased to dangerous levels, leading to his hospitalisation in the spring of 1957. In May he died of acute hepatitis, aggravated by cirrhosis of the liver. He literally drank himself to death at the age of forty-eight.

The usual planetary suspects

When we look at the planetary configurations, we see all the usual suspects. The Sun in Scorpio in the 7th is square Chiron in

Aquarius in the 11th house, suggesting not only the importance of others' acceptance, but also the sense of being isolated and marginalised by the collective. Uranus is angular, conjuncting the MC in Capricorn; McCarthy had a mission to remodel society according to his own vision. McCarthy's Saturn is in Aries in the 12th, trine the Moon in Leo. It may seem strange that we keep encountering important placements in Leo in these charts, since Leo is not usually associated with the psychology of the victim. But Leo is royal, and often, so is the scapegoat. And, as we have seen, Leonine pride can turn a scapegoat into a persecutor. The Moon and Chiron are in opposition in McCarthy's chart, and Chiron's placement in Aquarius echoes Chiron in Aquarius in David Koresh's chart. Both McCarthy and Koresh have the Moon in the 5th house, and both have Moon-Chiron contacts, as does Milosevic.

Neptune in Cancer at the IC is trine the Sun and opposition Uranus. This is a generational aspect reflecting a powerful collective conflict between the Uranian vision of social progress, based on authoritarian rule, and the Neptunian yearning for redemption through identification with racial and national roots. This generational aspect becomes a personal issue for Joe McCarthy because it straddles his meridian axis, suggesting that his parents' poverty and suffering, and the historical victimisation of the Irish in the previous century, may have exercised a great influence on his own psychological development. McCarthy's family had emigrated from Ireland in the mid-1800s, during the Great Famine, and like Joseph P. Kennedy, he inherited an ancestral memory of misery and persecution.

Audience: Wouldn't Uranus in the 10th be an anarchist?

Liz: McCarthy *was* an anarchist. His methods were utterly unethical, and he seemed to live in a different moral universe from his political fellows. His campaign of bullying, lying and terrorising effectively undermined freedom of speech in America, and unleashed a kind of madness in the collective psyche. That is what Miller portrays in *The Crucible*. Uranian anarchy is not always aligned with the political left. Uranus can also be ferociously, fanatically conservative, which is not surprising when it is placed in Saturn's sign and Saturn's house.

Audience: So he would see his public role as the creator of a perfect society.

Liz: Yes, exactly. The things he perceived as imperfect in the world are in some way connected with his family background or roots, as though his purging of the subversive elements and his creation of the perfect America were meant to redeem his parents' and grandparents' poverty and insignificance. Chiron in Aquarius in the 11th, square the 7th house Sun and opposition the Moon, also suggests a deep ancestral wound in relation to the collective. Chiron's natal placement often draws on family issues that go back long before one's birth. McCarthy's own feelings of being alien and unacceptable were transformed into the persecution of those he believed were alien, unacceptable and dangerous to his ideal of the perfect American society. His campaign began when transiting Neptune arrived at the Descendant and formed squares to the natal Uranus-Neptune opposition. This suggests that the overpowering sense of mission which drove him in the early 1950s was deeply connected to that opposition and its links to the family past.

Aries is rising and, like Milosevic with his Mars in Aries trine the natal Sun, McCarthy cast himself in a heroic role. According to his biographers, he behaved like a classic Aries on a bad day: bad-tempered, aggressive and domineering. He could never play the victim's role, despite the feelings of powerlessness described by Mars in Libra square Neptune. He was certainly locked into the scapegoat complex, but it was inevitable that he would wind up playing the persecutor. The emphasis in Martial signs, along with the angular Mars and the Leo Moon, would point to a tendency to scapegoat others rather than suffer the humiliation of being scapegoated himself.

Audience: Would the Moon's north Node in the 3rd describe his dogmatism?

Liz: By itself, the north Node in the 3rd does not indicate dogmatism. It suggests a need to develop rational thinking and the ability to communicate clearly. But in McCarthy's chart it conjuncts Pluto, which is also in Gemini in the 3rd. And Pluto in the 3rd *can* be obsessively dogmatic. McCarthy's survival instincts were connected with his framework of ideas. The ferocity of his convictions had something to do with that Pluto-Node conjunction in the 3rd. It is dogmatism of an emotional and deeply obsessive kind, as though his survival – and the survival of his collective – depended upon proving that he was right. If American society during the 1950s had been amenable to the sort of dictatorship that existed in the Soviet Union, I am sure that McCarthy would have exterminated anyone he deemed to be a communist.

Here an ideology is used to serve the complex. McCarthy had courage, tenacity and a great deal of intelligence and insight. But instead of expressing this in a creative way, his subtle and powerful mind was enlisted to serve his unconscious pathology. The complex ruled everything, and his mission was to hunt out all those elements in Anerican society which he believed were threatening to destroy it. Ultimately, these elements within himself destroyed him.

Transits that trigger the complex

Audience: What triggers that kind of behaviour? You said transits could trigger an understanding of the scapegoat pattern.

Liz: They can. But transits can also trigger the acting out of the complex. It depends on whether one is willing to do the hard work of becoming conscious. As we have seen, Neptune was transiting over McCarthy's Ascendant-Descendant axis and squared his Uranus-Neptune opposition during the period when he was at his most virulent. Uranus was transiting through Cancer at the same time, and soon arrived at his IC, running along in square with transiting Neptune during the four years in which he exercised power. Saturn moved into Libra and reached his Descendant in 1952, eventually conjuncting transiting Neptune and squaring transiting Uranus in 1953. And transiting Chiron was in Capricorn, right on his natal MC and Uranus, forming a T-cross in the heavens with transiting Uranus and Neptune. Throughout this time, all McCarthy's angular planets were triggered, including natal Mars and Venus, which form a T-square with natal Uranus and Neptune. Probably the external political and economic situation was mirroring a deep unconscious rage at his own and his family's isolation and impotence, but he couldn't bear to deal with the feelings, so he acted them out through projection.

He seems to have gone quite mad under those transits, but at the same time he was the mouthpiece for a kind of madness in the American psyche. We might recall that, in the natal chart of the USA, the Sun is at 13° Cancer in the 7th house, square Saturn at 14° Libra in the 10th. The same transits that triggered McCarthy's chart also triggered that Sun-Saturn square in the national chart. Everyone was building bomb shelters in preparation for an imminent Russian missile attack, and many Jewish families had to change their names in order to find jobs because anti-Semitism was ubiquitous. The collective psyche was afflicted by serious paranoia. McCarthy, like so many other scapegoats turned persecutor on the world's stage, could not have risen to power without the collusion of the collective to which he was so deeply bound.

When he was discredited in 1954, transiting Saturn arrived in Scorpio, first squaring his natal Moon-Chiron and then conjuncting his natal Sun. By this time transiting Uranus and Neptune had reached the last degrees of their respective signs, and had finished knocking his natal planets about. Transiting Chiron then moved into Aquarius and began creeping into opposition with his natal Moon, and transiting Uranus entered Leo and began applying to conjunct the natal Moon. This seems to have coincided with the savage increase in his drinking. Neptune went into Scorpio in 1956, and he died when it arrived on his natal Mercury. McCarthy's meteoric rise and fall were bracketed by transiting Uranus, Neptune and Chiron triggering the natal angles and the cardinal T-cross. Yes, it could have been an opportunity to become conscious. But Joe McCarthy was not a reflective man.

A question of choice

Audience: What would you see in a chart that would indicate an ability to work consciously with the scapegoat pattern?

Liz: I don't believe this is something we can identify in the chart. An openness to the collective is an important element of the scapegoat pattern, and this is certainly represented in the chart. A sense of woundedness is also an important element, and that too is represented in the chart. But we cannot know from the chart what any individual will do with either the receptivity or the suffering. Individual choice must be considered. All the charts we have looked at reflect both collective receptivity and a feeling of damage. Joe McCarthy's Chiron in Aquarius in the 11th tells us that he was very sensitive to what was wrong in society. The climate of the times was full of fear, and the global political situation was very unstable. He didn't make that up. And there certainly were communist infiltrators and spies at work during the Cold War, as there were in every Western country, including Britain. But McCarthy's solution to the problem was deeply personal and reflected his own pathology.

The magic ingredient that might have allowed him to question his own actions and motives is not described by the birth chart. The attitudes of the culture in which he lived are relevant. But no individual is forced to identify entirely with the values of their culture. They can, and perhaps must, learn to formulate their own values, for otherwise they can never develop their individual potential. We are back to the issue of choice, and the willingness to do the inner work required to understand one's needs, conflicts and aspirations. Milosovic has a choice, and I don't mean the one that NATO keeps going on about. He has always had a choice. David Koresh had a choice. So did Joe McCarthy. There are moments throughout life when we can decide to fight our own destructive compulsions, even if it hurts. That is what myth portrays as the heroic quest. Or we can choose to ignore that still, small voice and continue to indulge the complex, even if we know others are being injured. Often we don't even notice when these critical moments occur. We make a whole series of small choices without paying attention, and then, when the consequences arrive, we are amazed and claim it has nothing to do with us.

McCarthy served as a mouthpiece for certain elements in American society. Those who are receptive to the collective may, if they are capable and ambitious, rise to prominence because they embody the voice of the current *Zeitgeist*. The scapegoat too can rise to prominence in this way, especially when the collective itself is feeling scapegoated, as America was in the early 1950s. As we have seen, individuals who play such roles on the world stage usually have powerful links with the chart of their nation. Saturn is dominant in the American chart, and McCarthy plugged right into it with his T-cross of Uranus at the MC, Neptune at the IC and Mars-Venus at the Descendant. Saturn in the chart of the USA may be related to the American ideal of being the "policeman of the world", ensuring that justice – Saturn in Libra – is done everywhere and at all times. It is interesting to note that the nation, according to its own mythology, was founded by scapegoats. American school children are taught that the Puritans set sail for America because they were fleeing persecution in Britain. The reality was somewhat different. The Puritans were angry because, after the Restoration, Charles II would not permit them to scapegoat those who did not espouse the Puritan religious attitude, as they were wont to do under Cromwell's rule. So they left in a huff and decided to form their own theocracy in the New World. However, despite the usual hall of mirrors effect, the myth is one of scapegoating, and this myth is powerful in the American collective psyche. It presents us with a story of the creation of a free nation by the victims of oppression. Joe McCarthy instinctively understood that myth, and invoked it by reminding people that they were in danger of losing the freedom they had worked so hard to create. He never stopped to think that he himself was curtailing their freedom. All those who feel themselves to be victims are always at risk of becoming persecutors in one form or another. To untangle the knot is lengthy, difficult and painful, and it requires a great deal of honesty. What one achieves in the end is not escape from the complex, but a different and more life-enhancing way of living it.

The parent as scapegoat and persecutor

Inherited patterns of abuse

Before we look at a chart from the group, I would like to spend a bit more time on the issue of the parent as scapegoat and persecutor. This theme has come up several times during the day, but I feel it might be valuable to examine it more deeply. Parental abuse of children is one of the most disturbing, destructive and painful of all the possible manifestations of the scapegoat complex within families and within individuals, and its close cousin, paedophilia, seems to be on the rise, in part because of the availability of child pornography on the internet.

Whenever the subject comes up in a seminar, someone always asks whether it is possible to see childhood abuse in a chart. My response is invariably to say that I do not believe it is possible to see abuse in a literal sense. One can recognise inherited psychological patterns of a difficult and sometimes violent kind, and we will explore some of these astrological patterns in a few minutes. But we can never be sure whether violence or sexual abuse is enacted physically or remains invisible as an emotional undercurrent bubbling away in the unconscious atmosphere of the family environment. Abuse can take many subtle forms, including the kind of psychological coercion which demands that the child fulfil the parent's expectations or suffer the penalty of isolation and withdrawal of love. And sexual abuse is ultimately a symbol of a broader kind of cruelty, linked with issues of potency and powerlessness. The same may be said of rape: the rapist invariably suffers from feelings of impotence. But whether childhood abuse has been enacted physically or psychically, when we learn more about the individual's background we usually find the scapegoat theme at work in the family psyche for more than one generation.

We know that people who are abused in childhood may grow up to abuse their own children. Although not all abused children become abusers, most abusers have themselves been victims of abuse. Our understandable determination to find a scapegoat for our moral outrage at child abuse is made more difficult by the fact that, in such cases, the family history of scapegoating, when we track it back into the past, fans out from a specific family to a collective milieu. Behind the individual stands the family, and behind the family stands the collective. Eruptions of scapegoating in the collective do not just produce immediate victims. That is bad enough. But the repercussions embed themselves in the psychic fabric of individual families for many generations. We know that the 12th house can often give clues about this kind of ancestral inheritance, although it cannot tell us whether ancestral scapegoating has taken the form of physical abuse within the immediate family. Although I obviously cannot give you statistics on how many abusive parents belong to families who were, at some earlier point in time, scapegoated for racial, religious or economic reasons, I have heard enough stories over the years to be convinced that no individual springs into being as a full-blown abuser without trailing a long family and collective history of scapegoating behind them.

The father's legacy

Abuse does not spontaneously erupt out of a healthy family psyche. It is the by-product of a long history of conflicts and injuries which stretch back into the past and usually involve scapegoating on a collective level at some point in the family history. We have seen this kind of collective inheritance in the charts of both Milosevic and Joe McCarthy. Both these men experienced scapegoating in childhood, but they also inherited patterns of scapegoating from a much more distant past. Sexual abuse in childhood is horrific, and may take many years of therapeutic work to heal. Although it does not necessarily mean one will grow up to be an abuser, or even that one will attract actual abuse from others in later life, the scapegoat pattern, if it is present in the psyche, is crystallised by such an experience, and there is usually a tendency to wind up victimised on one level or another or, at the least, to carry a sense of shame, damage and rage. In the case of a strong personality – such as that of Milosevic or McCarthy – one may wind up scapegoating others.

Either parent may display violence toward a child, and either parent may also perpetrate sexual abuse. But the majority of cases of sexual abuse are linked with the father, or with a stepfather or male relative. Therefore we need to look at what planets might be found in the 4th house or in strong aspect to the Sun. Fathers who abuse their children are not just individuals who behave in a destructive way. They are carriers for a pattern of collective victimisation, and we will often find either Chiron, Neptune or Pluto in the 4th house as a reflection of this pattern. Less often, Uranus may be involved. The theme of father as victim may also be suggested by the Sun in the 12th, but in that case we will usually find that the Sun is in hard aspect to either Neptune, Chiron or Pluto, and one or more of these planets may also be in the 4th house or conjunct the IC from the end of the 3rd. Usually these themes of victimisation are stated more than once: for example, Neptune might be in the 4th square the Sun in the 12th.

A planet in the 4th or 10th suggests that the relevant parent is more than a person. He or she is the carrier of an archetypal principle, and this principle will usually be found to be active over many generations. It is a kind of daimon passed down through the mother's or father's line. In essence the daimon is not pathological. It is a family myth or family gift which could be expressed in creative ways. But time and human blindness eventually distort the daimon so that its expression becomes increasingly destructive. This is what the Greeks understood as a family curse. When an outer planet is involved, the archetypal principle related to the parent is connected with the collective, and in the case of Neptune, it is often the collective victim, the sacrificial goat. Neptune may also describe the father as an artist or a mystic. But even if he is able to express Neptunian qualities in positive creative form, the suffering victim is usually not far away.

Chiron and Pluto are linked with the exiled goat, and we have seen that these planets can reflect great rage against the collective because they carry the collective projection of outsiders and even outlaws. It is interesting to recall the chart of Robert F. Kennedy in this context: he had Pluto exactly at the IC, and the tragic history of his family, including his father's tyranny and links with bootlegging and the criminal elements in American society, are somehow encapsulated in this natal placement. Joseph P. Kennedy, driven by his own ancestral background of starvation and suffering during the Great Famine in Ireland, was determined to make one of his sons president of the United States, and in a sense he abused all his children psychologically by coercing them into enacting his obsessive vision of what they should become. All four of Joe Kennedy's sons became victims of tragedy, and two, including Bobby, were murdered. I do not believe Bobby Kennedy was sexually abused by his father. It is possible that he was beaten as a child, although I do not know for certain. But he was certainly psychologically abused, and used, as was his brother John, as an instrument of his father's revenge for a much longer family history of social and religious scapegoating.[10]

The role of Mars in child abuse

While these planets may speak of scapegoat themes, it takes more than that to generate the kind of violent energy needed to act out the pattern as abuse within the family. Whether the abuse is physical or psychological, we will also usually find Mars as a father-significator, linked with the Sun or in the 4th house and often in combination with Neptune, Chiron or Pluto. When Mars appears as a father-image, the father may be Martial in some way: he may have Sun, Moon or Ascendant in Aries, or the luminaries in strong aspect to Mars, or Mars may be angular in his chart. In the ordinary run of things, a Martial father is energetic, forceful and perhaps domineering. But when Mars is linked with Chiron, Neptune or Pluto, the father is portrayed as having a deep split in his nature. This split comes down through the father's line, and reflects a collective inheritance of frustration and scapegoating. I will repeat once again that finding something like Mars-Neptune in the 4th house does not indicate that the father was physically abusive. But it does indicate that the father carries a profound inner conflict whose roots lie in the past.

He is portrayed by two opposite images, the Neptunian victim and the Martial fighter. Any individual with such a polarity has a big problem, and few men are able to reconcile the conflict, especially when they are young. In recent years it has become more possible for a man to work toward greater understanding of himself before he fathers children. But earlier generations, especially if the family was being driven from one place to another by economic hardship, social ostracism or a hostile political regime, did not have the luxury of introspective pursuits such as psychotherapy. The men who carry such patterns simply pass them down to their sons and daughters, and act out an

---

[10] See my article about the Kennedy family, "The Oracle and the Family Curse", first published in *Apollon*, Issue 4, CPA Press, December 1999, and now available on www.astro.com.

archetypal theme that has its roots in centuries of collective scapegoating. Sexual abuse, as I have said, is a symbol as well as a violently destructive physical act. The father who sexually abuses his son or daughter is driven by a gnawing inner sense of rage, humiliation and impotence, which he acts out on the helpless child who has become a symbol and constant reminder of his own helplessness.

Cases of abuse in families are disturbingly common, but as I have said, abuse is not always physical. It can be emotional or intellectual, and that kind of abuse, while still extremely destructive, leaves no scars and no specific memories because it is so subtle. It is often the most gifted children who are subjected to abuse of one kind or another because these are the children who inadvertently inspire envy, rage and desire in their parents. We would all like to find a culprit to blame because the consequences are so terrible. Even if we have not experienced abuse in childhood, hearing about the experiences of others stirs up all our own feelings of victimisation. It would be very easy to say, "This father is evil. He is entirely to blame," without looking at the context. But people do not just spring into being behaving that way. There is always a psychological inheritance, and it is usually described quite precisely by planets in the 4th house and planetary aspects to the natal Sun.

Parental dichotomies

Audience: Would you know from a chart that the person was abused by the father?

Liz: I just said, more than once, that the chart cannot tell us about physical abuse. It can, however, tell us something about a specific conflict present in the father and his family line which might result in tension and compulsive behaviour. If we know about the abuse, we can put two and two together and work out the possible psychological dynamics that fuelled it. Mars and Neptune are archetypal opposites, and if they are linked by a conjunction or hard aspect, a deep inner conflict is portrayed which concerns potency and will pitted against the archetypal theme of the sacrificial victim. When this conflict is related to the 4th house, it has come down through the father. Sometimes combinations such as Saturn-Neptune in the 4th with Sun square or opposition Mars reflect the same kind of deep inner conflict. It is unlikely that a father described by such extreme opposites is going to be able to handle them with any grace – particularly when he is young, and even more particularly if he himself was subjected to family or collective scapegoating.

The mother's legacy

When the father is represented with such a split, the mother is usually also portrayed with the same kind of dichotomy. When one parent acts out a scapegoat pattern, the other parent will be caught in it, and both parents' inherited patterns provide one of the chief reasons why they got together in the first place. A father who abuses his daughter often also abuses his wife, or the mother unconsciously colludes with the father's abuse of his child by "turning a blind eye", thus venting her own unconscious scapegoat's rage on the daughter toward whom she feels envy. We might find configurations such as the Moon conjunct Mars and also square Neptune, with Chiron or Pluto at the MC. Complex patterns such as this are not pathological in themselves, but their very complexity, when we consider it in terms of the general level of human unconsciousness, can perpetuate conflicts which are acted out blindly and compulsively within marriages and families. When there are two contradictory father-images in the chart, there are usually also two contradictory mother-images. How does one woman cope with such profound internal conflict, unless she is highly psychologically sophisticated and has done a lot of inner work before she becomes a mother? The likelihood is that she doesn't cope, and may herself enact the role of the scapegoat within the parental marriage. Sometimes the mother can also be an abuser, emotionally and sometimes sexually, at the same time as being a victim.

In the end, the person with such conflicting parental significators in the chart will initially act out the polarity in one way or another, because the split lies within that individual as well as within the parents. The victim of abuse who grows up to be an abuser is expressing the same violent internal conflict as the parents did, and the scapegoating pattern is passed down to the next generation. These patterns, which involve apparently irreconcilable opposites, are inherited, and we share them with our parents. Then we may become the scapegoat for the family, not just in the sense of being victimised by an abusive parent, but also in the redemptive sense. Even if we do not realise it, we are the *pharmakon*, the healing agent who faces the enormous challenge of healing these ancestral splits through our own inner work.

Audience: So it would be inevitable that the splits would be acted out for a while.

Liz: Certainly. How can a child, or even a teenager, find a way to reconcile them? The developing ego is not strong enough to take both sides on board. In the early part of life, one will be the victim of the ancestral inheritance. One side of the dichotomy will be acknowledged, and the other side will be suppressed, projected, and experienced outside. One may also flip back and forth between the two, acting out first one and then the other. In later relationships we might play the role of Neptune while our partner plays Mars, Chiron or Saturn. Or we might play the role of Mars while our partner plays Neptune, Chiron or Pluto. The synastry contacts between the two charts will usually involve the triggering of parental significators and scapegoat patterns in both charts. After a while it becomes possible to recognise that all the characters in the drama are within us.

Planetary opposites

Audience: Why are the opposites so extreme?

Liz: It is because of the nature of the planets involved. Mars and Neptune are archetypal opposites. Mars has antipathy toward any planet which thwarts it, and Chiron, Saturn, Neptune and Pluto are great thwarters. Not all hard aspects involve such extreme polarities. Some are much easier to manage. Saturn and Neptune are another pair of archetypal opposites. Any Saturn-Neptune combination, even the trine and sextile, takes a long time to develop in a creative way. Saturn defends its autonomy against the chaos of Neptune's waters by becoming hyper-critical and hyper-rational, and Neptune attempts to defend itself against Saturn's loneliness and separateness by becoming helpless and pathetic, and by secretly undermining Saturn's structures. It is possible to bring the two principles together, and then the combination can be immensely creative. But in early life, this is impossible. When the father is personified by archetypal opposites such as Mars and Neptune, it is likely that he has a deep split in his personality, swinging between aggressive anger and helpless impotence. It is unlikely that the father will have integrated these two sides of his personality during one's childhood, if he is portrayed in such a way in one's birth chart. This ensures that the split continues into the next generation, still waiting to be healed.

Audience: How can Mars and Neptune work together creatively?

Liz: One way is to channel Martial energy into the service of the weak. This aspect has a kind of Robin Hood quality: the person who works in a forceful, aggressive way to protect and provide support for Neptunian people or Neptunian things. We can see modern forms of this archetypal figure in such fantasy characters as Superman, Spiderman and Batman. Silly though these comic-strip characters are, they have enormous global appeal because they are mythic. Another sphere where the two planets can work together is in the arts. Mars-Neptune is often associated with theatre and music, because Mars' powerful passional energy can be translated into a form which touches the collective soul. But Mars-Neptune needs either an imaginative outlet or an idealistic cause. If neither is provided, the two will remain hopelessly opposed, and the person will identify with either the victim or the persecutor.

Repetition compulsion

Victimisation is addictive. When we identify with the victim, we may continually need a fix, but instead of drugs or alcohol, it is a fix of suffering and isolation. We may be repeatedly attracted to violent partners, or allow ourselves to be continually victimised in subtle ways within our relationships and our working lives. While there are situations like the present one in Kosovo where one can hardly attribute personal responsibility to the individuals being persecuted, there may also be many areas in our lives where the scapegoat complex ensures that we charge ahead blindly toward precisely those situations which are guaranteed to make us feel scapegoated.

As I have said, sometimes astrologers fall into this pattern. Historically, being an astrologer has not been collectively acceptable for a few centuries, and as a profession we have tended to be scapegoated by collective authorities. Once upon a time the persecutor was the Church. Now it is the scientific establishment. Not all astrologers identify with this historical role as outlaw and scapegoat. But many do, and, to the extent that we carry a personal scapegoat pattern inside, we love being scapegoated by the establishment. It gives us a sense of identity. We would be most unhappy if we were to become respectable. We try to prove our legitimacy to people who always have been and always will be incapable of recognising the value of what we do. We beg to be punched in the face, and then we turn the other cheek and say, "Punch me again!" We get into arguments with sceptics at parties, when any fool could see that the person isn't interested in learning anything of value. They just want somebody to vent their aggression on, because they too are carrying a scapegoat complex and have chosen to play the role of the persecutor.

In the same way, if we are identified with the scapegoat archetype, we will choose friends and partners who persecute us. We join groups where we know we will be pilloried. We actively pursue unhappiness if this pattern is dominating our inner life. There are many areas where we really do create our own suffering, because the unconscious inner persecutor needs a hook on which it can be projected. If we are in a repeating pattern of scapegoating, it is always worth asking, "Why have I put myself in this situation? Are there other options?" Begging to be accepted by the persecutor is one of the most compulsive dimensions of this pattern. If only we could get the acceptance of the person or group which rejects us, we believe we would be freed of our feelings of shame and sin. But it never works. It can't work, because the only way we can win the love of the persecutor is to face the one inside. If we can begin to do this, we may find that we don't encounter external persecutors with quite the same frequency.

When there is a repeating pattern of victimisation, it is urgent that we look at the inner issues. This is especially the case when we are locked into mental generalisations about other people, like the belief that all men are abusive or all women are victims. One may indeed have encountered a series of abusive partners, but there might be an element of unconscious choice involved, and one will unerringly find people who vindicate the belief and reinforce the pattern. As Ian Fleming tells us, "Once is chance, twice is coincidence, and three times is enemy action." And the enemy lies within.

The flight into the spirit

Aspects like Sun-Chiron, Sun-Saturn, Moon-Pluto and Moon-Neptune are parental significators relevant to the scapegoat theme, and so are certain planets in the 10th and 4th houses. We have seen that Mars connected with these parental significators can sometimes reflect the acting out of violence or abuse, physical or emotional, in the family environment. Other factors in the birth chart can exacerbate such family conflicts by suggesting a predisposition to escape it altogether through a flight into the spirit. Jupiter or Neptune in the 9th or 12th as well as Sun-Neptune and Sun-Jupiter contacts are characteristic of a longing to "transcend" the suffering and conflict of the family inheritance. These kinds of placements reflect genuine religious feeling, and this dimension of the personality does need to be expressed. But often the spiritual realm is used as a premature escape route away from the darkness of the ancestral scapegoat pattern. This is particularly the case in people who are drawn toward the esoteric world in the hope that they can somehow sidestep the onerous task of struggling to redeem the scapegoat pattern within the family.

One of the great dangers in this kind of sidestepping is that one may wind up scapegoated by a tyrannical guru or spiritual community. There are certain spiritual groups which make life extremely difficult for any member who dares to leave the group, and the members of some religious communities, like those formed by David Koresh and Jim Jones, become so caught in the archetypal scapegoat pattern that they wind up sacrificing their lives because of the enormous power of the archetype wielded by the leader. These communities, unlike the victims of the Holocaust or Milosevic's genocide, are comprised of individuals who have made a conscious choice to submit to a spiritual leader who plays the role of persecutor. Here we will usually find the family scapegoat pattern in individual charts, enacted in the outer world through the dynamics of the group. We are given a salutary reminder of the more dangerous side of this kind of repetition compulsion by Charles Manson, who called his group "The Family".

A chart from the group

Debbie: the anticipation of punishment

Now I would like to move on to a chart from the group, because we are running out of time. It is understandable that not very many people offered their charts today, as the theme is so sensitive and personal. This is Debbie's chart. Debbie, what did you want us to focus on?

Debbie: There have been things throughout the day – virtually everything that you've been talking about – that I feel is relevant to my life.

Liz: All right, let's look at the main themes in the chart. The Sun is conjunct Chiron in Capricorn at the MC, and opposes Uranus at the IC. The Sun is also square a Saturn-Neptune conjunction in Libra in the 6th house. You don't have a lot of options, do you? The Moon in Scorpio is in the 7th, square Pluto, sextile Chiron, opposite Jupiter and trine Uranus. There is a lot of outer planet activity involving the two luminaries, and Chiron is very powerful in this chart. Can you tell us something about how you feel scapegoated?

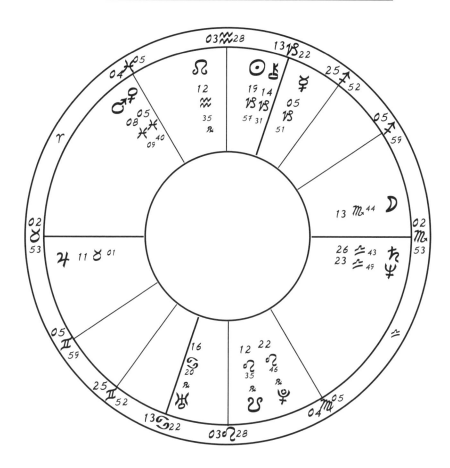

Debbie
(Birth data withheld for reasons of confidentiality)

Debbie: It really started in childhood. For some reason, people seemed to pick me out, and I never really understood why. It wasn't until I got into therapy when I was forty that I had a huge revelation about myself. I realised something in me was attracting it.

Liz: Can you tell us what you mean when you say they "picked you out"?

Debbie: It seemed as if, when I was in a group and an outsider came into the group, for some reason they would look at me and something would happen where I was victimised.

Liz: So you would always get picked on in group situations. Picked on for what? In what way?

Debbie: It could be a minor thing. For example, I could be with a group of friends in a park, and someone would come up and offer sweets. The sweets would always go to everybody else, and when it came to me, a game would be played about whether or not I could have a sweet. I could feel the hostility very powerfully, but I never knew why.

Liz: It sounds as though your feelings and the objective reality of the situation may sometimes have been rather different. That is characteristic of identifying with the archetypal scapegoat. The experience of being victimised was no doubt objective in particular situations, but the pervasive feeling of being an unwelcome outsider can mean that, even if no one was actually persecuting you, you interpreted their behaviour through the lens of the complex, and reacted accordingly. You may even have provoked being scapegoated because of your reactions. This is one of the most difficult issues around the scapegoat pattern, because there is usually a real experience of being scapegoated in early life, but the expectation that it will always happen ensures that it will always happen. Our complexes have a way of drawing similar complexes out of others, rather like a magnetic field. Even if your friends didn't initially want to give you a hard time, they found themselves being pulled into a behaviour pattern which suited both your scapegoat complex and theirs. And when we view others' behaviour through the lens of our own complex, we may also distort reality and attribute motives to others which do not actually exist.

There may be difficult issues in your family background that are linked with this identification with the scapegoat pattern. The Sun-Chiron conjunction opposite Uranus, which straddles the meridian axis, suggests that you are carrying conflicts and wounds for both parents. The Moon-Pluto square also hints at a sense of threat in the early environment. These aspects imply that there was conflict between your parents, and you may well have been expected to take sides – probably with your mother against your father – and were punished, subtly if not overtly, when you took the wrong side. The Sun conjuncts Chiron at the MC, which suggests that the scapegoat pattern was in both parents, and one or both may have unconsciously scapegoated you to alleviate their own feelings of victimisation. Of course you have also made your own contribution to the problem because, with that powerful Chiron, you always expect to be marginalised. Any situation that can be seen that way, will be seen that way. If the sweets run out before they get to you, your way of perceiving it is that the group is making a statement about your unworthiness. It would never have occurred to you that perhaps there just weren't enough sweets, nor could you have entered into the game with a light heart and a sense of humour. Where the scapegoat complex dominates, one interprets all situations in relation to one's own "badness", even though, on the conscious level, the persecutors are perceived as bad.

Debbie: Yes.

Liz: All this can create a certain amount of paranoia. The Moon in Scorpio square Pluto can sometimes reflect a sense of enemies everywhere. One always feels threatened. These feelings can be very intense at times.

Debbie: Yes, I feel that all the time.

Liz: There are many aspects in the chart that reflect your sensitivity to the collective psyche. There also seems to be a very deep need to be acceptable in the eyes of the collective, described by that Sun in Capricorn at the MC. It matters a lot to you what "they" think of you. Is this something you have worked on?

Debbie: Yes. The Uranus-Neptune conjunction went over my Sun ten years ago, and that really loosened me up. I didn't worry so much after that. I went into therapy at that time, and that also helped.

Liz: It seems that recognising the parental expectations you were supposed to fulfil is a fundamental place to begin working. Although both parents are involved, this applies especially to your mother, because the Sun is at the MC.

Debbie: I always thought my father expected too much from me.

Liz: His expectations may have been more obvious. A father represented in the chart by Uranus is often perceived as highly critical, and he may expect intellectual achievement from his child. Sometimes he conveys the message that ordinary instinctual and emotional needs are somehow "bad". You may remember that, in myth, Ouranos found his children repellent because they were imperfect, and forced them back into the womb of the underworld. But it is, after all, your Uranus, and it is also your own perfectionism which imposes those impossible expectations and makes you feel worthless and scapegoated. In your own eyes as well as your father's, you are supposed to be perfect. If you don't make the grade, you are unworthy. This is exacerbated by the Sun-Saturn square, which suggests a rather harsh inner judge. Life may feel like a perpetual exam, and any mistake, however small, constitutes a total failure.

Debbie: I can understand what you said about my father, because even when I passed exams he would always pick up on what I did wrong instead of what I did right. I could never get praise from my father. But I never picked up on those kinds of expectations from my mother.

Moon-Pluto: the depressed mother

Liz: I am not suggesting that your mother was critical in the way your father was. It is much more subtle. Moon square Pluto suggests deep unhappiness in the mother. Your mother may have been depressed in the early months of your life, because this is an applying square which became exact by progressed motion when you were around nine months old. Living with a depressed parent can feel very threatening to a small child, and it may sometimes seem as though one is surrounded by darkness and death. Although it is usually deeply unconscious, the message from the mother is that you, her child, must redeem her suffering. You must make her life worth living again, and if you fail, you are unworthy.

There may also be issues of unconscious resentment and jealousy directed toward a child who has her whole life in front of her. When this kind of thing occurs, it is usually unconscious, and it is not mutually exclusive with love. Probably both your parents loved you, but they suffered from their own complexes, and therefore they wanted far too much from you. The Sun-Chiron conjunction at the MC suggests that your mother was a strong and creative woman, but she was wounded by life and failed to fulfil her dreams and potentials. Perhaps she was too dominated by her own worry about what "they" thought of her, and lived her life trying to fulfil others' expectations. Whatever the reason, the image of the mother in your chart is a scapegoat figure, because of Chiron at the MC and the Moon square Pluto. And a victimised mother may inadvertently victimise her child.

Debbie: Yes, you are probably right.

Liz: With your watery Moon square Pluto, you are very sensitive to the unspoken emotional currents going on around you. Your mother's unhappiness was something you probably felt you had to fix, not only because her pain was real to you, but also because, if the caretaker dies, so does the child. It was a matter of survival. Think about it, because it may help you to understand your internal victim's pattern. If you felt your father was hyper-critical of you, your mother probably felt he rejected her as well, and suffered the same feelings of inferiority and victimisation. She may also have felt the same feelings of deep suppressed rage, which might have lain beneath her depression. Both these parents are inside you, and the conflict between them is your own internal conflict. The Uranian side of you beats up the Sun-Chiron in Capricorn, leaving you feeling that you will always be unacceptable in the eyes of others because you are not perfect.

The Sun at the MC suggests a very strong bond with the mother. Sometimes it takes a long time for a person with the Sun placed here to define their own values, because the identification with the mother is so intense. You might look at your relationships with other women to get some clues about the deeper dynamics of your relationship with your mother. Do you have a direction in which you can work with the scapegoat pattern creatively?

Debbie: Yes. I am teacher and counselling astrologer. That's where it is heading.

Liz: And how do you see your role? What do you want to give?

Debbie: I would like to be able to bring the knowledge I have to people who want to learn about astrology. But the counselling side is important, because I want to be able to help people.

Liz: Yes, I can understand that. There are many things in the chart which might incline you that way, not least the Sun in Capricorn, which has such a strong need to be useful. But do think about what I have said. There was a great weight of expectations placed on you in early life, and as a Capricorn you were peculiarly receptive to the unspoken demand that you do something about the unhappiness you felt around you. You are extremely sensitive to every dark or destructive undercurrent in the group, and you often assume it is your personal failure. You know about your issues with your father, but there is a missing piece to the puzzle, and understanding it could help you to be a more effective counsellor. More importantly, it could help you to avoid falling back into the scapegoat pattern.

Debbie: It is only now that I am fighting back.

Liz: Capricorns tend to flower late. Thank you for offering your chart for discussion. We have a couple of minutes left before the end. Are there any more questions?

Audience: If someone feels like a victim, isn't it right to devote their life to serving others? That would be using the pattern creatively.

The scapegoat and the helper

Liz: It may not be particularly creative if one is unconscious. Wherever there is an inner scapegoat, there is also an inner persecutor, even if there has been real persecution from the outside. If you put yourself in the service of others without any awareness of the scapegoat pattern within yourself, you may wind up perpetuating the pattern in a different way. Identification with an archetype is not creative. It is a means of escaping from the hard work and responsibility of owning oneself and mediating the archetype through individual choices and values. If you simply move from being your parents' victim to being the saviour of other victims, you will eventually feel victimised by the people you are trying to help, and you will end up exhausted and exploited. It is a common enough problem in the helping professions, but it is a problem which will not go away without consciousness. It is very important to find out where one's anger lies, and toward whom. A lot of dark stuff tends to float around in the place of the helpless victim, particularly anger, shame, guilt and a desire for revenge. Many people become helpers, not because they have a real sense of what they are working with, but because it is a way of trying to win back a sense of self-value. And it also smacks of what Freud called "repetition compulsion": a constant recreation of the original wound in the hope that somehow, magically, it will resolve itself.

Audience: Sometimes people who have been victims, whether of drugs or abuse or something else, get involved with helping other people who have the same problems. Is that what you mean? Is that part of the scapegoat pattern?

Liz: Sometimes. It is very natural to feel empathy toward those who have suffered in the same way one has oneself, and I would certainly not suggest that it is a "bad" choice. But I will repeat what I just said in response to the previous question. If you put yourself in the service of others without any awareness of the scapegoat pattern within yourself, you will wind up perpetuating the pattern in a different way. Sometimes the path of the helper is quite opposite to what the person really needs. A sense of self-worth is essential in working with a scapegoat pattern creatively, and if we try to find our sense of self-worth by devoting our life to helping other people, it may be a compensation rather than a true vocation for which one is genuinely temperamentally suited. If it is one's vocation, then of course it is the right thing, although it is still necessary to have some consciousness in order to avoid both inflation and victimisation. But if one has a 5th house Sun and lots of planets in fire, and there is a deep but unexpressed need to be creative oneself, taking on the healing role too quickly in order to heal one's feeling of being worthless may short-circuit the chance to feel that one has something special and important to offer.

Taking on the role of the helper can sometimes be the wrong thing to do. It depends on many factors. I have had many chart clients who say, "I really would like to help people." I do not doubt that most, if not all, are coming from a place of compassion. But they may also be coming from a place where they have been scapegoated and victimised for a long time, and have had no chance to spend time being the centre of their own universe. They don't really know what they are best suited to do. They have moved from being their parents' scapegoat-redeemer to being somebody else's scapegoat-redeemer, without ever learning to become selfish, self-nourishing and self-interested. It is very generous to offer our solar light to others, but the Sun has to shine first, before we can do that authentically. The scapegoat pattern isn't healed simply by helping people. It can actually be exacerbated. You might have a look at Howard Sasportas' seminar on the psychology of the helper, in which he explores some of these themes.[11]

Earlier, we were talking about Mother Theresa. We all need to have a sense that our life is worth something, whether we help other people in the literal sense or contribute to life in other but equally worthwhile ways. But if we use other people as a means of affirming ourselves, we are actually exploiting the very people that we are claiming to help. We are using them to fill our own empty space. It is a good idea to be very careful about this. I don't think there is a formula. Sometimes it is the right thing to do, but a lot of the time it isn't. It may be jumping out of the frying pan into the same old fire, albeit with

---

[11] Howard Sasportas, *Direction and Destiny in the Birth Chart*, CPA Press, 1996 (2002).

compassion. Only when there is a sense that our existence is worthwhile, that we are not merely a vessel for the sins of the collective, that we are not a reprehensible creature who must earn the air we breathe by sacrificing our life to others – only then does helping others become a real consecration. I would be very careful about advising someone with a scapegoat pattern to pursue the helper's path, and I would want to look at the whole chart. If I see a strong Mars, I might conclude that it may not, at least for a while, be appropriate for the person to move from Neptunian victim to Neptunian redeemer when they have never learned to express Mars. A lot of people who want to be in the helping professions probably shouldn't be, just as there are many people who are very gifted at it but could never imagine that it might be possible.

I think we have come to the end of the seminar now. I hope I have given you some food for thought, and perhaps also helped to raise some questions about things we so often take for granted about the black-and-white portrayal of persecutors and their victims. There are real persecutors in the world, and real victims, and they are often people who do not have a scapegoat's pattern individually, but are caught in a collective eruption about which they can do nothing. Jung suggested that the only antidote against such eruptions as collective scapegoating is to defuse the charge around one's own complex through constant efforts toward greater consciousness. The more individuals are able to do this, the fewer people there will be to participate in the kind of descent into mass brutality which we have seen so many times in our chequered human history. We will never see the end of the scapegoat pattern, because it is archetypal and will always rise up whenever the collective is caught in a split. And such splits are inevitable because we keep on growing and changing. But whatever we do in terms of individual inner work, it does, ultimately, make a difference.

Thank you all for participating.

About the CPA

Director: Liz Greene, Ph. D., D. F. Astrol. S., Dip. Analyt. Psych.

The Centre for Psychological Astrology provides a unique workshop and professional training programme, designed to foster the cross fertilisation of the fields of astrology and depth, humanistic, and transpersonal psychology. The main aims and objectives of the CPA professional training course are:

- To provide students with a solid and broad base of knowledge within the realms of both traditional astrological symbolism and psychological theory and technique, so that the astrological chart can be sensitively understood and interpreted in the light of modern psychological thought.
- To make available to students psychologically qualified case supervision, along with background seminars in counselling skills and techniques which would raise the standard and effectiveness of astrological consultation. It should be noted that no formal training as a counsellor or therapist is provided by the course.
- To encourage investigation and research into the links between astrology, psychological models, and therapeutic techniques, thereby contributing to and advancing the existing body of astrological and psychological knowledge.

History

The CPA began unofficially in 1980 as a sporadic series of courses and seminars offered by Liz Greene and Howard Sasportas, covering all aspects of astrology from beginners' courses to more advanced one-day seminars. In 1981 additional courses and seminars by other tutors were interspersed with those of Liz and Howard to increase the variety of material offered to students, and Juliet Sharman-Burke and Warren Kenton began contributing their expertise in Tarot and Kabbalah. It then seemed appropriate to take what was previously a random collection of astrology courses and put them under a single umbrella, so in 1982 the "prototype" of the CPA – the Centre for Transpersonal Astrology – was born.

In 1983 the name was changed to the Centre for Psychological Astrology, because a wide variety of psychological approaches was incorporated into the seminars, ranging from transpersonal psychology to the work of Jung, Freud and Klein. In response to repeated requests from students, the Diploma Course was eventually created, with additional tutors joining the staff. The CPA continued to develop and consolidate its programme despite the unfortunate death of Howard in 1992, when Charles Harvey became co-director with Liz Greene. Richard Aisbitt managed the administration until 1994, when the burden of increasing ill-health forced him to restrict his contribution to beginners' and intermediate classes. At this time Juliet Sharman-Burke took over the administration. Richard himself sadly died in 1996. Finally, in February 2000, Charles Harvey tragically died of cancer, leaving Liz Greene as sole director. In the new Millennium, the CPA continues to develop along both familiar and innovative lines, always maintaining the high standards reflected in the fine work of its former co-directors.

Qualifications

Fulfilment of the seminar and supervision requirements of the In-Depth Professional Training Course entitles the student to a Certificate in Psychological Astrology. Upon successfully presenting a reading-in paper, the student is entitled to the CPA's Diploma in Psychological Astrology, with permission to use the letters, D. Psych. Astrol. The successful graduate will be able to apply the principles and techniques learned during the course to his or her professional activities, either as a consultant astrologer or as a useful adjunct to other forms of counselling or healing. Career prospects are good, as there is an ever-increasing demand for the services of capable psychologically orientated astrologers. The CPA's Diploma is not offered as a replacement for the Diploma of the Faculty of Astrological Studies or any other basic astrological training course. Students are encouraged to learn their basic astrology as thoroughly as possible, through the Faculty or some other reputable source, before undertaking the In-Depth Professional Training Course. The CPA offers introductory and intermediate courses in psychological astrology, which run on weekday evenings.

THE CPA DIPLOMA DOES NOT CONSTITUTE A FORMAL COUNSELLING OR PSYCHOTHERAPEUTIC TRAINING. Students wishing to work as counsellors or therapists should complete a further training course focusing on these skills. There are many excellent courses and schools of various persuasions available in the United Kingdom and abroad.

Seminars in Zürich

Certain seminars from the CPA programme are available in Zürich. Please write to Astrodienst AG, Dammstrasse 23, CH-8702 Zürich-Zollikon, Switzerland, www.astro.com for details. However, those wishing to enter the In-Depth Training Course will need to attend seminars and supervision groups in London in order to obtain the Diploma, and should apply through the London address.

Individual Therapy

In order to complete the In-Depth Professional Training, the CPA asks that all students, for a minimum of one year of study, be involved in a recognised form of depth psychotherapy with a qualified therapist or analyst of his or her choice. The fee for the CPA training does not include the cost of this therapy, which must be borne by the student himself or herself. The basis for this requirement is that we believe no responsible counsellor of any persuasion can hope to deal sensitively and wisely with another person's psyche, without some experience of his or her own. Although it is the student's responsibility to arrange for this therapy, the CPA can refer students to various psychotherapeutic organisations if required.

Criteria for Admission

The following guidelines for admission to the In-Depth Professional Training Programme are applied:

- A sound basic knowledge of the meaning of the signs, planets, houses, aspects, transits and progressions, equal to Certificate Level of the Faculty of Astrological Studies Course. The CPA's own introductory and intermediate courses will also take the student to the required level of knowledge.

- Being able and willing to work on one's own individual development, as reflected by the requirement of individual therapy during the programme. Although a minimum of one year is required, it is hoped that the student will fully recognise the purpose and value of such inner work, and choose to continue for a longer period.
- Adequate educational background and communication skills will be looked for in applicants, as well as empathy, integrity, and a sense of responsibility.

Enrolment Procedure

Please write to the Centre for Psychological Astrology, BCM Box 1815, London WC1N 3XX, for fees, further information, and an application form. Please include an SAE and International Postage Coupon if writing from abroad. The CPA may also be contacted on Tel/Fax +44 20 8749 2330, or at www.cpalondon.com.

PLEASE NOTE:
- The CPA does not offer a correspondence course.
- The course does not qualify overseas students for a student visa.
- The course is for EU and Swiss residents only, although exceptions may sometimes be made.

About the CPA Press

The seminars in this volume are two of a series of seminars transcribed and edited for publication by the CPA Press. Although some material has been altered, for purposes of clarity or the protection of the privacy of students who offered personal information during the seminars, the transcriptions are meant to faithfully reproduce not only the astrological and psychological material discussed at the seminars, but also the atmosphere of the group setting.

Since the CPA's inception, many people, including astrology students living abroad, have repeatedly requested transcriptions of the seminars. In the autumn of 1995, Liz Greene, Charles Harvey and Juliet Sharma-Burke decided to launch the CPA Press, in order to make available to the astrological community material which would otherwise be limited solely to seminar participants, and might never be included by the individual tutors in their own future written works. Because of the structure of the CPA programme, most seminars are "one-off" presentations which are not likely to be repeated, and much careful research and important astrological investigation would otherwise be lost. The volumes in the CPA Seminar Series are meant for serious astrological students who wish to develop a greater knowledge of the links between astrology and psychology, in order to understand both the horoscope and the human being at a deeper and more insightful level.

The hardback volumes in the series are not available in most bookshops, but can be ordered directly from the CPA or purchased from Midheaven Bookshop, 396 Caledonian Road, London N1, Tel. +44 20 7607 4133, Fax +44 20 7700 6717, www.midheavenbooks.com. Paperback volumes may be ordered from Midheaven Bookshop or from The Wessex Astrologer, PO Box 2751, Bournemouth BH6 3ZJ, Tel/Fax +44 1202 424695, www.wessexastrologer.com.

Hardback volumes available in the CPA Seminar Series:

The Astrologer, the Counsellor and the Priest by Liz Greene and Juliet Sharman-Burke
The Family Inheritance by Juliet Sharman-Burke

Venus and Jupiter: Bridging the Ideal and the Real by Erin Sullivan

The Art of Stealing Fire: Uranus in the Horoscope by Liz Greene

Water and Fire by Darby Costello

*Where In the World? Astro*Carto*Graphy and Relocation Charts* by Erin Sullivan

Planetary Threads: Patterns of Relating Among Family and Friends by Lynn Bell

Relationships and How to Survive Them by Liz Greene

Earth and Air by Darby Costello

Astrology, History and Apocalypse by Nicholas Campion

Paperback volumes available in the CPA Seminar Series:

The Horoscope in Manifestation: Psychology and Prediction by Liz Greene

Apollo's Chariot: The Meaning of the Astrological Sun by Liz Greene

The Mars Quartet: Four Seminars on the Astrology of the Red Planet by Lynn Bell, Darby Costello, Liz Greene and Melanie Reinhart

Saturn, Chiron and the Centaurs: To the Edge and Beyond by Melanie Reinhart

Anima Mundi: The Astrology of the Individual and the Collective by Charles Harvey

Barriers and Boundaries: The Horoscope and the Defences of the Personality by Liz Greene

Direction and Destiny in the Horoscope by Howard Sasportas

The Astrological Moon by Darby Costello

The Dark of the Soul: Psychopathology in the Horoscope by Liz Greene

Incarnation: The Four Angles and the Moon's Nodes by Melanie Reinhart